THE
NATURAL
GOURMET

ANNEMARIE COLBIN

THE NATURAL GOURMET

DELICIOUS RECIPES FOR HEALTHY, BALANCED EATING

BALLANTINE BOOKS · NEW YORK

Library of Congress Cataloging-in-Publication Data
Colbin, Annemarie.
The natural gourmet.
Includes index.
1. Cookery (Natural foods) 2. Vegetarian cookery.
I. Title.
TX741.C65   1989   641.5'63   87-91858
ISBN 0-345-32771-3

Book design by Beth Tondreau Design/Gabrielle Hamberg

Manufactured in the United States of America

First Edition: March 1989

10   9   8   7   6   5   4   3   2   1

I dedicate this book to
The Natural Gourmet Cookery School/
Institute for Food and Health,
its dedicated staff and enthusiastic students,
in the hope that together we can contribute to
bringing in the new Age of Light that
we all long for.

Contents

Acknowledgments

This book is truly a collaborative effort, even though only my name is on the jacket; it would never have seen the ink of print if it had been left totally to me. My thanks, therefore, first of all to the graduates of my first Teachers' Training Program, whose names you will find in various places in this book. Without their enthusiasm and cooking skills, terrific recipes, initial writing help, and recipe testing, there would have been no book. I'm also grateful to Elizabeth Karaman for further recipe testing; to Linda Haelters for patiently typing the first version of the recipes, and to Gloria Greaves for typing the subsequent ones and actually making sense out of the corrections.

My thanks to Jack Garvy, N.D., for his teachings on the Five Phases of Food, a concept that gives a whole new meaning to cooking and menu planning, let alone healing through food. This latter subject, although not center stage in this book, is always in the background for me, as context and measure of my cooking style.

Another indispensable collaborator has been Virginia Faber, who in her role as editor-cum-reader found all the obscurities, inconsistencies, and unfinished thoughts in this book, helped me to harmonize the writing, and kept after me to make sure I got it all done. Thanks once again to Joëlle Delbourgo, editor-in-chief, and Ballantine Books, for their unwavering enthusiasm about my work, unflagging patience with my slow writing this time around, and for sparing neither time nor expense to produce the best possible book we can create together. James Harris, the art director; Beth Tondreau, the designer; Laura Maestro, the illustrator; and Dodie Edmands, the copy editor were all major players in this effort.

Finally, I wouldn't bother doing any of this if it weren't for the joy and strength I find in my support group. I'm grateful to my daughters, Shana and Kaila, for being always patient, undemanding, and supportive of my work, especially in the last three years since I moved the school out to the house; to Rod Colbin, their father, for being there for them when I am not; to Lissa De Angelis, my colleague and right hand at the Natural Gourmet Cookery School, for help and support far beyond the call of duty; to Bernie Gavzer, for everything; and to my many friends who I don't see enough, for love and friendships that never wane.

THE
NATURAL
GOURMET

Introduction

The relationship between food and health has fascinated me since the early fifties, after my parents took my brother and me to a spa. It was time, they had decided, to get healthy, so the whole family went on a vegetable-broth-and-fruit-juice fast. My parents stayed on it for twenty-one days; I, just turned eleven, stayed on it eleven days, and my five-year-old brother, five.

That fast made me acutely conscious of the connection between food and health. After the experience, my family remained mostly vegetarian. From a weak, whiny child, I became healthier and stronger. More importantly, I learned to choose my food so as to feel well.

In 1964 I discovered the macrobiotic way of eating. This was the Japanese version of the vegetarian and natural-healing ideas I had grown up with; but instead of whole wheat, lentil soup, raw vegetables and fruits, dairy products, garlic, parsley, and lemon juice, macrobiotics offered brown rice, miso soup, sautéed vegetables, pickles, cooked fruit, tofu and other soyfoods, ginger, sea-weed, and umeboshi plums. What's more, the macrobiotic system was rooted in a well-defined philosophy of how the world works. In terms of food choices, macrobiotic theory takes into account general energy flow, intrinsic food quality, relationships between nutrients, plus the traditions and physical health of your ancestors, the condition of your general health, the influence of your environment, your current work, and your spiritual direction. I am inclined toward philosophy, and an eating style based on firm philosophical principles makes more sense to me than one based on constantly changing scientific data.

As a Westerner adopting this diet, however, I eventually began to see a basic contradiction. Although I was supposed to eat like my European ancestors, a macrobiotic diet is based mainly on Oriental foods, ingredients, cooking techniques, and home remedies. Since I agreed with the basic philosophy, I began little by little to integrate my Western heritage with the macrobiotic dietary ideas.

For the rest of the sixties and early seventies I spent a lot of time reading both esoteric and orthodox books on nutrition, health, food, and cooking. My dual interest kept my reading on parallel tracks. While I plowed through unorthodox nutrition writers such as Arnold Ehret, Paavo Airola, Dr. Vander, George Ohsawa, Herman Aihara, Dr. Henry Bieler, Weston Price, J. I. Rodale, and George Watson, I was also devouring cookbooks like *The Joy of Cooking*, along with the works of Julia Child, James Beard, and Beatrice Trum Hunter. I also read Michel Abehsera and every vegetarian and macrobiotic cookbook on the market, and attended numerous workshops and as many cooking classes as I could, although in those days there were very few of any kind available.

Eventually all this mental gluttony needed a constructive outlet. As the Japanese say, "One grain planted returns ten thousand": Soon I found myself compelled to teach what I had learned. After a two-year stint as vice president of the New York East West Center for Macrobiotics, I opened my own cooking school in my apartment on November 22, 1977, and called it The Natural Gourmet Cookery School. I taught a basic set of ten cooking classes that I called health-supportive, using ideas from both Eastern and Western unorthodox nutritional thinkers, rearranged in my own way.

As I developed my own approach, my book learning became rounded out by my own real-life experiences, by those of my two growing daughters, and of course, by my students. The feedback I received from them about their reactions to different foods and systems has been one of my major sources of information. I found, for example, that not only do sick meat eaters get healthier when they turn vegetarian, but weak vegetarians often become stronger when they reincorporate fish or fowl into their diets. People with digestive disturbances often do better avoiding all raw foods, but others need a regular dose of fresh salad or raw fruit. The initial strict macrobiotic slant of my classes relaxed as I began to use more and more herbs, spices, and fresh and raw vegetables while cutting down on soy foods and salty condiments. My cooking style returned to a more Western approach. However, I did not reincorporate refined sugar, white flour, and dairy products, as I found health suffered whenever I used these foods.

In 1979, I wrote my first cookbook, *The Book of Whole Meals*, in which I taught readers how to put together dinners, breakfasts, and lunches based on whole grains and beans. The book is meatless and wholly dairy- and sugar-free but does contain several fish and egg recipes. Curiously enough, I received completely opposite comments about that book, in addition to the many positive ones: strict adherents of macrobiotics consider it "too wide," while mainstream nutritionists think it is "too restricted." Fortunately enough people find it useful so that it continues to sell and be reprinted.

In 1982 I signed up for a week-long seminar called "The Five Phases of Food," given by John Garvy, a naturopathic physician and longtime friend. In that course I learned a most fascinating viewpoint on food, gleaned from the Five-Element Theory of Chinese medicine. It would take me another two years to really begin to work with it, but the course greatly expanded my vision about how food works. It also helped me in the area of menu planning, and it is there that I find its main usefulness in my cooking classes.

My continued studies of the relationship between what we eat and how we feel found expression in my next book, *Food and Healing*, where I attempted a sort of unified field theory of all dietary systems. That is, I first laid out a basic philosophical model, then I examined the Standard American and Recommended American diets, vegetarianism, high-protein diets, the Pritikin regime, low-caloric diets, the fortified natural-foods diet of Adelle Davis and others, macrobiotics, and the "health-supportive" eating style, comparing them to that model, to discern discrepancies and points in common. The third part of the book shows how to use the same philosophical model to help heal minor health complaints, headaches, fevers, colds, skin problems, and the like, using food remedies.

HOW THIS BOOK CAME TO BE

When I started teaching, I hadn't anticipated how much fun it would be. Now I found myself more and more excited not just about the content of my classes, the actual information I was passing on, but about the process of teaching itself.

In September 1984 I added a new course to the school's curriculum, the Teacher's Training Program, or TTP. It was my intention to train natural-foods cooking teachers in all aspects of the craft: advanced cooking techniques, theories of food and healing, the art of teaching, running the business, keeping books, marketing, public relations, planning courses, and so on. In short, I wanted to pass on everything I had learned in my twenty years of whole-foods cooking, which included twelve years of teaching and counseling people about healthy eating and eight of running a profitable natural-foods cooking school.

Ten highly motivated women signed up for the course, which took place over one weekend a month for ten months. They came from all over the country: Johnna Albi and Phyllis Johnson, both experienced macrobiotic cooks, from Boston; Janie Jacobson, who had been studying with me during the three years since she had completed high school, from Virginia Beach, Virginia; Diane Korzinsky, who found that a knowledge of food and healthful cooking was an asset in her bodywork practice, from New Jersey; Joan Kopetski, a registered nurse with a strong commitment to natural healing, and Gail Vandy Bogurt Hansen, the owner of a health food store called Laughing Gull Organics, both from Long Island; Janice Florendine, who had been studying the Pritikin system intensely and was considering opening a health spa, from western Canada. They joined three local New Yorkers: Minx Boren, with classic training in French and international cooking, who had begun to study with me the year before to help improve her son's asthma; Jenny Matthau, who had signed up for the year-long apprenticeship with me as well; and Carol Amoruso, with extensive experience in both vegetarian and Italian cooking.

Our first weekend together we did a hands-on improvisational class called Creative Cooking. We decided on a menu and ingredients, making sure all five food phases were represented (more on the Five-Phase Theory later), then we all went shopping to Fairway, our magnificent local market, and picked the best-looking produce we could find. Back at the school, we wrote our menu on the blackboard, put on aprons, and got to work preparing the meal. Each dish was assigned to two people; most of what we cooked we made up on the spot.

I watched the timing, checked the seasonings, and made sure all the recipes harmonized. Then we sat down to eat our feast.

We loved it. Not only were we delighted with the recipes that emerged from our collaboration, we loved the whole experience of working together. And we agreed that we had to do something to share our food with the world. The result is *The Natural Gourmet.*

One of its main features is that it classifies dishes according to the Chinese Theory of the Five Phases. We've been using this concept at the school since 1983; I find consistently, and without exception, that balancing meals according to this theory is, if not exactly the simplest, without a doubt the most effective way to make sure the meal leaves the diner with a feeling of well-being.

What you will find in this book, then, is a chapter on how the Five-Phase Theory works, with each recipe classified according to its major and minor phases. For your convenience, the recipes have been organized into categories. However, for those times when you may need a fully balanced menu, you can turn to the menu section at the back. Since each student presented an individual class, at the end of the book you will find menus devised by each of the ten graduates under their individual names; you'll also find menus from several "International Vegetarian" classes and those from the best of our "Creative Cooking" workshops. To round out the book, I added a number of dishes from my general repertoire; Lissa De Angelis, associate director of the Natural Gourmet Cookery School, contributed the recipes for her homemade pasta and her course on "Easy Summer Lunches," as well as many of those in the fish chapter; and I also have included variations of recipes contributed by Melanie Raneri, John Boyajy and Bernie Gavzer. The recipes in this book conform to the eating style I dubbed health-supportive whole-foods cooking in *Food and Healing*: that is, they are based on natural ingredients; seasonal produce and fruit; whole grains and beans as your protein base; fish on occasion; the judicious use of herbs, spices, and soy foods for flavor and extra nutrition; and natural sweeteners, such as maple syrup and barley malt, in the desserts. Perhaps the biggest difference between this book and my earlier cookbook is the occasional use of butter, especially in baking. That came about because I had found, and the experience of many of my students corroborated this, that cakes and cookies made with oil feel heavier on the digestion than those made with butter. Cravings for fats are also lessened when we added a small amount of butter to our diets. I think it's important to pay heed to such physiological responses when deciding what foods are best for us.

Most of the dishes are vegetarian, not because I feel that everyone should eat that way, but because in our society there is little information on how to put together a satisfying and balanced meatless meal for those who want it as an option. When you study the meal combinations, you'll get an idea of what goes with what. The recipes are not always simple, for this is not a beginners' cookbook; yet they are not excessively complicated either. Some ingredients may be unfamiliar to you; we have used them because they balance this cooking style in both nutrition and taste and because of their high quality. Please make sure to look them up in the "Ingredients" section.

I hope you enjoy cooking from this book as much as we have enjoyed "cooking it up."

Annemarie Colbin
New York City
September 1988

IS THIS BOOK FOR YOU?

A "gourmet" is a lover of good food. Hence, a "natural gourmet" is either one who loves good food by nature or one who loves good natural food. Perhaps both. People who fit either definition will be interested in this book. In addition, vegetarians, macrobiotics, those who cook for them, those with allergies to dairy and sugar, and those who are trying to avoid the ravages of illness and old age will also like a lot of these recipes. Last but not least, the gastronomic adventurers in search of new tastes, new exotic ingredients, and unusually delicious food combinations will find plenty of recipes to excite their palates.

The dishes in this book are meatless, with only a few exceptions. It is possible to be a healthy vegetarian provided you eat whole-grain-and-bean combinations *daily* and a variety of vegetables of all colors. *It is also imperative that you avoid the use of white table sugar and the foods containing it.* Refined sugar is a pure carbohydrate, lacking in all other nutrients; therefore it creates a relative deficiency, or nutrient debt, by *not* providing the fiber, protein, minerals, vitamins, and water present in the original sugarcane. Since the body is most naturally prepared to consume nutrients in their natural context, it responds to such a lack with a deficiency syndrome. A meatless, dairy-free diet that includes sugar will therefore weaken and demineralize you. If you decide to continue consuming sugar, please go back to eating meat, fish, or fowl. Interestingly enough, I've found many cases where a vegetarian's intense sweet cravings disappeared once animal-protein foods were reintroduced into the diet. This has led me to believe that such cravings are often a sign of protein deficiency.

It is not, however, essential that you "be" a vegetarian. If you label yourself as such, deviations from your dietary standards, which are sometimes unavoidable, will cause you anguish and guilt. It is much more sensible to choose to eat foods that keep you feeling healthy, whatever those may be. Many people today are finding that a largely natural-foods diet, sugar- and dairy-free, with accents of fish, fowl,* or perhaps an occasional egg, keeps them in excellent health.

In my experience, and in that of many of my students, a lactovegetarian diet

---

* However, there are no chicken recipes included in this book. Chicken today is shot with so many hormones and antibiotics to facilitate mass production that we have generally avoided its use at the school. Organic, or free-range chicken is acceptable, but often hard to come by. Perhaps, as demand increases, so will availability.

with heavy emphasis on cheese, yogurt, and milk, does not promote health: it seems to be associated with overweight, asthma, allergies, colds, and other disorders of the respiratory system. According to Christiane Northrup, M.D., a Maine gynecologist who works a lot with diet, such a regime is especially harmful to women; the consumption of dairy products is associated with overweight and many disorders of the female reproductive system. The problem with milk products, incidentally, is not the fat content; rather it is the excess protein and calcium: cow's milk contains about four times as much of either as mother's milk. This may seem like a nutritional bonus, but experience has convinced me otherwise. All that protein and calcium, intended to help calves grow into cows, is too much for us humans. It is excreted (via pimples, infections, or various mucus discharges) or accumulated (as excess weight, tumors, cysts, fatty deposits, or calcium deposits).

Interestingly enough, cow's milk and mother's milk contain roughly the same amount of fat—4 percent of weight. Thus, only when used in excess does butter cause the problems associated with the intake of excess fats. Since we require a minimum amount of fat in our food, a meatless diet based on whole grains and beans—foods that have a relatively low fat content in and of themselves—can afford a tablespoon or two of additional fats per day, either saturated or unsaturated. Therefore, along with olive oil and unrefined sesame oil, you will find modest amounts of butter used in the recipes in this book.

If getting an adequate amount of calcium is a particular concern of yours, rest assured that your calcium needs will be met. In the first place, you will be avoiding the main foods—sugar and excess animal protein—that deplete calcium from the body. Secondly, you'll be consuming lots of vegetables, leafy greens, seeds, beans, and sea vegetables—all of which are valuable sources of calcium.

Creating healthy meals, either for your family or for entertaining, is not terribly difficult once you understand the principles of food selection. These are outlined fully in my book *Food and Healing* (Ballantine Books, New York, 1986). I'll restate them briefly here. In addition, the Five-Phase Theory will provide you with a sophisticated and fascinating menu balancing tool, to use when you wish. Learning and utilizing these concepts will take some time and effort on your part, yet I assure you it's worth it. When you exercise not just your esthetic sense but also your intelligence when you cook, food takes on a profound new meaning.

The Principles of Food Selection

Healthy food is more than merely fuel we put into our bodies to make them work at peak efficiency. Properly chosen, the food we eat nurtures mind and spirit, too. To derive a centered and harmonious feeling from your meals and to achieve a state of all-around good health, choose, whenever possible, food that is:

- *Whole*, therefore, no fragmented (that is, refined or processed) foods, such as sugar, white flour, white rice—all of which have had major nutrients removed. Some fragmented foods may be used as condiments, cooking aids, and flavor enhancers; these include oils and fats, mild sweeteners such as barley malt or maple syrup, fruit juices, tofu. (Note: tofu is considered a fragmented food because it is made by coagulating soy milk, which in turn is obtained by cooking soybeans and discarding the pulp.) Some fragmented foods are considered healthy: wheat germ, bran, blackstrap molasses, extracted juices. Though these foods may be rich in nutrients, they are nevertheless unbalanced, because they are lacking many of the nutrients present in the original food from which they are derived. The latest scientific research shows that whole foods, such as carrots or broccoli, contain health-giving and medicinal qualities. These qualities diminish or disappear when their individual nutrient constituents—such as beta carotene—are used instead.

- *Fresh*, or if not, then perhaps dried or pickled. Canned, frozen, or chemically preserved foods undermine our energy because their nutrient content is greatly diminished, and they are unpleasant to eat when served just plain or lightly steamed. As a test of this concept, imagine yourself being a 100 percent vegetarian and living *only* on unseasoned canned or frozen vegetables. You don't even have to do it to get the idea.

- *Local*, whenever possible. Locally produced foodstuffs are usually fresher and more flavorful, and also more economical.

- *Seasonal*, whenever possible, or at least from a similar climate. Eating tropical fruit during a cold northern winter prepares your body for hot weather. If it happens to be 15 degrees Fahrenheit outside, it will require more effort for your body to adjust to the cold. Many people on high fruit diets have trouble coping with winters. Of course, some leeway is called for here, because even in the winter we live at 68 degrees most of the time; therefore, springlike foods such as green vegetables and salads are generally appropriate year-round in our centrally heated and cooled society.

- *In harmony with ancestral traditions.* A tricky proposition, because in our society our ancestors come from many different places. For the majority of our food choices, it is a good idea to use cooking styles and seasonings that our great-grandmothers used. Another rule of thumb is that our major daily choice of whole-grain-and-bean combinations should be that of the continent of our ancestors: rice, soybeans, aduki beans from the Orient; wheat, barley, rice, split peas, kidney beans from northern Europe; oats, barley, lentils from the British Isles; wheat (including bulgur and couscous), chick-peas and lentils from the Mediterranean countries; kasha (buckwheat) and white beans from eastern Europe and Russia; millet and chick-peas from Africa; and corn and black-eyed peas from America. Does this mean that we should never eat ethnic meals from other countries? On the contrary—perhaps the key to international understanding may come precisely from such friendly food sharing. What it does mean is that it may not be a good idea to drop your own ancestral eating habits and adopt those of another country entirely. Every country in the world has its healthy, healing foods, and each person's body manifests the adaptive mechanisms set up by its forebears. Fresh, wholesome, natural foods prepared in a traditional manner, without modern chemical colorings, flavorings, and preservatives, provide the best foundation for health.

- *Balanced.* To understand fully the concept of balance as it applies to food, please consult my previous book, *Food and Healing.* For the purposes of this cookbook, it will help you to think of balancing meals according to:

  1. *Color.* Include something green, something red, something yellow, something white, and something brown in the meal.

  2. *Flavor.* A satisfying meal should offer the five flavors: sour, spicy, salty, bitter, and sweet. Two flavors can be combined in one dish (sour and spicy, for example). The bitter flavor is the hardest to obtain—most people get it from coffee, or perhaps bitter chocolate. In this book you'll find it mostly in bitter greens.

  3. *Nutrient complementarity.* Choose a grain-and-bean combination for protein and complex-carbohydrate complementarity. For acid/akaline balance, your daily diet should consist of about 40 to 45 percent vegetables and fruit, 35 to 40 percent whole grain, and 15 to 20 percent beans (or animal protein if you're not a vegetarian) by volume. For a full complement of vitamins and minerals, include vegetables that grow up (green leafy vegetables, such as lettuce, kale, and parsley), down (root vegetables, such as carrots, onions, and parsnips), straight (celery, broccoli), even sideways (squashes, cabbages, tubers).

  4. *Texture and shape.* Include a crunchy food along with the softer ones in a meal (nuts, raw vegetables). Also, avoid having a meal of mixtures: an example of such a confusing combination would be minestrone soup, rice and bean salad, and fruit medley. A better balance with similar ingredients would be minestrone soup, rice croquettes, refried beans, salad, and baked apples; textures and shapes in this case complement one another more harmoniously.

And finally, last but not least, healthy food should be:

- *Delicious.* If it's not delicious, why bother? Dutifully consuming food that is "good for you" overlooks the fact that eating is much more than a mechanical refueling of the body. It must also be pleasing to the senses, soothing to the soul. Healthy eating can be a robust and joyful event, or at the very least quite pleasant. Let's celebrate the miracle of life by enjoying and appreciating that which gives us sustenance.

The Five-Phase Theory

Early Chinese philosophers described the world in terms of the movement of energy. Upon emerging from Infinity, energy first split into two opposing forces, Yin (the moon, coldness, the female principle) and Yang (the sun, heat, the male principle). The energy flow of these two opposite but complementary principles was then further subdivided by points where it changed direction. The Chinese called these points Wood, Fire, Earth, Metal, and Water and assigned to them various characteristics. Wood symbolizes growth, Fire represents maximum function before the decline begins, Earth is balance or neutrality, Metal suggests a declining state, and Water typifies maximum rest before growth.

Diagram I: NOURISHMENT CYCLE

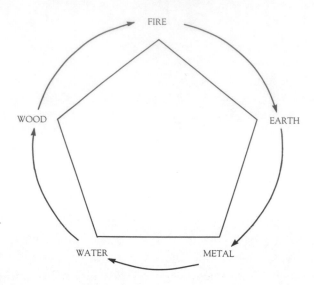

The relationship between these points were considered nourishing, or one of "mutual production," when going in clockwise order: Wood nourishes Fire, which nourishes Earth, which nourishes Metal, which nourishes Water, which in turn nourishes Wood again. On the other hand, in order to keep the energy from becoming excessive, there is also a relationship of "mutual control," where

Diagram II: NOURISHMENT AND CONTROL CYCLES

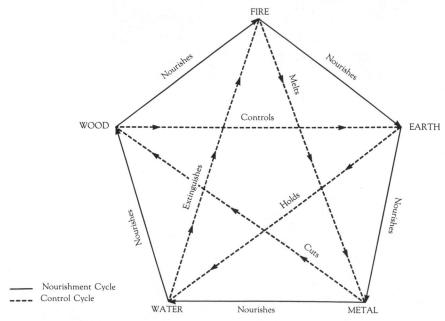

——— Nourishment Cycle
- - - - Control Cycle

each point controls its opposite: Wood controls Earth, which holds Water, which extinguishes Fire, which melts Metal, which in turn cuts down Wood.

Various phenomena were then classified according to these five phases (translated by some scholars as "elements" and by others as "transformations"); the system evolved into one of relationships and correspondences and it found a niche within both Chinese philosophy and Chinese medicine. What follows is a chart of some of these correspondences, which include the categories of seasons,

CHART I

The categories are in this order: a) SEASONS, b) ORGAN SYSTEMS, c) FLAVORS, d) COLORS, e) POSITIVE EMOTIONS, f) NEGATIVE EMOTIONS, g) CELL CONSTITUENTS, h) MAJOR VITAMINS, i) MINERALS, j) ENDOCRINE GLANDS.

WOOD

a) Spring
b) liver/gallbladder
c) sour
d) green
e) planning and decision making
f) anger, irritability, impatience
g) fats
h) A, B_{12}
i) copper, iron
j) gonads.

FIRE

a) Summer
b) heart/small intestine
c) bitter
d) red
e) making things happen, manifesting, joyfulness
f) anxiety
g) electrolytes/stimulants
h) B_3, B_5, C
i) potassium, sodium
j) pituitary.

EARTH

a) Indian summer
b) stomach/spleen-pancreas
c) sweet
d) orange, deep yellow
e) imagination, sympathy
f) worry
g) carbohydrates
h) B_1, B_6
i) manganese, zinc
j) thymus.

METAL

a) Fall
b) lung/large intestine
c) sharp, pungent
d) white
e) creating order
f) grief, melancholy
g) protein
h) E
i) phosphorus
j) thyroid

WATER

a) Winter
b) kidney/bladder
c) salty
d) black, blue, brown purple
e) perseverance, will, vitality
f) fear
g) water
h) D
i) manganese, calcium
j) adrenals.

organ systems, flavors, colors, positive emotions, negative emotions, cell constituents, major vitamins, and minerals. (Chart I) In the Five-Phase system used in Chinese medicine, there are a great deal more, but for our purposes they are not needed. Although it is well beyond the scope of this book to delve into the intricacies of this fascinating and effective system, experience has shown us a fairly simple way of taking advantage of its best features.

Foodstuffs themselves can be classified according to these phases in two ways: in terms of cell constituents (protein, carbohydrates, fats, electrolytes, stimulants), and as individual grains, beans, vegetables, fruits, nuts, seeds, and animal foods. In addition, cooking techniques and food-preserving methods can be classified in this manner as well. (Chart II)

MEAL BALANCING
ACCORDING TO
FIVE PHASE THEORY

Basically the idea is that balance is attained when energy flows smoothly from one phase to the next, neither blocked nor hastened. Theoretically, we should eat more or less equal amounts from all the phases—about 20 percent from each, so as to equally nourish the different organ systems and thereby achieve balance in both the nourishment and the control cycles of our energy flow.

In actual practice, however, each person has a different energy pattern, and will be more naturally attracted to the foods in some of the phases and less, or not at all, to the foods in others. This idiosyncrasy is appropriate as long as the individual remains in good health and feels comfortable. However, at times we fall into dietary patterns of imbalance that do not support our health. For example, if you eat a lot of foods that are high in fat (Wood), you may become cranky or irritable. Though not necessarily always, the same may happen if you eat a lot of bread (Wood) and salad (Wood). You may then develop a craving for food in the phase controlled by the food you have eaten in excess. Thus if you have eaten excess Wood you may develop a craving for Earth foods (sweets). If you feel uncomfortable, or unbalanced, in spite of eating a nutritionally adequate diet according to the Principles of Food Selection (fresh, natural foods, whole grains, beans, vegetables, fruits, some animal protein), it may help to evaluate your food choices according to the Five Phases. People who keep a Five Phase food diary for a week or more often find that they are choosing most of their foods from just two or three phases.

CHART II

In this order: 1) grains and tubers; 2) dry beans and legumes; 3) vegetables; 4) fruits; 5) seeds; 6) herbs; 7) nuts; 8) dairy products; 9) seafood; 10) fowl; 11) meat; 12) miscellaneous; 13) cooking techniques.

WOOD

1) barley, oats, rye, triticale, wheat
2) green lentils, mung, black-eyed peas, split peas, peanuts
3) artichoke (globe), bell pepper (green), broccoli, carrot (raw), knotweed, lettuce (Bibb, Boston, romaine, curly), parsley, green beans, green peas, rhubarb, summer squash (pattypan, zucchini)
4) apple (sour), cherry (acerola), avocado, currant (sour), coconut, crab apple, grapefruit, kiwi, lemon, lime, orange (sour), pineapple, plum, pomegranate, quince
5) alfalfa
6) alfalfa root, saffron, caraway, cumin, marjoram, bay leaf, dill, nutmeg, tarragon, cloves, gumbo filé
7) Brazil nuts, cashew nuts, litchis
8) butter, cream, egg yolk, mayonnaise, sour cream, yogurt (sour)
9) freshwater clams, softshell crabs, eel, trout, mackerel
10) chicken, liver (chicken)
11) fats, liver (beef, lamb)
12) lard, nut butters, oils, olives, sour pickles, sauerkraut, seitan (wheat gluten), vinegar, wheat bran, germ, wheat grass, yeast
13) frying

FIRE

1) amaranth, corn (yellow), popcorn, sorghum
2) red lentils
3) asparagus, arugula, bell pepper (red), bok choy (greens), broccoli rabe, brussels sprouts, chicory, chives, collard greens, dandelion (root and leaves), endive (Belgian), escarole, kale, lamb's-quarters, mustard greens, okra, snow peas, scallions, Swiss chard, turnip tops, tomato
4) apricot, guava, kumquat, loquat, persimmon, raspberries, strawberries
5) hing (asafetida), hops
6) apricot kernels, sesame, sunflower
7) pistachios, bitter almonds

9) shrimp
10) squab
11) heart (beef), lamb
12) beer, coffee (bitter), chocolate, ketchup, liquor, tobacco, wine
13) roasting, barbeque, grilling

EARTH

1) millet, sweet potato, yam
2) chick-peas
3) artichoke (Jerusalem), bamboo shoot, calabash, corn on the cob (sweet), crookneck squash, eggplant, kuzu (kudzu), mallow, parsnip, pumpkin, rutabaga, spaghetti squash, winter squash (acorn, butternut, buttercup, hokkaido, hubbard, etc.), tapioca
4) apple (sweet), banana, breadfruit, cantaloupe, cassava, coconut milk, currants (sweet), dates, figs, grapes (sweet), honeydew melon, mango, mulberries, muskmelon, orange (sweet), papaya, plantain, prunes, raisins, sweet cherries, tangelo, tangerine
5) pumpkin
6) allspice, achiote, anise, cardamom, cinnamon, licorice, turmeric, vanilla
7) almonds, beeches, filberts, pecans, pine nuts, macadamia nuts
8) fresh cheeses (cottage, farmer's, ricotta), ice cream, milk, yogurt (sweet)
9) anchovies (fresh), carp, salmon, sturgeon, swordfish, tuna (canned)
10) pheasant, quail
11) mutton, pancreas (beef), rabbit
12) carob, honey, barley malt, maple syrup, rice syrup, sherbet, sugar (brown and white), sweet chocolate
13) boiling

METAL

1) rice (brown and white), sweet rice, taro potato, white potato
2) great northern, navy, lima, soybean, tempeh, tofu
3) bok choy (whites), cabbage, capers, cauliflower, celeriac, celery, chili, Chinese cabbage (nappa), cress, cucumber, daikon, eggplant, garlic, ginger, iceberg lettuce, kohlrabi, leeks, lotus root, onion, radish, rape, shallots, spinach, turnips, watercress, water chestnuts
4) peach, pear
5) dill
6) basil, cayenne, coriander, fennel, fenugreek, mint, horseradish, black pepper, white pepper, thyme, sage
7) hickory, walnut
8) sharp aged cheeses, egg white
9) cod, flounder, haddock, halibut, herring, perch, scrod
10) turkey
11) beef
12) mochi (cooked molded sweet rice)
13) baking

```
┌─────────────────────────────────────────────────────────────┐
│                        WATER                                  │
│  1) buckwheat                                                 │
│  2) aduki, black soybeans, black turtle, kidney, pinto        │
│  3) agar-agar, beets, beet greens, burdock, dulse, hiziki,    │
│     Irish moss, kelp, kombu, mushrooms, nori, radicchio,      │
│     red cabbage, salsify, wakame, water chestnuts             │
│  4) blackberries, black raspberries, blueberries,             │
│     boysenberries, concord grapes, cranberries, watermelon    │
│  5) chia, black sesame                                        │
│     ─────                                                     │
│  7) chestnuts                                                 │
│  8)                                                           │
│  9) caviar, abalone, bluefish, catfish, clam, crab,           │
│     cuttlefish, lobster, mussel, octopus, oyster, sardine,    │
│     scallop, squid, turtle                                    │
│ 10) duck                                                      │
│ 11) ham, kidney, pork                                         │
│ 12) coffee (decaffeinated), sesame salt, miso, pickles        │
│     (brine cured), salt, soy sauce, umeboshi plums,           │
│     umeboshi vinegar, bancha tea                              │
│ 13) steaming, salt pickling                                   │
└─────────────────────────────────────────────────────────────┘
```

(Adapted from John Garvy, *The Five Phases of Food*)

The ideal is to eat from all phases, so as to allow the energy to move around. A well balanced meal in terms of this system has each phase represented either as a major—the principal foodstuff of a dish—or as a minor—as secondary foodstuff, condiment, or cooking style. If all the phases are offered in a healthful meal, often the natural appetite of the diners will lead them to select dishes whose phases will balance them individually.

To take advantage of the Five Phase theory in cooking, all you need to know is what is the major phase of each dish, and to make sure that all the phases are represented in your meal. The major phase of a dish is the one of the main ingredient; if it contains equal amounts of two or more ingredients, the dish will have two or more major phases. The minor phase(s) of a dish are determined by other noticeable ingredients; flavors and cooking styles can be considered as well. Not all dishes will have a minor phase.

To plan a balanced meal, choose your main dish—say the whole grain entrée—from one of the major phases, and then pick beans, vegetables, soup, and dessert from other major phases. If you have fewer than five dishes in a meal—very common, for sure—then use the minor phases to achieve balance. That's all.

For example, say you pick Polenta (Fire) as the main dish; you could then complement with Black Bean Feijoada (Water), Onion Soup (Metal), Green Salad with Miso-Coriander Dressing (Wood), and Pumpkin Pie (Earth). An unbalanced meal would be brown rice (Metal), with miso soup (Water), aduki beans (Water), onion-cabbage-tofu sauté (Metal) and oatmeal cookies (Wood—Earth): in this meal you're missing Fire energy, and will then be attracted to coffee and cigarettes (both Fire).

But if you only have soup and salad for lunch, pay attention to the minor phases: pick something like Clear Broth with Garlic and Escarole (Fire—Metal and Water) and Pasta Salad with Zucchini and Chickpeas (Wood—Earth); theoretically, with this meal you'll need nothing else to be in balance.

When cooking for others, make sure all the phases are represented. It's easiest, though not crucial, if each dish has a different major phase; then the people around your table can make their own choices for individual balance. It usually works out just fine. Take a look at the menu section at the end of this book to see how meals can be assembled by looking not only at nutritional balance (protein complementarity, color, flavor, texture, shape) but also at the Five Phases.

Have fun. It may take you a little while to get used to this system. In fact, you may even ignore it when you first encounter it! I did, for sure; and it took me a few years to get the hang of using Five Phases. However, my students and I have all found that it beats every other system when it comes to menu planning and giving zest to your meal. To learn more about this fascinating theory, consult the Five-Phase bibliography at the back of this book.

HOW TO KEEP
A FIVE PHASE FOOD DIARY

If you're curious to see what you're eating in terms of the Five Phases, keep a week-long diary in the form of a grid: divide the page lengthwise into five sections and label each with one of the phases. Then divide the page horizontally into seven days with room for three meals plus snacks in each day. Then place everything you eat in the right day under its phase (refer to the charts to find the latter). After a week take a look. You'll begin to see the patterns emerge.

If you really want to have fun, keep the diary as above but also keep a record of moods and feelings in the same timeframe. You may learn some interesting things about yourself. Some people discover that they miss an entire phase (maybe Fire or Water) from their diet. When they make a conscious effort to add more of the missing foods, they find they feel better, clearer, more energetic.

Breakfast: Oatmeal/raisins, mint tea
Lunch: Pinto Bean Salad, Corn Bread
Dinner: Escarole Soup, Baked Whitefish, Crunchy Fennel, Salad, Brown Rice, Almond Flan
Snack: Popcorn

		WOOD	FIRE	EARTH	METAL	WATER
MONDAY	B	✓				
	L		✓	✓	✓ ✓	✓
	D		✓		✓ ✓	✓
	S		✓			
TUESDAY	B					
	L					
	D					
	S					
WEDNESDAY	B					
	L					
	D					
	S					
THURSDAY	B					
	L					
	D					
	S					
FRIDAY	B					
	L					
	D					
	S					
SATURDAY	B					
	L					
	D					
	S					
SUNDAY	B					
	L					
	D					
	S					

The above is a one-day set of meals. The major phases of the dishes have been marked by a check in the appropriate boxes. You will see that there is a higher amount of checkmarks in the Metal and Fire phases. If you continue with the diary, you will find out what your own pattern is; if quite unbalanced in terms of phases, you may want to rebalance and see what happens.

Ingredients

GRAINS

These include all unpolished cereals, whole, cracked, or ground into flour: brown rice, whole wheat, barley, oats, millet, buckwheat (kasha), corn, and rye. With the exception of rye, these grains are used throughout the book. Lately a few more exotic—and expensive—grains have appeared on the market: brown basmati rice, hato mugi (a variety of barley), quinoa, amaranth. You can find the first three in a couple of recipes here as well.

Commonly available whole-grain products include bulgur (cracked, steamed, and dried whole wheat) and whole wheat or buckwheat pasta. "Artichoke," "spinach," and other interesting pasta variations are usually made with white flour. Couscous is an unbleached-white pasta product used as a grain side dish or in desserts.

Whole grains are composed of starch, bran, and germ. They contain complex carbohydrates and protein in their starches; protein, fats, minerals, and vitamins in the germ; and minerals and fiber in the bran. Whole grains are an excellent source of the B-vitamin complex necessary for healthy nerves. They are also the best source of dietary fiber. Because the fiber in the whole grain is balanced with the other nutrients, they are more effective than pure bran in normalizing the digestive system.

Kasha (roasted buckwheat groats) is done cooking in about 15 minutes. Millet and quinoa need 40 minutes. Brown rice and barley need about 1 hour of cooking. Whole wheat berries and whole oats need soaking overnight and about 1½ hours' cooking time. Whole dry corn is quite complicated to prepare. The traditional method calls for the use of lime (a calcium compound) or wood ash, both of which help soften the grain and make the nutrients more assimilable. Cornmeal is easier to use, and you will find it in several of the recipes.

BEANS

Hearty and delicious, beans are known the world over as builders of strong bodies. In combination with whole grain, they are the major source of protein in a vegetarian diet; it is essential that any conscientious vegetarian consume a reasonable amount of beans daily. Unfortunately beans have a bad reputation, because they are difficult for many people to digest. Those who are used to consuming animal protein may lack some of the intestinal flora necessary to digest beans. It may take several months of regular consumption for the body to adjust. In the meantime, the practice of long presoaking and discarding the soaking water, sometimes twice, helps make beans more digestible. Cooking beans with herbs and spices, as is done in Indian cuisine, is another common practice helpful to the digestion. In macrobiotic cooking it is recommended to add a piece of kombu seaweed when cooking beans, which will add valuable minerals and nutrients.

The fastest-cooking legumes need no soaking. Red lentils are done in 15 minutes. Green, or brown, lentils and green and yellow split peas are next, requiring 1 hour of cooking time. Aduki beans take 1½ hours. All other beans require presoaking before cooking. For more information on proper handling of beans see page 39 in Kitchen Basics.

You will not find any recipes in this book with whole soybeans; I find their taste too unpleasant, and tend to believe some research that indicates they may contain oxalates and other elements that prevent nutrient absorption. Soybean products such as miso, shoyu (the natural soy sauce made with wheat), tamari (a wheat-free natural soy sauce), tofu, and tempeh, on the other hand, are delicious; tofu and tempeh are good protein sources when combined with the grains. You will also find the condiments miso and shoyu or tamari used in many of the recipes.

VEGETABLES

The protein and starch in beans and grains help in the buildup and replacement of cells. On the other hand, the vitamins and minerals present in vegetables and fruits help in the metabolic exchanges resulting in breakdown and elimination of waste matter. Vegetables are therefore extremely helpful for people who have eaten a lot of meat, fat, and cheese during most of their lives and very effective as cleansers and healing aids. A diet consisting *solely* of vegetables, however, promotes breakdown without a counterbalancing protein buildup; hence, it is not uncommon for longtime strict raw-food vegetarians to show signs of protein and calcium deficiencies. A healthy middle ground—40 to 60 percent of the diet consisting of vegetables and fruits, the rest of grains and beans or animal protein—seems to be, in my experience, the healthiest and most sustainable way to eat in our society.

Eat fresh vegetables whenever you can. If you can't get fresh, the next best choice is dried. After that, pickled vegetables often have valuable nutrients to contribute—but only when pickled in brine, not in vinegar (vinegar is too acidic). Frozen and canned vegetables taste flat and lifeless and are not helpful in a well-balanced, healthful, and tasty diet.

For people with arthritis, it may be advisable to refrain from consuming the nightshades: potatoes, tomatoes, eggplant, and peppers of all colors (red, green, yellow, hot, Tabasco, paprika, chili, and so on). There are many who have found that avoiding those vegetables helps diminish, and in some cases eliminate, joint pains. For those on a nondairy diet, the nightshades are problematic in any event, for in large amounts they may tend to draw calcium out of the system. However, I have not found that eating them occasionally causes any noticeable problems in reasonably healthy people. Therefore you will find recipes using tomatoes and other nightshades in this book, as they are such marvelous flavor enhancers. If you feel that the condition of your health necessitates it, you may wish to avoid them.

In our society we have it easy in terms of acquiring our food: we just pick it up at the grocery store, instead of slaving for months in the garden or field. We also have most vegetables available year-round, instead of only seasonally. Still, it's not a bad idea to cook according to the seasons, choosing, for example, more leafy vegetables in the warm weather and more starchy vegetables in the cold. For anyone looking to feel more centered and anchored, enriching his or her diet with root vegetables (carrots, turnips, parsnips, rutabaga, radishes), yams, and winter squashes would be very helpful. Those same vegetables are also a blessing if you are struggling with a sweet tooth: baked yams are an especially good snack to replace a cookie or candy bar.

SEA VEGETABLES

Very popular in Japanese cooking, seaweeds have also been used in the British Isles, in the U.S. northern coastal regions, in Hawaii, and in other islands. The ones most easily found are Japanese varieties, such as kombu (kelp), nori (used in sushi making), hiziki, arame, and wakame; and dulse, alaria, porphyra, and sea palm, which are harvested these days on the east and west coasts of the United States.

These plants are an excellent source of minerals, especially iodine, which is needed by the thyroid gland; I find it interesting that many people diagnosed as hypothyroid usually adore sea vegetables. Conversely, those who thoroughly dislike them may have an overactive thyroid gland. Sea vegetables also contain appreciable amounts of calcium, iron, magnesium, vitamins A, B complex (possibly including some B_{12}), and C.

FRUIT

Some people have found that eating raw fruit at the end of a meal that contains vegetables and starches does not agree with them. Cooked fruit, on the other hand, poses no problem. When in doubt about your own responses, test by consuming raw fruit on an empty stomach and then at the end of a meal and note how you feel.

Choose fruit that is generally fresh, seasonal, and, whenever possible, grown without pesticides: pears and apples in the winter; peaches, strawberries, bananas, kiwi fruit, and such in the summer.

NUTS AND SEEDS

These are wonderful as accents in main dishes and desserts. Besides a rich and rounded taste, they provide extra protein and fatty acids, both quite necessary in a mostly vegetarian regime. The ones used most often in these recipes are almonds, walnuts, cashews, filberts, and sesame, sunflower, and pumpkin seeds. They're best when freshly shelled, and keep well in the freezer.

SWEETENERS

Maple syrup, barley malt, and rice syrup are the natural sweeteners you will find in most of the dessert recipes. Fresh and dried fruit, fruit juices, and fruit juice concentrates are also used, as these all are rich in taste and satisfying to the sweet tooth.

CONDIMENTS AND SEASONINGS

These are the secret ingredients that help the artistry of the cook shine at its maximum. A touch of nutmeg in the greens, a bit of tarragon and ginger in the soup, and even the most humdrum dish becomes an exciting event. In fact, without condiments, there would be no art in cooking!

You will see that salt is used in these recipes, even though salt has had such bad press during the past few years. (The real culprit in causing health problems has been sodium, which is widely used in various food additives, such as baking powder—sodium bicarbonate—preservatives, monosodium glutamate, and extraneous additives to salt itself, such as sodium silico aluminate and yellow prussiate of soda.) The salt we use is plain sea salt, with no additives; and we'll be using it in small amounts, just enough to bring up the taste in the food. If you wish, you can eliminate it. Several of the recipes in this book call for vegetable seasoning salt. There are one or two brands available in natural foods stores that contain just sea salt and various dried vegetables and kelp—no yeast and no hydrolyzed vegetable protein or other additives. Vegetable seasoning salt gives added dimension to soups and sauces when you aren't using stock.

Marvelous natural flavoring agents, contributed by many countries, have found their way into these recipes. Among them are:

- *Miso*—a rich fermented soybean paste made with white rice, brown rice, corn, or barley that comes, unpasteurized, in several varieties from sweet white to dark red.
- *Shoyu*—a natural soy sauce made from soybeans, wheat, water, salt, and culture, unpasteurized and aged in wooden barrels for 18 months; it has also been called tamari, but "genuine tamari" is a natural, flavorful, aged wheat-free soy sauce; darker and heavier. For cooking purposes, shoyu and tamari may be used interchangeably.
- *Umeboshi plums*—or plums pickled in brine, prized for their tart/salty taste and their ability to counter indigestion and hangover headaches. Also available as paste.
- *Umeboshi vinegar*—the juice left over from the plum-pickling process. Umeboshi vinegar helps to lighten any soup or casserole containing starch or grain. Its salty flavor eliminates the need to add extra salt to salad dressings. If umeboshi vinegar is not available, a mixture of fresh lemon juice and sea salt makes a satisfactory substitute. 1½ tablespoons lemon juice + ½ teaspoon sea salt = 1½ tablespoons umeboshi vinegar.
- *Mirin*—a cooking wine made from sweet brown rice (can be replaced by dry sherry).
- *Brown rice vinegar*—mild and delicious, less corrosive than white or wine vinegar, excellent in sauces and dressings. Apple cider vinegar makes an acceptable substitute.
- *Whole-grain mustard*—such as Pommery, is used exclusively in salad dressings.
- *Kuzu*—a starch extracted from the Japanese kuzu plant (known as kudzu in the southern United States); it thickens like cornstarch, but also has a soothing effect on the digestive system and nerves, which makes it the better choice in spite of its higher price.
- *Arrowroot*—another thickener for puddings and pie fillings; it imparts a velvety texture.
- *Agar or kanten*—a sea vegetable that has a jelling effect much like gelatin, with a high mineral content and amazing versatility.
- *Herbs*—or the aromatic leaves of certain plants, which include basil, oregano, thyme, rosemary, marjoram, sage, tarragon, chives, parsley, and the like.
- *Spices*—or aromatic seeds, roots, and barks, including cinnamon, mace, nutmeg, allspice, turmeric, fenugreek, ginger, anise, dillseed, coriander, caraway, cumin, cardamom, and others.

COOKING FATS AND OILS

There is much concern over the excess fat in the diet nowadays. However, a small amount of fat is necessary to maintain health. It is our experience that when cooking with natural, high-fiber foods, in a semivegetarian, dairy-free diet, a fat intake of about 1 to 2 tablespoons per day (per person) works just fine.

The oils you will find used most in this book are unrefined sesame oil and extra-virgin olive oil. These are the only two that, to our knowledge, do not go rancid. Most other oils do become rancid sooner or later, a problem that some researchers have linked with the development of cancer. In a few recipes we use cold-pressed vegetable (sunflower or soy) oil, mostly because cold-pressed oils have no strong taste; they also don't smoke when used at frying temperatures of 300° to 350°F.

For baking, we have found that, on the whole, unsalted butter (raw if available) works much better than oil. Cakes and cookies made with butter and whole-grain flours seem lighter and less cumbersome to digest. Ghee, or clarified butter, is another fat that does not go rancid and, when properly prepared, can be kept at room temperature for a long time.

❧Equipment❧

POTS AND PANS

The best cooking pots have either a stainless-steel or a porcelain interior; several brands of stainless pots feature aluminum around the outside all the way to the top rim, either sandwiched between two layers or along the outside by itself. The stable steel or porcelain is best when in contact with the food, while the aluminum exterior ensures the smooth diffusion of heat. In pots like these, food doesn't stick or burn as readily, and is easy to soak off when it does.

Glass is also a good material for cooking, especially for baking and casseroles. In fact, the only materials to avoid are aluminum and nonstick plastic surfaces, both of which are unstable and can get into the food, either by being scratched, by combining with certain foods, or by being exposed to high temperatures. Copper is an excellent heat conductor, but dangerous when in contact with food, so it needs to be lined with tin; the tin wears off easily, and therefore copper pots must be periodically retinned.

You will need saucepans with covers in several sizes, from 1 quart to 8 or 10 quarts; baking sheets, loaf pans, and pie plates, one or two each, which could be made from tin or black steel. One or two heavy cast-iron skillets are essential, as is a good wok, preferably one with a long wooden handle.

MACHINES

A good blender is essential for making cream soups and other smooth-textured dishes. A food processor helps greatly with quantity chopping or slicing chores and with mixing very thick blends, such as pastry dough or nut creams, as well as thick sauces. For grinding spices or small quantities of grain, an electric coffee grinder is excellent. And for the occasional large batch of batter, an electric mixer can be a great help. (For further information on proper use of the blender and the food processor, see page 44, in Kitchen Basics.)

KNIVES

Find a good sharp knife you're comfortable with. In the school we use an 8-inch stainless Japanese vegetable knife with a rectangular blade; we find it can do everything, so we use it for slicing, chopping, peeling, scooping up, flattening, whatever. You may also get a few small paring knives and a good sharpening rod, either in steel or porcelain. Incidentally, while stainless steel holds up well, it is also more difficult to keep it sharp; carbon steel keeps an edge better, but rusts easily and chips; molybdenum sharpens easily when stroked against unglazed pottery or a porcelain sharpening rod and doesn't rust.

SMALL ESSENTIALS

To help your cooking, you need some wooden spoons, a garlic press, peeler, grater, apple corer, melon baller; ladles, spatulas, strainers, measuring cups and spoons; a lemon juicer, and perhaps some oddities like a cherry pitter and strawberry picker. You'll need a mortar and pestle, either in marble or wood, or even better, the Japanese "suribachi" version; a rolling pin, cheesecloth, and of course dish towels and pot holders and oven mitts.

·Kitchen Basics·

Before you start cooking, there are certain prepa-
rations to be made to ready your ingredients. I have
my own favorite ways of pureeing soups, slicing
vegetables, and so on.

WASHING GRAINS

Nowadays the whole grains you buy packaged or in bulk are clean; that is, they contain no stones, twigs, or other debris. Still, grains should be washed to clean away dust or an occasional leftover bit of chaff and—in the worst scenario—to flush out bugs if there are any. To wash, place the measured amount of grain in a bowl or saucepan, cover with about three or four inches of tap water, and swirl thoroughly. If you're artistically inclined, you can swirl the water in a counterclockwise pattern, the direction water circles down the drain in the northern hemisphere (it flows clockwise south of the Equator). Some people think that will harmonize you with the cosmic energy flow. In any case, it can't hurt.

The swirling will loosen dirt, chaff, and insects if any, all of which will float to the top. Pour off all floating debris including stray grains; catch the rest in a strainer or colander just before it comes tumbling out of the pot. If the water looks very dirty, repeat the procedure.

This technique cleans more thoroughly than putting your grain in a colander and running it under the tap; using the latter system will not remove all of the dust, chaff nor, of course, the insects if any, which may create a problem for vegetarians.

COOKING GRAINS

Grains vary as to cooking times and handling. Here are the techniques for five of the grains frequently called for in this book.

Brown Rice: To cook 1 cup of brown rice, wash the rice and combine it with 1¾ cups water and a pinch of sea salt in a 2- to 3-quart sauce pan. Cover, bring to a boil, then reduce heat to very low (using a heat deflector if necessary), and continue cooking for 55–60 minutes, until tender. Allow the cooked rice to rest 10 minutes off the heat. If you have a pressure cooker, you will need only 1½ cups water to cook 1 cup of brown rice. Wash the rice, drain, and combine with water and a pinch of sea salt in the pressure cooker. Seal and place over high heat until it comes up to pressure. Reduce heat to very low (using a heat deflector if necessary) and continue cooking, maintaining pressure, for an additional 20 minutes. When the rice is done, remove from the heat and bring the pressure down under cold running water before opening cooker.

Barley: Cook as for rice.

Millet: Wash 1 cup of the grain and drain well. Dry roast in a stainless pan or cast iron skillet until fragrant and a few grains begin to pop, about 10 to 15 minutes. Add 2–2¼ cups water or stock, a pinch of sea salt, and bring to a boil. Lower the heat, cover, and simmer 40 minutes. Fluff with fork before serving. The grain should be just slightly sticky when it's done, otherwise it's too dry. For pressure cooking, reduce the water ⅓ cup, and cook at 15-pound pressure over low heat for 20 minutes. Yields 4 servings.

Kasha: Bring 2 cups of water or stock to a boil with pinch of sea salt. Pour in 1 cup of the kasha, bring back to the boil, lower flame, cover, and cook over low heat until all the water is absorbed and top grains have burst open, about 15 minutes. Yields 4 servings.

Quinoa: Wash well 1 cup of the grain, drain, then wash again, and drain well. Add 2 cups of water or stock, a pinch of sea salt, bring to a boil, cover, and simmer 15 minutes until the grains swell. They'll look like Saturn, with a little ring around them.

WASHING BEANS

Beans need more careful picking over, as they very often have stones in their midst; kidney beans, pinto beans, and, especially, chickpeas are notorious in this respect. Red lentils are, however, the worst of all; if you buy split red lentils from Middle-Eastern stores, you can spend almost as much time picking them over as cooking them. You may want to spend the extra money, as I do, and buy clean whole red lentils from the natural food store. These don't need any picking over.

To wash beans, use the same technique as for grains (page 38). Once again, red lentils require special handling: wash them very quickly and just before cooking. They absorb water immediately. If allowed to sit in a bowl or colander when wet, they tend to clump together and dry out, which makes them harder to cook.

SOAKING AND COOKING BEANS

In general, the following legumes need no pre-soaking: red lentils, green lentils, split yellow and green peas, and aduki beans. Most other beans need soaking before they are cooked in order to minimize gas-producing acids, and to facilitate the cooking.

Place the beans in a bowl or saucepan covered with about three inches of cold water. Let them stand at room temperature for about 8 hours. If circumstances prevent you from initiating the cooking after the 8 hours, place the beans with their water in the refrigerator, in order to avoid fermentation. If you still don't get around to cooking them after 24 hours, drain the beans, transfer them to a colander or a bowl, and return them to the refrigerator. This allows them to dry somewhat and prevents sprouting. If by any chance your beans do sprout, use the sprouts as vegetables in a soup.

To insure faster cooking of the beans, do not salt them until 10–15 minutes before the end of the cooking time. Handled this way most beans will cook within an hour or so. The exception may be black beans and chickpeas; occasionally these may be old, in which case they can take two or three hours to become tender. Then they need to be pressure cooked in order to soften. If you prefer not to salt your beans at all, this is fine, but remember that beans cooked without salt tend to disintegrate more easily; this is great for soups, but a decided disadvantage when you are making bean salads. Judge the timing of your salting accordingly: The more whole you'd like your beans, the earlier you salt them; at times you may need to cook them longer.

CLEANING AND PEELING VEGETABLES

Hard root vegetables such as carrots, parsnips, radishes, etc. with edible skin are best cleaned by scrubbing with a stiff bristled brush. It is not necessary to peel them. However, if they look particularly discolored you can trim or peel them with a vegetable peeler. Do the same with squashes you plan to bake.

Vegetables with edible peels that have been waxed must be peeled with a vegetable peeler: cucumbers, butternut squashes, rutabagas (yellow turnips) are commonly treated this way. Also, if you have the suspicion that your vegetables have been treated with chemical pesticides, peel them if possible.

To peel tomatoes (this is advisable so as to avoid little curled-up tomato peels in your soup or sauce) make a 1-inch slit across the skin on the bottom of each tomato, then drop in boiling water for 10–15 seconds. Remove the tomatoes from the water and allow to cool. The skin will pull open at the slit. Peel the skin from there, and it will slip right off.

To peel garlic, place the garlic clove on your chopping board, place the flat side of your knife on the garlic, angling the sharp edge downward a bit, and give the knife a good whack with your other hand. The skin will burst open and the clove can be easily removed. It is now ready to chop.

To clean leafy greens, such as spinach, kale, collards, mustard greens, and the like, trim about 1½ to 2 inches from the root end; this will separate most of the leaves. Plunge the leaves into a sinkful of cold water, and dunk and swirl them around energetically to dislodge the sand, dirt, and insects if any and allow them to settle on the bottom. The leaves will float, and can be easily retrieved and placed in a colander, basket, or strainer, leaving the dirt behind.

To clean leeks, slice them lengthwise once and then crosswise into ½-inch pieces; drop the pieces in a bowl of water and treat the same as for greens. This is the best method I have found for cleaning these very dirty vegetables.

CUTTING VEGETABLES

Pay special attention to vegetable cutting. Together with menu planning and seasoning, proper vegetable cutting helps create the artistic beauty that is so important in satisfying meals. Make sure you have a good sharp knife that you find comfortable to handle; in the school we use the Japanese vegetable knife, but a good 8-inch French utility knife works beautifully, too.

For all round vegetables (onions, turnips) first slice the vegetable in half,

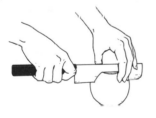 

north to south (pole to pole); place the vegetable cut side down on your work surface. The next cut is also pole to pole (stem end to root end), depending on the type of cut and size you want. For *Half Moon Slices*: adjust thickness by changing the distance between cuts.

For *Large Chunks*: make two or three pole to pole cuts, then a half-turn and two or three more cuts side to side (east to west).

Medium and *Small Dice:* cut in the same manner as for large chunks—first pole to pole, then crosswise from side to side—except reduce the distance between cuts to make smaller pieces. *Mince:* same as above, making the cuts very close together; if necessary, you may do some additional chopping.

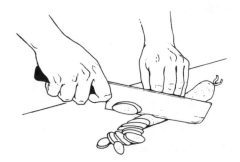

To make onion *Rings*, cut only crosswise, thinly or thickly according to choice.

For root vegetables (carrots, parsnips, burdock), the basic cut is on the diagonal. These diagonal slices can then be stacked and cut. *Half Moons:* cut the slices in half.

Julienne (match sticks): cut them lengthwise into thin strips.

Dice, all sizes: cut the root into 2-inch lengths; make two or more lengthwise cuts (you'll get slabs), then give the vegetable a quarter turn and cut two or more lengthwise cuts again (this will give you sticks); now cut crosswise, spacing evenly, and you'll get dice.

Roll Cut: used mostly with root vegetables, this means making one diagonal cut, rolling the vegetable over 90 or more degrees, and making another diagonal cut. This is an especiallly attractive cut for soups.

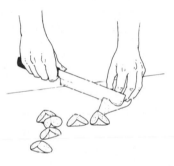

For cylindrical vegetables (yams, butternut squash, daikon), first cut crosswise into round slices, then stack the slices. *Half Moons:* cut the slices across once. *Julienne:* cut the slices into thin strips. *Dice:* cut the slices into strips, then crosswise into dice, adjusting the distance between cuts according to the size you wish. Use this system to mince ginger: slice, stack, cut into thin slivers, then across to make minuscule dice.

To chop leafy greens: stack the leaves in the same direction, cut lengthwise once or twice, then crosswise however much is necessary to get the size you want.

In a soup or stew, try to cut all vegetables to about the same size: It's most disconcerting to have a stew with large chunks of carrot and tiny bits of onion. Generally when a recipe instructs you to "chop the onion," it means medium dice, except where another cut is specified.

BLENDER AND FOOD PROCESSOR USE

A creamy texture is very pleasant for most of us Westerners, and a blender is the best appliance for obtaining it. For salad dressings, as well as vegetable or bean cream soups, then, I only use a blender; the food processor has more of a chopping action, and does not create a truly creamy consistency with vegetables.

In order to save the motor, always start the blender at its lowest speed; increase the speed only if necessary to keep the food moving around. Start by filling the container no more than two cups full; that way you will avoid a large splash when you start it. If you need to blend several batches, you can add more soup to the blender while it's running, practically up to the top; remember to put the cover on before you stop the machine, to avoid a final bubble and splash. If you're up to a high speed, reduce the speed to low before stopping.

The food processor works best for chopping, blending dough, and working with thick pastes or consistencies; I use it mostly for dips, thick nut creams, pastry dough. With the grating and shredding blades, it's a godsend for quantity vegetable cutting. Remember, by the way, that to chop garlic in the processor you need to start with a clean and dry bowl and blade, and drop in the garlic piece by piece while the processor is running: If you were to add garlic to an already full bowl of, say, tofu dip, you'd end up with very large pieces of garlic.

There are a few instances in the book where either appliance will do the job adequately; the recipe will tell you.

BUYING AND HANDLING FISH

When buying whole fish, look for bright eyes, firm flesh, red gills to indicate freshness. When buying fillets, make sure that they are moist and don't flake easily.

Really fresh fish does not smell fishy; however, fresh fish that is kept wrapped in paper and in a plastic bag may develop an odor within an hour or two; thorough rinsing and perhaps a half hour soak in water with a sprinkle of salt and a splash of vinegar will remove the odor.

When preparing fish, never place it on a wooden surface: work on a plastic cutting board, or even on a cookie sheet. Wood may absorb the juices, which then will spoil and become attractive for bacteria; you could get food poisoning from an onion chopped on a wood board that's had fish or seafood on it the day before. Always wash your hands with soap after touching fish and before you touch anything else.

THE ART OF SEASONING

There is nothing so individual in cooking as the preferred level of seasoning, and I don't mean just salt. Seasoning allows a great deal of leeway for personal taste, and the measure of a good cook is in coming up with the taste that will please a majority of the people at table. The five major tastes (sour, bitter, sweet, spicy, and salty) correspond, according to the Five Phase Theory, to the different organ systems (liver/gallbladder, heart/small intestine, stomach/spleen-pancreas, lung/large intestine, and kidney/bladder); therefore, either liking or disliking strongly a particular flavor may indicate something about the functioning of the corresponding organ. I believe that we should listen to these indications, and generally go with our tastes, as long as we pay attention to the results in our health and well-being.

Salt use is highly suspect today; however, only a few people ought to eliminate it altogether. Everyone else can have from a few grains to a modest dose of *sea salt*, free of additives and iodide. (If you're concerned about getting enough iodine for thyroid function, use some seaweed regularly, either as vegetable or as condiment.) Many of the recipes in this book call for "sea salt to taste"; that means add a bit at a time until you arrive at the taste that makes you happy. It's a good idea to add salt only to the cooking pot, and allow it to cook into the food; adding salt at the table, especially if done without tasting the food first, may be harder on the system.

The spicy taste is attractive to many; there are those, however, who can't tolerate it. Therefore, freshly ground pepper, which is always optional, should be added last, again to taste.

Herbs lend interest to many dishes. Be careful, however, not too use them to excess, as an overpowering herb taste can totally ruin a dish. Among the herbs to be most careful with are tarragon and sage. The same goes for spices: A small amount makes a dish, a large amount breaks it. When in doubt, use less first.

If you end up with seasoning problems, there are a few things you can do to repair the dish. If it is:

- too salty: add liquid (water, stock), or fat (oil, tahini, butter), or something bland (potatoes, grain, bread), or wash off the salt.
- too bitter: add fat, or something sweet (rice syrup, fruit juice), or something sour; avoid salt, which will intensify the bitter taste.
- too sweet: add liquid, fat, or salt.
- too spicy: add fat, or something sweet, or something bland, or something sour.
- too sour: add fat, salt, liquid, or something sweet.
- burnt: use only the upper unburnt part if grain, bean, or stew; if it's soup, however, discard it. Some things cannot be fixed.

❧ Appetizers ❧

Appe-teasers, they're also called—a hint of the meal to come, a bite to dull the edge of ravenous hunger, some color, flavor, crunch—ah! The nibblers could make a meal of these and feel satisfied and nourished. For the others, small portions only, please.

Aduki Bean Dip

Phase: Water

Yield: About 2 cups

The burnished red of the aduki beans give this flavorful dip great color. Serve it in a pale-colored bowl, surrounded with pita triangles and corn chips. Aduki Bean Dip is also delicious with crudités. Celery, blanched broccoli, snow peas, endive, and carrots are especially nice.

1 cup aduki beans
3 cups water
5 -inch piece kombu seaweed
2 tablespoons cold-pressed safflower oil
1/8 teaspoon cayenne pepper
1 to 1 1/2 tablespoons grated fresh ginger root
1 tablespoon umeboshi paste, or to taste
1/4 teaspoon sea salt, or to taste

1. Place the water, beans, and kombu in a 4-quart pot. Bring to a boil, reduce heat, and cook, covered, for 1 1/2 hours. (You can also pressure-cook beans for 1 hour in 2 1/2 cups water.) Remove the kombu. Drain the beans, reserving the cooking water.
2. Puree the beans in a food processor or mash to a thick paste in a bowl or mortar. Add some of the reserved cooking water to get a dip consistency.
3. Add the oil, cayenne, ginger, and umeboshi paste to the beans and mix well. Add the salt. Serve.

Black and White Aioli Dip

Major Phase: Metal
Minor Phase: Water

YIELD: About 1 cup

*P*owerful, *strongly flavored stuff! Tofu has come a long way. This dip is excellent with whole-grain crackers, or with crudités. Raw zucchini and yellow squash are good choices.*

2 to 3 cloves garlic
  ¼ cup extra-virgin olive oil
  8 ounces soft tofu
  2 tablespoons fresh lemon juice
  ½ teaspoon sea salt, or to taste
     Freshly ground black pepper to taste
  ¼ cup oil-cured black olives pitted and cut into slivers
  ⅛ cup small capers, drained

1. Peel and mince the garlic . Add the oil, tofu, lemon juice, salt, and pepper and process until very smooth. Taste and adjust the seasonings. Transfer to a bowl.
2. Stir in the olives and capers just before serving.

Curried Sesame-Peanut Dip

Major Phase: Wood
Minor Phase: Fire

YIELD: About 1⅔ cups

*T*he nutty, *spicy taste of this flavorful dip is terrific with raw cauliflowerets.*

½ cup chunky peanut butter
½ cup tahini
2 tablespoons maple syrup
5 tablespoons shoyu or tamari, or to taste
2 to 3 cloves garlic, finely minced (optional)
⅓ to ½ cup water (approximately)
10 to 12 drops hot sauce or ⅛ teaspoon cayenne pepper
1 teaspoon curry powder
1 teaspoon ground cumin seed
1 teaspoon ground coriander
1 teaspoon ground dill seed
1 tablespoon cold-pressed sunflower, peanut, or sesame oil

1. In a small bowl, mix together the peanut butter, tahini, maple syrup, shoyu, and garlic with a wooden spoon, adding the water gradually until the desired consistency is reached.
2. Measure out the spices. In a small skillet, heat the oil over high heat and sauté the spices for 5 seconds. Add to the peanut butter/tahini mixture and blend well.

Easy Guacamole

Phase: Wood

Yield: About 1¼ cups

Corn chips are the traditional accompaniment to guacamole, but it is equally good with whole-grain crackers. Blue corn chips are great, too.

2 ripe Haas avocados
1 tablespoon fresh lemon juice
⅓ teaspoon sea salt
A few drops hot sauce or chili oil, to taste

1. Mash all the ingredients together in a bowl with a fork. Adjust the seasonings and serve.

Spicy Guacamole

Major Phase: Wood
Minor Phase: Fire

YIELD: About 1 cup

2	large ripe Haas avocados
1½ to 2	tablespoons fresh lime juice
1½	medium tomatoes
3	tomatillos
½	medium onion
¼ to ½	chili pepper, to taste, depending on spiciness
1½	tablespoons fresh coriander leaves
¼ to ½	teaspoon sea salt

1. Using a fork, mash the avocados with the lime juice.
2. Finely chop the tomatoes, discarding the seeds and juices. Mince the tomatillos, onion, chili pepper, and coriander by hand, reserving about 1 teaspoon of the chopped coriander for garnish. Blend into the avocados.
3. Taste and adjust seasonings if necessary. Garnish with the remaining coriander and serve.

Avocado Mousse

Major Phase: Wood
Minor Phase: Fire

YIELD: 12 to 16 servings

Colorful, dramatic, unusual, this delightful mousse is a pleasant change from the traditional guacamole. Make sure to adjust the spiciness to your taste before you pour it into the mold. It goes well either with crackers or with corn chips, or serve it, sliced and garnished, by itself.

½ to 1	teaspoon hot sauce or Tabasco
4	ripe Haas avocados
¼	cup fresh lemon juice
1	bar agar-agar or 3 tablespoons (packed) agar flakes
1	sweet red pepper
1½	cups water
1	teaspoon sea salt
1½	tablespoons balsamic or brown rice vinegar
1	teaspoon umeboshi vinegar

1. Cut the avocados into chunks (you should have about 4 cups). Combine with the lemon juice and set aside. Rinse the agar bar under hot water to soften.
2. Dice the red pepper. Boil the water and blanch the red pepper in it for 3 minutes. Drain, reserving the cooking water. Remeasure the water so that you have 2 cups, heat to boiling, and shred in the softened agar or sprinkle in the agar flakes; simmer until dissolved, about 3–4 minutes. Set aside.
3. In a food processor, process the avocado chunks with the salt, vinegars, hot sauce, and the lemon juice the chunks were sitting in. Add the agar and continue processing until smooth.
4. Oil a 6-cup ring mold and put in a ring of red pepper pieces around the bottom. Fold the remaining red pepper pieces into the avocado puree. Pour the mixture into the mold. Chill for 2 hours in the freezer or 4 hours in the refrigerator.
5. To unmold, run a knife around the edges of the mold, then set it in a pan of hot water for 1 minute, to loosen. (Hot water expands the mold.) Place a serving

plate on top of the mold and invert. You may need to give it a shake or two. Serve.

❧ · ❧

Broccoli Aspic with Red Pepper

Major Phase: Wood
Minor Phase: Fire

YIELD: 8 to 10 servings

Here is a light and refreshing summer appetizer that lets you incorporate sea vegetables into your diet in an unobtrusive way.

    2 bars agar-agar or 5 tablespoons agar flakes
    1 quart water or Light Vegetable Stock (page 72)
1 to 1½ tablespoons shoyu (or tamari), or to taste
    1 teaspoon grated fresh ginger root
    1 large bunch (1⅓–1½ pounds) broccoli
    1 sweet red pepper, diced
       Parsley and radishes for garnish

1. Rinse the agar bars under cold water until soft. In a 2-quart saucepan, combine the agar bars or flakes, the water or stock, shoyu, and ginger. Bring to a boil, reduce heat, and simmer for a few minutes, or until the agar is thoroughly dissolved. Taste and correct the seasoning.
2. Pour the mixture into a mold or bowl with a 6-cup capacity and place in the refrigerator for 15 to 20 minutes, or until the agar begins to thicken.
3. Separate the broccoli into florets. You should have 2 cups. Steam florets briefly, just until they turn green in color. Steam the red pepper for 5 minutes. Using your finger or a chopstick, push the broccoli into the thickening aspic in a pleasing pattern; intersperse with the red pepper. Chill until well set, about 3 to 4 hours.
4. To unmold, run a knife around the edges and place the mold briefly in a pan

of hot water to loosen. Invert the mold onto a serving plate and tap it lightly with a knife. The mousse should slip out easily. Decorate with sprigs of parsley and cut radishes and serve.

Vegetable Pâté

Major Phase: Wood
Minor Phase: Water

YIELD: 10 to 12 servings

This beautiful dish may be served either as an appetizer or as a side dish. Try it with a garnish of feathered scallions. For best results, use a food processor.

2	bunches broccoli (about 2 pounds)
1 to 2	teaspoons sea salt, to taste
1	pound carrots, scrubbed and trimmed
2	pounds mushrooms, including stems
⅔	cup whole shallots
2	tablespoons unsalted butter or extra-virgin olive oil
2	tablespoons mirin (sweet rice wine) or dry sherry
3	bars agar-agar or ½ cup agar flakes
½	pound firm tofu
1	teaspoon fresh lemon juice
2	tablespoons chopped fresh dill, plus additional dill for garnish

1. Trim ends of broccoli stalks; peel. Cut the stalks into 1-inch pieces and separate the florets. Slice the carrots.
2. Bring 2 quarts water to a boil, add 1 teaspoon of the salt, and cook the broccoli at a slow boil for 8 to 10 minutes. Remove with a slotted spoon and set aside. Return the water to a boil, add the carrots, and cook for 20 minutes. Drain, reserving 1½ cups of the cooking liquid.
3. Wipe the mushrooms with a damp paper towel and chop the mushrooms finely in a food processor. Place them in a cloth dish towel and squeeze to remove excess liquid; set aside. Peel and mince the shallots; set aside.

4. In a heavy 2-quart saucepan heat the butter or olive oil and sauté the shallots over medium heat until transparent, about 2 to 3 minutes. Remove half the shallots and reserve. Add the mushrooms to the saucepan and sauté on medium-high heat to remove all excess moisture, about 4–5 minutes. Add the mirin and stir for a few moments. Remove from the heat.

5. Soften the agar bars under cold running water. In a 2-quart saucepan, simmer in the reserved vegetable cooking liquid until dissolved, about 3 minutes. Keep warm on the stove, covered.

6. Puree the cooked broccoli in a food processor. You should have about 2 cups. Cut the tofu into 3 equal pieces. Add the reserved shallots, 1 piece of the tofu, ½ cup of the dissolved agar, sea salt to taste, and the lemon juice. Process again briefly to taste and adjust the seasonings. Spread this mixture in the bottom of a well-oiled 6-cup pâté mold or 9-inch × 5-inch loaf pan.

7. In a food processor, combine the sautéed mushrooms with a piece of the remaining tofu and ½ cup of the dissolved agar; puree. Taste and adjust the seasonings. Spread this mixture over the broccoli in the mold, pressing down well.

8. Puree the cooked carrots in a food processor. You should have about 2 cups. Add the remaining tofu and agar and blend. Stir in the chopped dill. Taste and adjust the seasonings. Spread this mixture over the mushrooms, pressing down well.

9. Chill the pâté until well set, about 3 hours. Unmold onto a platter, garnish with dill sprigs, and serve.

❧ · ☙

Baked Garlic on Pita Toasts

Major Phase: Metal
Minor Phase: Wood

YIELD: 4 to 6 servings

If you have never tried baked garlic, you are in for a real treat. This is participatory eating, with each guest squeezing the softened, mild garlic cloves out of their skins onto the pita toasts. Sometimes I put tiny bowls of sea salt and extra-virgin olive oil nearby, for a sprinkle and a drop. You can also squeeze all the garlic cloves into a bowl yourself, season to taste, and spread onto crackers or toast, which you then heat before serving.

> 1 head garlic
> Extra-virgin olive oil to taste
> 3 whole wheat pita breads
> Sea salt to taste

1. Preheat the oven to 400°F.
2. Slice off the top of the garlic head evenly, cutting off a thin slice of the cloves themselves. Leave the root end intact. Do not peel. Place the garlic head in a baking pan and drizzle about ½ tablespoon of the oil over it. Bake for 30 minutes. After approximately 15 minutes, drizzle about another ½ tablespoon oil over the garlic to keep it moist. (You should use a total of about 1 tablespoon or less.)
3. To prepare the pita toasts, split each pita into 2 disks, then stack the disks on top of each other and cut into quarters. Spread them on a baking sheet and place in the oven with the garlic. Bake for 4 minutes, or until crisp.
4. Serve the toasts and garlic together. Season with salt if desired and a few drops of oil.

Daikon Radish Canapé

Major Phase: Metal
Minor Phase: Water

YIELD: About 36 canapés

These have become standard fare in almost every party we do at the school. The secret of their appeal is that the sharp taste of the raw daikon provides a tangy contrast to the salty, rich tahini topping. While either flavor alone may be too strong, the two together are a perfect blend. Black olive paste, available in Italian delis, also makes a nice topping.

         5 tablespoons tahini
         1 tablespoon miso, preferably light red barley or brown rice
         2 tablespoons water
         1 large daikon radish, about 8 to 10 inches long
   15 to 20 Kalamata olives, pitted and halved

1. In a small bowl, mix the tahini, miso, and water together until smooth.
2. Scrub the daikon and slice it into ¼-inch circles. You should have 30 to 40 slices.
3. Place a small amount (about ½ tsp) of the tahini/miso mixture in the middle of each daikon circle and place an olive half on top. Arrange the circles on a serving plate and serve.

Celery Stuffed
with Green Bean and Walnut Pâté

Major Phase: Wood
Minor Phase: Metal

YIELD: 4 to 6 servings

A tasty dairy-free variation on conventional cheese-stuffed vegetables, these may be made up to 3 hours in advance. Once again, make sure to adjust the spiciness to your taste.

         ¼ pound green beans
         1 small onion
         1 tablespoon unrefined sesame oil
         ¼ teaspoon sea salt, or to taste
         ½ cup walnuts
         ½ tablespoon white miso or 1 teaspoon lemon juice
            Freshly ground black pepper to taste
         6 stalks celery
            Carrot or red pepper matchsticks for garnish
            Capers for garnish

1. Wash the green beans and snap off the tips. In a medium saucepan over low heat, steam the green beans, covered, in ½ inch of water until tender, about 10 to 12 minutes. Drain. Set aside.
2. Meanwhile, slice the onion thinly. You should have about ½ cup. Heat the oil in a skillet over medium heat. Add the onions and sauté for 3 minutes. Add the sea salt, reduce heat, and cook, covered, for 5 to 7 minutes, or until soft. Uncover, raise the heat to high, and cook for about 10 to 15 minutes, or until well browned, stirring often.
3. Grind the walnuts in a food processor. Add the cooked green beans and onions and process until thoroughly blended. Add the miso or lemon juice and the pepper and process for a few seconds longer, or until blended. Taste and adjust seasoning. Transfer to a bowl.
4. Cut the celery ribs into 2-inch pieces and fill each piece with the pâté. Garnish with a carrot or red pepper matchstick and a caper and serve.

Mushrooms Stuffed with Garlic and Rosemary

Major Phase: Water
Minor Phase: Wood

Yield: 24 stuffed mushrooms

These are a standard in my "French Vegetarian" class. I make them last and serve them first, straight out of the oven. They may be filled 2 or 3 hours in advance and baked just before serving.

24 medium-large mushrooms suitable for stuffing
 3 tablespoons extra-virgin olive oil
 3 large cloves garlic
⅛ teaspoon sea salt
⅓ teaspoon powdered rosemary
½ cup whole wheat bread crumbs
½ cup parsley sprigs (loosely packed)

1. Preheat the oven to 375°F.
2. Wipe the mushrooms with a damp paper towel and separate the stems from the caps. Place the caps underside up on a cookie sheet, drop a couple of drops of the oil into each one, and bake for 5 minutes. They will shrink a bit and release some of their moisture; set aside.
3. Peel and finely chop the garlic. Mince the mushroom stems by hand or in a food processor.
4. Heat the remaining oil in an 8–9-inch skillet. Add the garlic, then the mushroom stems; sprinkle on the salt and the rosemary. Cook over medium heat, stirring until the mushrooms shrink and release their liquid, about 4 to 5 minutes. Add the bread crumbs and stir until they soak up all the mushroom liquid. Remove from heat.
5. Chop the parsley. Mix with the mushroom stem mixture. Using 2 teaspoons, work quickly and fill all the mushroom caps: scoop up some filling with one spoon, then tap it down and scrape into the mushroom hollow with the other. Pat down to pack.
6. Just before serving bake for 7 to 8 minutes, or until warm. Serve.

Stuffed Grape Leaves

Major Phase: Metal
Minor Phase: Wood

YIELD: 8 to 10 as an appetizer
4 to 5 as a main dish

A Middle Eastern staple, stuffed grape leaves are always popular. This version uses brown rice instead of the traditional white. Grape leaves, packed in jars, are available in Greek and Middle Eastern food markets.

4	medium shallots
½	pound mushrooms
1	tablespoon extra-virgin olive oil
	Sea salt to taste
3	tablespoons chopped parsley
1	teaspoon dried oregano
	Freshly ground black pepper to taste
⅔	cup cooked brown rice (page 38)
16 to 20	grape leaves
1	cup mirin (sweet rice wine) or dry sherry
½	cup water or Light Vegetable Stock (page 72)
1	tablespoon fresh lemon juice

1. Peel and mince the shallots. Wipe the mushrooms with a damp paper towel and chop them in a food processor.
2. Heat the oil in a large skillet, add the shallots, and sauté for a few minutes over medium-high heat. Add the mushrooms and salt and sauté until all the liquid the mushrooms release has evaporated, about 4 to 5 minutes. Stir in the parsley, oregano, and pepper. Remove from the heat and stir in the rice, mixing well.

3. Preheat the oven to 375°F. Oil a 9-inch × 14-inch shallow baking pan.

4. Place one grape leaf on your work surface, shiny side down. Place a heaping tablespoon of the filling crosswise along the lower half of the leaf,

fold up the bottom leaf to cover the filling,

then fold each side toward the center and roll from the bottom up. Place seam side down in the pan. Repeat with the remaining leaves.

5. In a small bowl or 2-cup measuring cup, mix the mirin or sherry, water or stock, lemon juice, and ¼ teaspoon of the salt. Pour over the stuffed leaves, making sure the top of each one gets moistened. The liquid should come up two-thirds the level of the leaves. Cover the pan with aluminum foil. Bake for 25 minutes. Serve hot or cold.

Vegetarian Norimaki

Major Phase: Metal
Minor Phase: Water

Yield: 24 pieces

Also known as sushi. These hold up well for 24 hours, and are terrific to take on a picnic. Six or eight pieces make a nice light entrée. In traditional sushi making, the freshly cooked white rice is sprinkled with a mixture of rice vinegar, sugar, and salt. This recipe and the one for Norimaki with Fish that follows use brown rice and either sauerkraut or brown-rice vinegar and mirin, achieving a similar but more balanced effect.

    4 scallions, each about 8 inches long
    1 carrot
    ½ cup sauerkraut
    4 sheets fine-quality pretoasted sushi nori*
    3 cups pressure-cooked short-grain brown rice** (page 38)
    4 teaspoons umeboshi paste

1. Wash and trim the scallions; set aside.
2. Peel the carrot and cut into long ¼-inch thick strips. Steam in a covered saucepan with an inch or so of water over medium heat until just tender, about 5 minutes. Drain, rinse with cold water, and set aside.
3. Rinse the sauerkraut, if you wish, to remove excess salt and press well in a colander until quite dry.
4. To assemble the norimaki rolls, have handy a small bowl of water and a sushi mat. The mat allows you to make the rolls neatly and firmly, as the nori itself

---

* Obtainable in Japanese food stores or natural-foods stores.
** Brown rice should be sticky for norimaki. If you aren't making it in a pressure cooker, knead it for about 5 minutes.

is very fragile. (If you have no sushi mat, use a strong paper towel that has been moistened and squeezed dry.) Place the mat or towel on a clean, dry surface and place the nori, shiny side down on top.

Place two ice-cream scoops of rice, or about ⅔ cup, on the sheet of nori. Dampen your fingers lightly in the water and press the rice out evenly (as illustrated in figure 1), making a slight groove or depression across the middle of the rice, and leaving about a 2-inch strip of the nori uncovered.

5. Place the assembled sheet of nori on the sushi mat with the extra margin of nori furthest away from you. Spread the teaspoon of umeboshi paste across the rice with your finger and then add a bit of sauerkraut, a carrot strip, and a scallion leaf neatly in a row (figure 2).

Pick up the edges of the mat and nori together and begin to roll, tucking firmly into the center while bending the mat slightly up, taking care not to catch it in the roll (figure 3). If you're using a paper towel, follow the same procedure; make sure, after rolling it up, to squeeze the middle of the cigarlike roll to avoid a bulge and make it even.

7. Complete the roll, holding it tightly in the mat a moment to help seal the edges. The moisture from the filling will enable the nori to stick together (figure 4). You may leave this roll seam-side down for a few minutes before cutting while you assemble the rest.

8. Using a wet sharp knife, cut each roll into six slices with a back and forth sawing motion; dip the blade occasionally into the water. Serve with Dipping Sauce (see below) and additional wasabi paste if desired. Best if served immediately, but it will hold well for several hours.

Norimaki with Fish

Major Phase: Metal
Minor Phase: Water

Yield: 24 pieces

Make sure you buy the freshest fish available from a fishmonger you trust, and use it the same day you buy it. Steam or poach any leftovers and make fish salad.

    2   tablespoons brown rice vinegar
    2   tablespoons mirin (sweet rice wine)
    3   cups hot cooked short-grain brown rice (page 38)
    ½   pound or less raw fish, filleted (use only seasonal fresh fish:
        porgy, tuna, striped bass, fluke, mackerel, sea bass)
    4   scallions, each about 8 inches long
    1   tablespoon wasabi powder (Japanese green horseradish)*
    4   sheets fine-quality pretoasted sushi nori*

Dipping Sauce

    ⅓   cup shoyu or tamari
    ¼   cup mirin
    1   -inch piece fresh ginger root

1. Combine the vinegar and the mirin and stir quickly into the hot rice. Cool the rice to room temperature before using.
2. Cut the fish into long, thin strips; set aside on a plate in the refrigerator. Wash the cutting board and knife.
3. Wash and trim the scallions.
4. Mix the wasabi powder with just enough water (½ teaspoon or so) to make a thick paste.
5. *To make the dipping sauce:* Combine the shoyu and mirin in a small, attractive

---

* Obtainable in Japanese food stores or natural-foods stores.

serving bowl. Grate the ginger root, put it into a garlic press, and squeeze the juice into the sauce. Discard the pulp.

6. *To prepare the rolls:* Follow the procedure on page 62, spreading the wasabi on the cooked rice instead of the umeboshi paste. Arrange the scallion and strips of fish across the rice, then roll up. Cut each roll into six or eight pieces. Serve with Dipping Sauce and additional wasabi paste on the side.

Tofu and Spinach Turnovers (Spanakopitas)

Major Phase: Wood
Minor Phase: Metal

YIELD: 60 to 75 pieces

In our version of these classic Greek turnovers, we substitute tofu for the traditional feta cheese. You won't miss it! But we have tried using oil instead of butter, and it just doesn't work. Butter is still better for baking; it creates good texture and feels easier on the stomach.

   1 pound fresh spinach
   1 pound soft tofu
  ½ bunch parsley, chopped
   1 tablespoon extra-virgin olive oil
   1 onion, finely chopped
   1 teaspoon sea salt, or to taste
      Freshly ground pepper to taste
  ½ pound phyllo dough (strudel leaves),
      removed from refrigerator 2 to 3 hours before using
  ½ pound (2 sticks) unsalted butter

1. Preheat the oven to 425°F.
2. Wash the spinach in several changes of water. Place in a pot with only the water

that clings to the leaves and cook, covered, over medium heat for 2 to 3 minutes; drain. When cool enough to handle, chop fine.

3. In a large bowl, mash the tofu, then add the chopped parsley; set aside.

4. In a medium frying pan, heat the oil and sauté the onion until soft. Add the salt, pepper, and cooked spinach and cook for 2 to 3 minutes to dry the spinach. Add the spinach mixture to the tofu mixture. Stir well to blend. Taste and adjust the seasonings; set aside.

5. Melt the butter over low heat. Open the phyllo dough and unroll carefully. Cut lengthwise into 3 equal sections. Keep covered with a very slightly damp towel.

6. Remove 1 sheet of phyllo. Place on a flat surface. Working quickly, brush melted butter over the entire sheet, then fold the long sides toward the middle, making a 2-inch-wide strip. Brush with butter again.

7. Place 1 tablespoon of the tofu-spinach mixture in the bottom right-hand corner of the strip and fold it over into a triangle shape. Continue folding until all the pastry is used up. Butter the outside and lay on a cookie sheet. Repeat with the remaining filling.

8. Bake for 20 minutes, or until golden brown. Serve warm.

❦ • ❧

Bernie's Gravlax

Phase: Earth

Yield: 20 to 25 servings

*E*asy to make and remarkably delicious, this great party dish is a hit whenever it is served. The main thing is to remember to make it three days in advance. Serve it with whole-grain crackers or dark rye bread. Use leftovers for brunch the morning after the party.

2 tablespoons coarse sea salt or kosher salt
1 tablespoon maple sugar crystals
1½ tablespoons freshly ground white pepper
2½ tablespoons chopped fresh dill
One 2- to 2½ -pound piece of fresh whole salmon, about 6 to 8 inches long, cut from the center of the fish, boned and scaled, skin *not* removed

1. In a small bowl, blend the seasoning ingredients together thoroughly.
2. Wipe the outside of the salmon on both sides, using a damp cloth or paper towel; do not wash it. Open the two halves of the fish and place it flesh side up on a platter or cookie sheet; spread the seasoning mixture on each half of the salmon, making sure to cover the entire fish. If you have any leftover sprigs of fresh dill, make a bed of them on one side.
3. Press the two sides of the salmon together again. Wrap snugly in plastic wrap and place in a 9-inch × 14-inch baking dish. Put a 12-inch chopping board on top of the fish, then a weight—a brick is ideal—and refrigerate for at least two days, preferably three.
4. To serve, wipe the seasoning mixture off the fish; discard the dill bed. Cut into very thin diagonal slices, leaving them on the skin if you wish, for serving.

❧ • ❧

Spiced Pecans

Phase: Earth

YIELD: 2 cups

2 tablespoons unsalted butter
¼ teaspoon paprika
¼ teaspoon five-spice powder* or cinnamon

---

* Obtainable in Chinese or natural-foods stores.

¼ teaspoon Szechuan peppercorns or coriander seeds, ground
⅛ teaspoon freshly ground white pepper
¼ teaspoon sea salt
2 cups pecans

1. Preheat the oven to 350°F.
2. In a small saucepan, melt the butter. Stir in the spices and salt, and remove from the heat.
3. Place the nuts in a shallow baking pan and drizzle the butter mixture over them; toss until well coated.
4. Bake in the preheated oven for 15 minutes. Allow to cool before serving.

Sesame–Whole Wheat Wafers

Major Phase: Wood
Minor Phase: Fire

YIELD: 1 dozen crackers

These paper-thin wafers are made quickly in a toaster oven, but they need careful watching to avoid burning. Stored in an airtight container, these will stay fresh for several days.

1 clove garlic
2 cups whole wheat bread flour
½ teaspoon sea salt
2 tablespoons sesame seeds
2 tablespoons extra-virgin olive oil
  or unrefined sesame oil
½ cup water

1. Peel and mince the garlic.
2. In a 3-quart bowl, combine the flour, salt, garlic, and sesame seeds. Add the oil and rub it into the flour mixture with your fingers. Quickly stir in the water,

still using your hands. Add a bit more water if the dough is too crumbly to hold together. Place the dough on your work surface and knead until smooth.

3. Divide the dough into 12 balls of equal size. Roll each ball out evenly with a rolling pin until it is paper thin; they will each be 3 to 4 inches in diameter.

4. Preheat a toaster oven to 400°F.

5. Place the crackers on the rack in the toaster oven; or bake on an oiled cookie sheet in the regular oven. Bake just until the crackers are lightly browned and a bit puffy; then remove them from the oven, flip, and toast the other side. Watch carefully, as they will be done in only minutes.

6. Cool to room temperature before serving.

❧Soups❧

There are soup people, as opposed to salad people or dessert people, for example. I count myself among the former. Whenever I'm in doubt about what to cook, I make soup. When I eat out, it's the first thing I look for on the menu. A meal without soup just doesn't seem complete. Clear soups balance a hearty meal, thick soups can be a meal in themselves with only a light accompaniment. And then, of course, there are those "hodgepodge" soups you create by mixing various leftovers and seasoning them creatively, maybe pureeing them in a blender. Here is a selection of my favorites for your dinner table.

Light Vegetable Stock

Phase: Wood

Here is a good, all-purpose stock. It contains no salt or oil, and is excellent for use in recipes that contain quantities of either. You'll find it used frequently throughout this book. It keeps well in the refrigerator if brought to a boil every several days. Freeze for longer storage.

Use the following scraps and peelings:
Onion peels (not too many)
Carrot peelings
Celery trimmings—strings, leaves
Ends of green beans
Corn cobs (kernals removed)
Parsley stems
Broccoli stalks
Pea pods

Bouquet garni:
½ teaspoon dried thyme
½ teaspoon dried marjoram
1 bay leaf
8 peppercorns
One 5- to 6-inch piece kombu seaweed

1. Place the vegetables and bouquet garni in a large stock pot. Add water four times the volume of the vegetables.
2. Simmer for 35 to 40 minutes.
3. Strain. Discard vegetable scraps.

❦ • ❧

Rich Vegetable Stock (Salt-Free)

Phase: Wood

Yield: 12 cups

Here is a slightly richer stock, containing a small amount of oil. Use it whenever you want a greater depth of flavor. It is an especially good base for sauces. You can use leftover stock vegetables the next day; just mash them with a little olive oil or butter, some sea salt and pepper, and chopped parsley.

> 1/4 pound dried white beans, soaked
> 1/4 cup oil (olive oil is a good choice
>   because it will harden in the refrigerator
>   and can be easily removed
>   to degrease the stock)
> 5 large carrots, sliced
> 2 large onions, sliced
> 2 large leeks, sliced
> 1/4 pound mushrooms, preferably not too fresh, sliced
> 2 large cloves garlic, sliced
> 4 quarts water
>
> *Bouquet garni:*
> 6 sprigs parsley
> 2 teaspoons chopped fresh thyme
> 1/2 teaspoon crushed dried sage
> 1 large bay leaf
> 12 black peppercorns
> 12 allspice berries
>
> 1 tablespoon brown rice vinegar
> 1/2 cup white wine, mirin, or vermouth (optional)

1. Drain the beans and tie them into a large square of cheesecloth to make them easier to retrieve later. Set aside.
2. In a large soup pot, heat the oil and sauté the vegetables over medium heat until wilted. Do not let them brown.

3. Add the water, beans, and the bouquet garni. Bring to a boil, reduce heat, and simmer, partially covered, for 2 hours. At the end of this time the liquid should have reduced slightly. Remove the beans and add the vinegar and wine and simmer for another 30 minutes.
4. Allow the stock to cool, remove the tied herbs, and strain the stock through a sieve lined with cheesecloth.
5. If the stock is not to be used immediately, store it in glass bottles in the refrigerator. When it is well chilled, skim the oil off the top if you wish. The stock will keep in the refrigerator for 2 to 3 weeks if it is brought back to a boil every few days, or for up to 3 months in the freezer.

❧ • ☙

Bean-of-the-Orient Miso Soup

Phase: Water

YIELD: 8 to 10 servings

Here is an especially rich and flavorful miso soup, a great light beginning for a meal. It will also steady your stomach if you feel out of sorts.

½	pound fresh shiitake mushrooms
2	medium onions
2 to 3	cloves garlic
2	tablespoons unrefined sesame oil
10	cups water
8 to 10	-inch strip kombu seaweed
2	tablespoons bonita fish flakes*
1½	tablespoons vegetable seasoning salt
2	tablespoons unpasteurized red barley miso, diluted in 3 tablespoons water
½	cup finely slivered scallions

---

* Obtainable in Japanese or natural-foods stores.

1. Chop onions and garlic. Wipe the mushrooms with a damp paper towel. Cut off and discard the stems; slice the caps thinly.
2. In a 6-quart soup pot, sauté the onions and garlic in the oil for 5 minutes, or until the onions are softened but not browned. Add the mushrooms and sauté for another 2 minutes.
3. Place the water and the kombu in another pot and bring to a boil. Add the bonita flakes and let them sink to the bottom of the pan. Strain immediately into the pot containing the onions and mushrooms and simmer for 5 minutes. Season with the salt and the miso. Simmer one minute longer. Serve hot, garnished with the scallions.

Clear Broth with Garlic and Escarole

Major Phase: Fire
Minor Phases: Metal and Water

YIELD: 4 to 6 servings

What follows are three variations on consommé, or clear soup. They are excellent to start any meal that features a hearty entrée, or with any dish with a higher-than-usual fat content.

        6 cups Light Vegetable Stock (page 72)
3 to 4 -inch piece kombu seaweed
        2 large cloves garlic
        1 tablespoon unrefined sesame oil
      ½ bunch escarole, washed in two changes of water
   1¼ teaspoons sea salt
        Freshly ground white pepper to taste
        1 teaspoon toasted sesame oil

1. In a 4- to 6-quart stock pot, bring the stock and kombu to a boil, reduce heat, and simmer for 10 minutes.

2. While the kombu is simmering, chop the garlic finely. In a small skillet, sauté the garlic in the unrefined sesame oil for 30 seconds. Swirl a ladleful of stock into the skillet to mix it with the garlic and oil, then return it to stockpot. Remove the kombu, chop it finely, and return it to the soup.

3. Wash the escarole, chop it coarsely, and add it to the soup, along with the salt, pepper, and toasted sesame oil. Simmer for 5 minutes longer, or until the escarole is tender. Serve hot.

Clear Soup
with Shiitake and Mustard Greens

Major Phase: Water
Minor Phase: Fire

YIELD: 6 servings

6 cups Rich Vegetable Stock (page 73)
4 -inch piece kombu seaweed
¼ cup dried shiitake mushrooms
2 cloves garlic
2 ounces large fresh shiitake mushrooms
1 pound mustard greens
1 tablespoon extra-virgin olive oil
Sea salt to taste
1 tablespoon white miso
1 tablespoon fresh lemon juice
Freshly ground white pepper to taste

1. In a 4- to 6-quart stockpot, simmer the stock with the kombu and dried mushrooms for 10 minutes.

2. In the meantime, chop the garlic. Wash, trim and chop the mustard greens.

3. Remove the kombu and mushrooms from the stock. Chop the kombu very

finely; set aside. Cut off and discard the stems of both the dried and fresh mushrooms. Slice the caps lengthwise.

4. In a skillet, heat the oil, add the garlic and sauté for 10 seconds. Add the fresh and dried shiitake, stir, and sprinkle on 1/4 teaspoon of the salt. Sauté until the fresh mushrooms wilt, about 4 to 5 minutes.

5. Add the mushrooms to the stockpot. Swirl a ladleful of stock around the skillet to pick up all the flavors, then return to the stockpot. Add the chopped greens, the chopped kombu, and more sea salt to taste if needed. Simmer, uncovered, for 10 to 15 minutes.

6. Adjust the seasoning. Dissolve the miso in the lemon juice and a ladleful of the soup stock and return to the soup. Just before serving, add a few grindings of white pepper.

❦ • ❧

Shoyu Consommé with Enoki Mushrooms

Major Phase: Water
Minor Phases: Wood and Metal

YIELD: 6 to 8 servings

1 large or 2 small carrots
1/2 bunch enoki mushrooms
2 to 3 whole scallions
6 cups water
4-inch piece kombu seaweed
2 teaspoons bonita fish flakes (optional)*
1/2 teaspoon sea salt
1 tablespoon shoyu or tamari
1/2 cup watercress leaves (loosely packed)

---

* Obtainable in Japanese or natural-foods stores.

1. Julienne the carrot. Cut off the root part of the enoki. Trim and slice the scallions. Reserve each vegetable separately.
2. In a 3- to 4-quart saucepan, bring the water and kombu to a boil, reduce heat, and simmer for 2 to 3 minutes. If you are using them, add the fish flakes, letting them sink to the bottom of the pan. Strain the broth and season with the salt and shoyu.
3. Add the carrots to the broth and simmer for 5 minutes. Remove from the heat. Add the mushrooms and watercress to the hot broth just before serving. (The heat from the broth is enough to cook these delicate vegetables.)
4. Garnish each serving with 1 tablespoon of the scallions. Serve hot.

Collard-Miso Soup

Major Phase: Fire
Minor Phase: Metal

YIELD: 4 to 6 servings

    1   medium onion
    ½   pound collards
    ½   head garlic (about 6 to 8 cloves)
    1   tablespoon extra-virgin olive oil
    5   cups water or Light Vegetable Stock (page 72)
    ½   teaspoon sea salt, or to taste
  1½   tablespoons white miso, diluted in ¼ cup water

1. Slice the onion thinly lengthwise into crescents; set aside. Remove the stems from the collards and chop the leaves into bite-size pieces; set aside. Mince the garlic; set aside.
2. In a 3- to 4-quart pot, sauté the onion in the oil over medium heat for 5 to 6 minutes, or until softened, then add half of the minced garlic. Sauté 3 to 4 minutes longer.
3. Add the water or stock, the salt, and the collards. Bring to a boil, reduce heat, and simmer, covered, for 20 minutes. Add the rest of the garlic and the diluted

miso and simmer for 1 minute more. Taste and correct the seasoning. Serve immediately.

Gazpacho

Major Phase: Fire
Minor Phase: Wood

Yield: 10 to 12 servings

This refreshing cold soup is excellent on a hot summer day. Try it with Lissa's Rolled Flounder Fillets (page 226), corn on the cob, and perhaps Peach Pie (page 253), for dessert.

8 to 10	ripe tomatoes
1 to 2	teaspoons sea salt, for salting tomatoes
3	medium cucumbers
3	small green bell peppers
6	whole scallions
3 to 6	cloves garlic
3	slices sourdough whole wheat bread
¾	cup parsley (chopped)
3	tablespoons fresh basil
2¼ to 3	cups cold water
½	cup extra-virgin olive oil
⅓	cup fresh lime juice
¼ to ⅓	cup umeboshi vinegar
	Freshly ground black pepper (optional)

1. Cut the tomatoes in half crosswise, sprinkle the cut sides generously with the salt. Let sit for 30 minutes, salted side down.
2. Meanwhile, peel and seed the cucumbers and cut into 1-inch pieces. Place in a medium bowl.
3. Cut the green peppers in half and remove the white seeds. Chop into 1-inch pieces. Place in a separate bowl.

4. Trim the scallions and chop them into pieces about ½- inch long; set aside.

5. Peel the garlic cloves and put them through a press or mince very finely; add to the peppers.

6. Remove the crust from the bread and cut each slice into cubes; add.

7. Squeeze the seeds from the tomatoes and cut into quarters; add.

8. Put the tomatoes, half the cucumbers, bread, the green peppers, garlic, and ½ cup of the parsley into a blender, 2 to 3 cups at a time, adding a little water to each batch. Blend at medium speed until the vegetables and bread are pureed. Pour the puree into large bowl and add the oil, lime juice, umeboshi vinegar, and pepper. Whisk vigorously until well blended. Taste, and adjust the seasonings if needed. If the soup is too thick, thin with a little more cold water.

9. Place the remaining cucumber, parsley, and all the scallions in separate bowls to be used as garnishes. Chill the soup for several hours before serving. Pass the garnishes around the table as the soup is served.

Hungarian Asparagus Soup

Phase: Fire

Yield: 6 to 8 servings

Thickening soup with a roux—flour briefly toasted in butter or oil—is a classic technique of European cooking. In this Hungarian-inspired recipe, I've substituted whole wheat flour for the original white. You'll find it gives body and a more robust, nutty flavor to the soup.

1 medium turnip
1 medium carrot
1 medium onion
1 pound fresh, firm asparagus (about 18 to 20 stalks)
1 bay leaf
½ teaspoon dried marjoram
6 cups water or stock
1 tablespoon vegetable seasoning salt

1½ tablespoons unsalted butter or extra-virgin olive oil
2 tablespoons whole wheat flour
Sea salt to taste
Freshly ground white pepper

1. Wash and cut the turnip and carrot into large pieces. Chop the onion. Wash the asparagus, cut off the tender tips, and reserve; cut the stems into several pieces.
2. In a large stockpot, place the chopped turnip, carrot, onion, bay leaf, marjoram, water or stock, and vegetable seasoning salt. Bring to a boil, lower the heat, cover, and simmer for 40 minutes, or until the vegetables are quite tender.
3. Puree the soup in batches in a blender until creamy; strain to remove asparagus strings, if any; and return to the pot.
4. In a small skillet, heat the butter or oil, add the flour, and cook, stirring continuously, for 4 to 5 minutes, or until the mixture gives off a nutty fragrance. Ladle a bit of soup into the skillet, and stir it around until the roux has been incorporated. Pour the mixture back into the soup, scraping up the last bits with a rubber spatula. Simmer the soup for 10 minutes longer.
5. Taste, and adjust the seasonings. Add the asparagus tips, and simmer for 3 to 4 minutes more. Serve immediately, making sure each serving contains several of the asparagus tips.

Borscht with Beans and Greens

Major Phase: Water
Minor Phase: Metal

YIELD: 6 to 8 servings

This hearty soup, our version of the old Russian staple, will warm everyone up on a cold winter night.

Stock

½ cup dried navy beans, soaked
2 yellow onions
2 stalks celery, with leaves
1 large carrot
1 small parsnip
1 small white turnip
1 bay leaf
5 cups water

Soup

1 large tomato
1 small onion
1 tablespoon extra-virgin olive oil
1 medium carrot
⅛ small head cabbage (about 1 cup shredded)
4 medium beets with greens
2 tablespoons mirin (sweet rice wine) or dry sherry
1 teaspoon sea salt
Freshly ground black pepper to taste
1 to 2 tablespoons fresh lemon juice
6 tablespoons chopped fresh dill for garnish

1. *To make the stock:* Drain the beans, cover with fresh water, and bring to a boil. Reduce heat, cover, and simmer until done, 45 to 50 minutes; set aside.

2. Wash all the soup stock vegetables and trim the ends, but do not peel. Cut the vegetables into large chunks and place them with the bay leaf and water in a 6-quart stockpot. Bring to a boil, reduce heat, and simmer, covered, for 45 minutes. Discard the bay leaf; remove the vegetables with a slotted spoon and reserve for another use.

3. *To make the soup:* Drop the tomato into the stock for 10 to 15 seconds, or until the skin starts to split. Remove and place immediately under cold running water. Slip off the skin, and cut the tomato in half crosswise. Squeeze out the seeds, chop the tomato coarsely.

4. Peel and chop the onion and sauté it in the oil in a 5-quart soup pot over medium heat. Cut the carrot into medium dice and add to the pot. Shred the cabbage, add it to the pot, and continue sautéeing until the onion is soft and the cabbage starts wilting. Add the chopped tomato and sauté for 5 to 10 minutes more.

5. Meanwhile, peel and grate beets. Chop the beet stems. Add to the pot, along with 6 cups of the stock. Bring to a boil, reduce the heat, and simmer, covered, for 30 minutes.

6. Chop the beet greens and add to the pot along with the cooked navy beans, mirin or sherry, salt, pepper, and lemon juice. Simmer for 15 minutes more.

7. Taste the soup, adjust the seasonings, and serve. Garnish each bowl of soup with chopped dill.

Carrot-Beet Soup
with Tofu Sour Cream

Major Phase: Wood
Minor Phase: Water

Yield: 6 to 8 servings

Beets are a wonderful addition to carrot soup. You may blend them in or use them as a garnish on top of each serving—either way, this soup looks beautiful and tastes delicious.

       4 medium beets*
       3 medium onions
       ½ tablespoon unrefined sesame oil
       1 pound carrots
       2 medium zucchini
       ½ teaspoon ground thyme
       6 cups water or Light Vegetable Stock (page 72)
       1 tablespoon vegetable seasoning salt
         Sea salt to taste

1. Simmer the beets, covered, for 1 hour in a 4-quart pot in water to cover. When cool, peel, grate, and set aside.
2. While the beets are cooking, chop the onions. Heat the oil in a 6-quart pot. Add the onions, cover, and cook over low heat for about 15 to 20 minutes, to heighten their sweetness.
3. Wash and trim the carrots and zucchini and cut them into medium chunks; add to the onions. Season with the thyme. Add the water or stock, vegetable seasoning salt, and sea salt to taste. Bring to a boil, reduce the heat, and simmer, covered, for 20 to 25 minutes.
4. Puree the soup in batches in a blender until smooth. Return to the pot and adjust the seasonings.
5. Serve each bowl with 2 tablespoons of the grated beets and a dollop of Tofu Sour Cream (see below).

Tofu Sour Cream

Major Phase: Metal

YIELD: About 1½ cups

       1 pound soft tofu
       2 tablespoons cold-pressed safflower or sunflower oil
       1 tablespoon fresh lemon juice
       ½ teaspoon sea salt

---

* Beets will bleed less when you boil them if you do not peel them and leave about 1 inch of the stem attached.

1 teaspoon umeboshi paste
½ teaspoon umeboshi vinegar
Water as needed

1. In a 2-quart saucepan, combine the tofu with 2 cups water or enough to come halfway up the side of the pan. Bring to a boil, reduce heat, and cook, covered, for 5 minutes. Allow to cool.
2. In a food processor or blender, combine the tofu, oil, lemon juice, salt, umeboshi paste, and umeboshi vinegar and blend until smooth, adding water as necessary to arrive at sour cream–like consistency. Chill.

Dark Onion Soup

Phase: Metal

Yield: 6 servings

The secret of making really delicious onion soup lies not so much in the ingredients as in the proper browning of the onions. It takes a bit of time, but it's also worth the effort. If you have no stock, by the way, make some while you prepare the onions; use the onion peels, a carrot, a piece of celery, a bay leaf, and 8 cups of water. This soup would be a wonderful contrast to the Vegetarian Carbonada Criolla (page 193)

2 pounds Spanish onions
¼ cup water
2 tablespoons extra-virgin olive oil
6 cups Rich Vegetable Stock (page 73), hot
3 tablespoons shoyu or tamari
Sea salt to taste

1. Slice the onions into very thin half moons.
2. In a 3–4 quart saucepan, combine the onions and the water, and steam over medium-low heat, covered, for 4 to 5 minutes, or until the onions are limp. Drain, adding the water to the stock.
3. In the same pot, heat the oil then add the onions, and sauté over medium heat until thoroughly browned, about 25 to 30 minutes.

4. Add the hot stock, scraping up all the brown bits from the bottom of the pan with a wooden spoon. Bring to a boil, reduce heat to low and simmer covered, for 15 minutes. Season with the shoyu and sea salt to taste. Serve hot.

Corn Soup
with Pimiento Puree

Phase: Fire

YIELD: 6 to 8 servings

The pimiento puree swirled into the pale yellow soup gives it a cheerful, festive look.

Corn Stock

 3 leeks, green tops only
 4 coriander seeds
 5 peppercorns
 1 small bay leaf
 1 clove garlic
   Silk, husks, and cobs from 5 ears corn
 1 small carrot
 1 small onion
 2 quarts water

Soup

 1 tablespoon cold-pressed sunflower seed oil
 1 cup thinly sliced onions
 ⅓ cup rolled oats
   Kernels from 5 ears corn
 5 cups Corn Stock (see above)
 1 tablespoon vegetable seasoning salt

1. *To make the corn stock:* In a large pot, combine the stock ingredients and the water. Bring to a boil, reduce heat, and simmer for 30 minutes. Strain and discard the vegetables.
2. *To make the soup:* Heat the oil in a 4- to 6-quart soup pot and sauté the onions over medium heat for 5 minutes. Add the oats, corn kernels, stock, and salt. Bring to a boil, reduce heat, and simmer for 15 to 20 minutes, or until the corn is sweet and tender and the oats are softened.
3. Puree in batches in a blender and return it to the pot. Serve hot, at room temperature, or chilled. Garnish each serving with a dollop of Pimiento Puree (see below).

Pimiento Puree

Phase: Fire

Yield: About ⅔ cup

    2 large sweet red peppers
    1 tablespoon extra-virgin olive oil
    ½ teaspoon sea salt
      Freshly ground black pepper to taste
      A few drops hot sauce or chili oil, or to taste

1. Roast the peppers in a 400°F oven for 30 minutes or more until they are totally charred black.
2. Place them in a brown paper bag or a small pot with a cover for 20 minutes, so that they sweat out their moisture.
3. Then remove the peppers and peel them under running water over a strainer (to catch the charred peel). Cut the pulp into strips, discarding the seeds.
4. Combine the peppers and the rest of the ingredients in a food processor or blender. Process until you get a smooth puree. Transfer to a bowl and adjust the seasonings if necessary.

Leek and Potato Soup

Major Phase: Metal

YIELD: 6 to 8 servings

This is a family favorite. It's simple, quick, and really satisfying. Try it with the Poached Salmon (page 228), Japanese Barley-Rice (page 106), and the Zesty Salad (page 214) for a light supper.

    3 or 4 leeks
       ⅔ pound potatoes (about three medium)
        1 tablespoon extra-virgin olive oil
        6 cups Light Vegetable Stock (page 72) or water
        1 teaspoon sea salt or 1 tablespoon vegetable seasoning salt
           Freshly ground white pepper
        2 tablespoons chopped parsley for garnish

1. Cut the leeks lengthwise, then crosswise, discarding the tough outer leaves and using as much of the green as possible. Drop in a large bowl with cold water, swirl around to loosen the dirt, then scoop out with a slotted spoon and place in a colander.
2. Peel and dice the potatoes, and place them in a bowl of cold water.
3. In a 4-quart pot, heat the oil, then add the leeks and sauté over medium heat for 3 or 4 minutes, or until wilted. Add the stock or water, the potatoes, and the salt. Bring to a boil, lower the heat, cover, and simmer for 25 to 30 minutes.
4. Puree half the soup in the blender and return to the pot. Adjust seasonings, and serve hot, garnished with a few grindings of white pepper and 1 teaspoon parsley.

Simple Cream of Mushroom Soup

Phase: Water

Yield: 6 servings

When I was a child in Holland, my uncle once told me that elves and gnomes live in mushrooms. Perhaps for that reason I've always loved these vegetables—they have a hint of magic about them. Here's a soup I like to make often at home.

1 cup shallots
4 tablespoons butter or extra-virgin olive oil
5 tablespoons whole wheat flour
4½ cups hot Rich Vegetable Stock (page 73) or water
¾ pound white button mushrooms
1 tablespoon vegetable seasoning salt
½ tablespoon umeboshi vinegar
Freshly ground black pepper to taste
Parsley sprigs for garnish

1. Mince the shallots. In a 4-quart soup pot, heat the butter or oil and sauté the shallots over medium heat for 4 to 5 minutes, or until softened.
2. Sprinkle the flour over the shallots and continue to sauté, stirring continuously, until the flour begins to give off a nutty aroma.
3. Pour 1 cup of the hot stock or water over the flour-shallot mixture, beating rapidly with a whisk to incorporate all the flour. Add the remaining stock while you continue whisking, making sure no lumps of flour remain. Bring to a simmer.
4. Chop the mushrooms and add to the soup pot, along with the vegetable seasoning salt. Simmer, covered, for 15 minutes; stir occasionally. Puree in a blender and return to the soup pot.
5. Adjust the seasonings to your taste with sea salt and black pepper. Serve hot with a parsley sprig for garnish.

Chunky Cream of Mushroom Soup

Major Phase: Water

Yield: 6 servings

Stock

1 carrot
1 onion
2 stalks celery, with leaves
2 quarts water

Bouquet garni:
1 bay leaf
1 teaspoon dried oregano
1 teaspoon dried basil
4 black peppercorns
1 teaspoon dried rosemary
1 teaspoon chopped parsley

Soup

6 ounces fresh shiitake mushrooms
12 ounces white button mushrooms
2 tablespoons extra-virgin olive oil or unsalted butter
2 tablespoons whole wheat flour
6 cups stock (see above)
2 tablespoons shoyu or tamari
1 teaspoon sea salt, or to taste
Freshly ground black pepper to taste

1. *To make the stock:* Place the vegetables and bouquet garni in a 3- to 4-quart saucepan. Bring to a boil, reduce heat, and simmer 30 minutes, covered.
2. *To make the soup:* Cut off the stems of the shiitake and discard. Chop the caps coarsely; set aside. Chop the button mushrooms in a food processor; set aside.

3. In a 2-quart saucepan, heat the oil or butter, then add the flour and cook over low heat, stirring continuously, until toasted and fragrant, about 5 to 7 minutes. To this roux add all the mushrooms, stirring to mix well, then the hot stock. Whisk until thoroughly blended, add the shoyu, and simmer for 5 minutes. Season to taste with salt and pepper. Serve immediately.

❧ • ❧

Potage New York

Major Phase: Metal
Minor Phase: Earth

YIELD: 4 to 6 servings

Cream soups, I find, are always a hit with company. In this case, the creamy texture comes from a base of starchy vegetables and just enough stock to puree them in a blender.

> 1 leek
> ½ small butternut squash, (½ to ¾ pound)
> ½ head cauliflower
> 2 teaspoons extra-virgin olive oil
> 3½ cups water or Light Vegetable Stock (page 72)
> ¼ cup rolled oats
> Sea salt to taste
> Minced chives or dill for garnish
> Freshly ground white pepper to taste

1. Cut the leek into crosswise slices, discarding only the toughest parts of the green leaves. Place in a large basin of water. Swirl around once or twice, letting the dirt sink to the bottom of the bowl. Remove, using a slotted spoon, and place in a bowl. Peel the squash, seed it, and cut into chunks. Separate the cauliflower into florets, discarding the core.
2. In a 3- to 4-quart soup pot, heat the oil over medium heat. Add the sliced leek and sauté for 4 to 5 minutes, or until soft. Add the cauliflower and the squash, then add water or stock to cover. Add the rolled oats and salt. Bring to a boil, reduce heat, cover, and simmer for 30 minutes.

3. Puree the soup in a blender in at least two batches.
4. Serve hot, garnished with dill or chives and pepper.

Cream of Squash
and Parsnips Soup with Dill

Major Phase: Earth
Minor Phase: Wood

YIELD: 6 servings

  1 medium onion
  2 large carrots
  2 large parsnips
  ½ small butternut squash (about 1 cup cubed)
  1 tablespoon unrefined sesame oil
  ½ teaspoon dried thyme
  ½ teaspoon dried dill
  5 cups water or Light Vegetable Stock (page 72)
  ¼ cup rolled oats
  1 teaspoon sea salt, or to taste, *or* 1 tablespoon vegetable seasoning salt
  1 teaspoon umeboshi vinegar
  ⅛ teaspoon freshly ground white pepper, or to taste
  3 teaspoons fresh chopped dill

1. Wash, trim, and dice all the vegetables. In a 3- to 4-quart pot, heat the oil, then add the onion, and sauté over medium heat until transparent, about 3 to 4 minutes. Add the carrots, parsnips, butternut squash, thyme, and dried dill. Sauté for 4 to 5 minutes more, stirring.
2. Add the water or stock, the oats, and the salt. Bring to a boil, reduce heat, and simmer, covered, for 45 to 50 minutes.

3. Puree the soup in a blender in several batches and return to the pot. Add the umeboshi vinegar. Taste and adjust the seasonings. Add the pepper. Serve hot. Garnish each serving with ½ teaspoon fresh chopped dill.

Curried Apple-Squash Bisque

Major Phase: Earth
Minor Phase: Wood

YIELD: 6 to 8 servings

A lovely soup, delicate and with an unusual flavoring touch provided by the very tart Granny Smith apples.

1 medium onion
1 tablespoon unsalted butter or cold-pressed sunflower oil
1 tablespoon curry powder, or to taste
1 butternut squash (about 1½ pounds)
2 Granny Smith apples
5 cups Light Vegetable Stock (page 72)
1 tablespoon fresh lemon juice
1 teaspoon sea salt, or to taste

1. Chop the onion. In a 3- to 4-quart pot, heat the butter or oil and sauté the onion and the curry powder over medium heat, until the onion is translucent, about 10 minutes.
2. Meanwhile, peel and seed squash; cut into cubes. Peel and seed one of the apples; cut into cubes. When the onion is done cooking, add the squash, the cubed apple, and the stock to the pot, bring to a boil, reduce heat, and simmer, covered, for 20 to 30 minutes, or until the squash is tender. Add the salt and correct the seasoning.
3. Puree the soup in a blender. Peel the remaining apple, grate it, and toss in a bowl with the lemon juice. Serve hot or cold garnished with the freshly grated apple.

Tomato-Coriander Soup

Major Phase: Fire
Minor Phase: Wood

YIELD: 4 to 6 servings

The light, tropical flavors of this soup make it especially good on sultry summer days. Make it in July or August when tomatoes are at their peak.

1½ pounds very ripe tomatoes
    Sea salt, for salting tomatoes
2 medium onions
2 cloves garlic
    A large handful coriander leaves
2 tablespoons extra-virgin olive oil
¼ cup whole wheat flour
1 quart water or Light Vegetable Stock (page 72)
3 tablespoons shoyu or tamari
1 teaspoon grated fresh ginger root

1. Cut the tomatoes in half horizontally, salt well, and place salted side down on a board for 20 minutes. In the meantime, chop the onions and mince the garlic.

2. Squeeze the seeds out of the tomatoes and discard. Cut the tomatoes into medium-size chunks. Chop the coriander leaves.

3. In a 3- to 4-quart soup pot, heat the oil, and sauté the garlic and onion over medium heat until lightly browned, about 6 to 8 minutes. Add the flour and stir until it begins to exude a nutty aroma. Whisk in the water or stock, add the tomatoes, and bring to a boil. Add half of the chopped coriander to the soup, reduce heat, and simmer covered, for 30 minutes.

4. Strain out the vegetables, pressing them well against the strainer with a wooden spoon. Discard. Return the soup to the pot. Add the shoyu and ginger and cook for another minute. Cool to room temperature, then chill in the refrigerator. Serve cold, garnished with the rest of the chopped coriander.

Vegetable-Barley Soup

Major Phase: Wood
Minor Phases: Metal and Fire

Yield: 6 to 8 servings

This is the kind of soup I'd have for lunch on a day I'm puttering around the house and want something light yet filling—Mixed Salad with Fennel (page 206) and a piece of Apple-Cranberry Pie (page 245) with added roasted almonds would complete the meal and keep me humming till dinner-time.

1	quart water or Light Vegetable Stock (page 72)
½	cup whole barley
1	carrot
1	medium onion
2	stalks celery, with leaves
2	ounces mushrooms
1	tablespoon extra-virgin olive oil
½	teaspoon dried oregano
1	teaspoon vegetable seasoning salt, or to taste
1	bay leaf
	Sea salt or shoyu or tamari to taste
	Freshly ground white pepper to taste
6	tablespoons chopped scallions for garnish
6	sprigs watercress for garnish

1. In a 4-quart pot, combine the water or stock and barley. Bring to a boil, reduce heat, cover, and simmer for 30 to 40 minutes, or until the barley is tender.
2. Meanwhile, wash, then dice the carrot and celery. Chop the onion. Cut the mushrooms into quarters.
3. Heat the oil in a large skillet and add the onion. Sauté for 2 to 3 minutes, or until transparent. Add the celery, carrot, and oregano, and sauté for another 3 to 4 minutes.
4. Add the skillet contents to the cooking barley, scraping it out of the pan with a spatula. Then add the mushrooms, vegetable seasoning salt, pepper, and bay

leaf. Cook, covered, over low heat for 1 hour. Remove the bay leaf and season to taste with sea salt or shoyu. Serve hot, garnished with chopped scallions and watercress.

Japanese Red Bean Soup

Phase: Water

<small>YIELD:</small> 8 to 10 servings

This hearty soup makes a great meal served with Focaccia (page 118) and the Radish-Watercress Salad (page 209).

1	cup dried aduki beans
4 to 6	-inch piece kombu seaweed
5	cups water or Light Vegetable Stock (page 72)
2	shallots
1	small carrot
1	small white turnip
2	teaspoons unrefined sesame oil
½	teaspoon sea salt, or to taste
1	tablespoon grated fresh ginger root
	Freshly ground black pepper to taste
3	whole scallions, chopped

1. Combine the beans, the kombu, and the water or stock in a 3- to 4-quart saucepan. Bring to a boil, cover, and simmer for 45 minutes, or until the beans are tender.
2. Meanwhile, mince the shallots; dice the carrot and the turnip. In a large skillet, heat the oil and sauté the vegetables, adding them to the skillet one by one in the order given. Cook each one for 2 to 3 minutes before adding the next. Scrape into the beans with a spatula. Deglaze the skillet by adding a ladleful of hot bean-cooking liquid, swirling around to pick up all the flavorings; return

it to the soup pot. Cover the pot and continue simmering for another 30 minutes.

3. When the beans are soft, add the salt and stir with a wooden spoon to blend well. If the kombu has softened, break it up and blend it in, too. Simmer for 15 minutes longer. Add the ginger during the last 2 minutes of cooking. Add freshly grated black pepper to taste. Serve hot, garnished with scallions.

❧ • ☙

Phyllis's Bean Soup with Arugula (Zuppa di Fagioli con le Bietole)

Major Phase: Metal
Minor Phase: Fire

YIELD: 4 to 6 servings

A rich, nourishing soup; it's also a good way to get people to eat their greens. Kale, collards, mustard greens, all can be used according to availability.

1 cup dried white navy beans, soaked
1 bay leaf
1 quart Light Vegetable Stock (page 72)
1 teaspoon sea salt
1 tablespoon shoyu or tamari
1 pound tomatoes
1 small onion
2 to 3 cloves garlic
1 tablespoon extra-virgin olive oil
1 teaspoon dried oregano
1/4 teaspoon dried marjoram
Freshly ground black pepper
1 bunch arugula or 1/2 pound fresh spinach

1. Drain the beans and place them in a pressure cooker or 4- to 6-quart saucepan. Add the bay leaf and stock; pressure-cook for 20 minutes or simmer for 45 to

60 minutes. Ten minutes before the end of cooking time, add ½ teaspoon of the salt and the shoyu; set aside.

2. *To blanch the tomatoes:* Make a shallow slit in the bottom of each tomato. Place the tomatoes in rapidly boiling water for 10 to 15 seconds. (You can blanch them in soup stock if you happen to be making it at the same time.) Remove and allow to cool slightly before peeling. The skins should slip off easily. Cut them in half crosswise and squeeze out the seeds. Chop coarsely and set aside.

3. Chop the onion finely; mince the garlic. In a large pot, sauté the onion and garlic in the oil until translucent. Add the tomatoes and herbs and stir well. Cook for a few minutes to incorporate flavors, then add the navy beans with their cooking liquid, adding more water or stock if the soup seems too thick. Season with the remaining sea salt and the pepper. Simmer for 10 minutes.

4. Wash the arugula or spinach. Remove any thick or tough stems and tear into bite-size pieces (you should have about 3 cups, loosely packed), then add to the soup and simmer for a minute or two more. Serve immediately.

Garden Green Soup with Chick-peas

Major Phase: Earth

Minor Phase: Fire

Yield: 6 servings

½ cup dried chick-peas, soaked
1 clove garlic
3 small white onions or shallots
3 ounces mushrooms
1 tablespoon extra-virgin olive oil
½ teaspoon dried savory
   Pinch dried sage
5 cups water
1 bay leaf
1 or 2 teaspoons vegetable seasoning salt, to taste
   Sea salt to taste
   Freshly ground white pepper to taste
   Several leaves each of collard greens and kale

1. Drain the chick-peas and place them in a medium saucepan. Add water to cover, bring to a boil, reduce heat, and cook, covered, for 1 hour.
2. While the chick-peas are cooking, finely chop the garlic and onions or shallots. Wipe and slice the mushrooms.
3. In a 3- to 4-quart saucepan, heat the oil, add the garlic and onions, and stir over low heat until the onions wilt, about 3 to 4 minutes.
4. When the chick-peas are done, drain and add them to the onions. Add the sliced mushrooms, the savory and sage and sauté for a few minutes more to blend the flavors.
5. Add the water, bay leaf, and vegetable seasoning salt. Bring to a boil, reduce heat, and simmer for 45 minutes to 1 hour. Taste and adjust the seasoning if necessary with additional sea salt and white pepper.
6. Wash the collard greens and kale and cut them into thin strips. Add the greens and simmer with only half the pot covered, for another 15 to 20 minutes, or until the greens are wilted. Serve immediately.

Black-eyed Pea Soup
with Turnips and Coriander

Major Phase: Wood
Minor Phase: Metal

YIELD: 6 servings

1 cup dried black-eyed peas, soaked
1 bay leaf
5 cups water or Light Vegetable Stock (page 72)
1 medium onion
½ pound carrots
1 medium turnip
1 tablespoon extra-virgin olive oil
½ teaspoon sea salt, or to taste
 Freshly ground white pepper to taste
2 tablespoons umeboshi vinegar or brown rice vinegar
2 tablespoons chopped coriander leaves

1. Drain the black-eyed peas and place them along with the bay leaf in a 3- to 4-quart saucepan with the water or stock. Bring to a boil, cover, reduce heat, and simmer for 30 minutes.
2. While the beans are cooking, chop the onion, carrots, and turnip.
3. Heat the oil in a large skillet, and sauté the vegetables, adding them to the skillet in the order given. Cook each one for 2 to 3 minutes before adding the next.
4. Scrape the vegetables into the cooking beans, cover, and cook for 1 hour more. Add the salt, pepper, and vinegar. Stir well, cover, and cook for another 10 minutes.
5. Remove and discard the bay leaf. Puree 1 cup of the soup in a blender and return to the pot. Stir well, taste, and adjust the seasoning.
6. Sprinkle each serving with 1 teaspoon chopped coriander and more freshly ground white pepper to taste. Serve immediately.

❦ • ❦

Black Bean Soup

Major Phase: Water

YIELD: 6 servings

½ pound dried black turtle beans, soaked
1 quart water
1 large onion
3 medium cloves garlic
1 tablespoon extra-virgin olive oil
1 tomato
¼ teaspoon dried oregano
½ teaspoon ground cumin
2 teaspoons chili powder
1 bay leaf
2 tablespoons mirin (sweet rice wine)
  or 1 tablespoon dry sherry
1½ tablespoons brown rice vinegar
  Sea salt and freshly ground black pepper to taste
¼ cup chopped whole scallions for garnish

1. Drain the beans and place them in a 6-quart soup pot with the water. Bring to a boil, skimming the foam that rises to the surface until it almost ceases to form, then reduce heat, cover, and cook for 45 minutes.
2. While the beans are cooking, chop the onion fine and mince the garlic. In a medium skillet, heat the oil and sauté the onion and garlic over medium heat for 4 to 5 minutes.
3. While onion and garlic are sautéing, drop the tomato into the bean pot for 30 seconds; remove using a slotted spoon. Peel. Cut in half crosswise and squeeze out the seeds. Chop coarsely and add to the skillet, along with the oregano, cumin, and chili powder. Cook, stirring for 2 or 3 minutes.
4. Scrape the contents of the skillet into the soup pot. Add the bay leaf. Cover the pot and simmer for 1 hour more.
5. Add the mirin or sherry, vinegar, and salt and pepper and continue to simmer for another 30 minutes. If you wish, puree 2 to 3 cups of soup in a blender or food processor to create a thicker, smoother texture.

6. Remove the bay leaf. Ladle into soup bowls and serve, garnished with chopped scallions.

❧ · ❧

Black and White Bean Soup

Major Phase: Water
Minor Phase: Metal

Yield: 6 to 8 servings

Surprisingly simple to make, this makes quite a dramatic presentation when served. Serve it in soup plates, not bowls, for full effect. I like to put the white bean soup in first, then carefully ladle the black bean soup right into the center; however, you can reverse the colors if you like. This soup is excellent with Jalapeño Corn Bread (page 133).

2 cups dried black beans, soaked*
2 cups dried white beans, soaked*
10 cups water or Light Vegetable Stock (page 72)
12 cloves garlic, peeled and crushed
½ cup fresh coriander leaves
¼ cup extra-virgin olive oil
    Sea salt to taste
5 tablespoons red wine vinegar or brown rice vinegar
1 fresh jalapeño pepper

1. Drain the beans and place them in separate pots. Add 5 cups water or stock to each pot .
2. To the black beans add 6 cloves of the garlic, the coriander, and half the oil. Simmer until the beans are tender, about 50 minutes. Puree in several batches in a blender or in a food processor. Return to the pot. Season to taste with the salt and cook 5 minutes longer.
3. To the white beans add the remaining garlic, the vinegar, the jalapeño pepper, and the remaining oil. Simmer until the beans are tender, about 50 minutes.

---

* Soak the beans separately.

Thin with more water or stock if necessary. Puree the beans in a blender until creamy. Return to the pot. Season to taste with the salt and cook 5 minutes longer.

4. To serve, ladle ¾ cup white bean soup into a shallow soup plate, then carefully ladle ¾ cup black bean soup into the center of the white bean soup. Serve immediately.

❧ · ❧

Joan's Red Lentil–Lemon Soup

Major Phase: Fire
Minor Phase: Wood

YIELD: 6 servings

Here is a light, easy soup. It cooks quickly, which is great for a soup with legumes. It would go well with the Barley Croquettes (page 116) and the Radish-Watercress Salad (page 209)

2 medium onions
2 cloves garlic
½ teaspoon sea salt
1 tablespoon unrefined sesame oil
1 teaspoon ground cumin
1 cup dried red lentils
5 cups Light Vegetable Stock (page 72) or water*
1 bay leaf
2 thin strips lemon rind
1 tablespoon fresh lemon juice
6 thin slices of lemon for garnish

1. Chop the onions into medium pieces. Chop the garlic. On a cutting board, mash the garlic into the salt with the side of the knife blade to make a paste.

---

* If you use water instead of stock, you may want to add 2 teaspoons of vegetable seasoning salt after the lentils have softened.

2. In a 3- to 4-quart soup pot, heat the oil over medium heat. Add the onions and sauté until translucent, about 3 to 4 minutes. Add the garlic paste and cumin and cook until the onion is golden, about 6 to 7 minutes longer.

3. Meanwhile, pick over the red lentils carefully; discard any stones. Rinse. Add to the onions with the stock or water and bring to a boil, skimming off the foam, if necessary. Reduce heat, add the bay leaf and lemon rind, and simmer, covered, for 25 minutes. Discard the bay leaf and lemon rind.

4. Add the lemon juice to the soup and stir. Pour into bowls and garnish each with a slice of lemon.

Cantaloupe Soup with Blueberries

Major Phase: Earth
Minor Phase: Water

Yield: 6 to 8 servings

This cooling soup may be served as an appetizer or dessert. Try it also as a refreshing and low-calorie afternoon snack.

> 1 ripe peach
> 1 cantaloupe
> ¾ cup unfiltered apple juice
> 2 teaspoons fresh lemon juice
> ¼ teaspoon vanilla extract
> 2 tablespoons fresh mint leaves, chopped
> ½ pint blueberries for garnish

1. Peel and chop the peach; cut the cantaloupe into small chunks. Place the fruit in a medium saucepan, and add the apple juice. Cook over medium heat until the fruit is soft, 7 to 8 minutes. Stir in the lemon juice and vanilla.

2. Puree the soup in a blender or a food processor. Transfer to a bowl and fold in the chopped mint leaves. Chill for 2 hours. Garnish with blueberries and serve.

❦ Grains ❧

In a mostly vegetarian eating style, cereal grains and beans are the pivot upon which the whole meal turns. Grain-based dishes are hearty and centering; they steady our nervous system and keep our blood sugar stable. The fiber in them has been shown to keep our digestive system and arteries in good working order. Grains are our daily bread, fruit of the earth, gift of the gods. Let's be grateful for them.

Japanese Barley-Rice

Major Phase: Metal
Minor Phase: Wood

YIELD: 6 servings

Janice learned this recipe from a Zen monk, who said it was the most digestible grain combination he knew. That is because, according to the Theory of the Five Phases, rice tonifies the lung/large intestine and sedates the liver/gallbladder, while barley tonifies the liver/gallbladder and sedates the spleen and stomach.

½ cup barley
½ cup short-grain brown rice
½ cup white rice
3 cups water
Pinch sea salt
3 to 4 slices pickled ginger*

1. In a 2- to 3-quart saucepan, combine the grains, water, and salt. Bring to a boil, reduce heat to low, and simmer, covered, for 1 hour.
2. Turn off the heat and without removing the cover, let the grains rest undisturbed for 15 minutes. Chop the pickled ginger.
3. Add the chopped ginger to the rice, fluff with a fork, and serve in individual rice bowls.

---

* Obtainable in health-food stores that carry Japanese products.

Bulgur Pilaf with Mushrooms

Major Phase: Wood
Minor Phases: Metal and Water

YIELD: 6 to 8 servings

A light and pleasant dish, especially good with bean salads.

3½ cups water
½ teaspoon sea salt
2 cups bulgur
¾ pound fresh mushrooms
1 medium onion
2 tablespoons unrefined sesame oil
¼ cup currants
⅓ cup toasted pumpkin seeds
Shoyu or tamari to taste

1. In a 2-quart saucepan, bring the water to a boil with the salt. Add the bulgur and return to a boil; then turn off the heat, cover the pot, and set aside until all the water has been absorbed, about 30 minutes.
2. In the meantime, wipe and slice the mushrooms thinly. Chop the onion fine. In a large skillet, heat the oil over medium-high heat. Add the mushrooms and sauté until they are slightly browned, about 5 minutes. Add the currants and pumpkin seeds and mix well.
3. When the bulgur has absorbed all the water, remove the cover and fluff the grain with a fork. Scrape the contents of the skillet into the bulgur and toss well to combine. Serve immediately.

Mamaliga (Polenta with Cheese)

Major Phase: Fire

Yield: 5 to 6 servings

In traditional American Indian cooking, cornmeal is treated with lime (as in limestone) or cooked with wood ash to increase its calcium and vitamin B content. Regular cornmeal does not undergo such treatment, and for that reason I find that this dish, a Romanian version of polenta, needs cheese for balance. Although tofu, with its lower calcium content, doesn't work as well, it certainly may be used as a substitute.

2 cups freshly ground cornmeal*
4 to 5 cups cold water or Light Vegetable Stock (page 72)
1 tablespoon vegetable seasoning salt
1½ tablespoons unsalted butter or cold-pressed sunflower oil
1 teaspoon sea salt
½ pound mild-flavored raw-milk cheese, such as raclette, Monterey Jack, or Muenster, or substitute crumbled seasoned tofu

1. Preheat the oven to 350°F.
2. In a heavy 4-quart pot, dissolve the cornmeal in the cold water or stock. Add the vegetable seasoning salt and bring to a boil over high heat, stirring constantly. The cornmeal will thicken as it cooks.
3. As soon as it has thickened and is heaving, lower the heat to medium, cover, and cook for 25 minutes, lifting the lid frequently to stir. Add more water if it becomes too thick to stir. Halfway through the cooking time, add the butter or oil and salt.
4. Slice the cheese thinly. In an oiled 4-quart heavy ovenproof casserole, layer the cornmeal and cheese in 3 to 4 layers, ending with a top layer of cheese. (This can also be done in little individual casseroles.)

---

* Cornmeal that is over 5 to 7 days old sometimes tastes bitter when cooked. If fresh ground cornmeal is not available, use "high-lysine" cornmeal, obtainable in health food stores. It does not go bitter.

5. Bake, covered, for 40 minutes; uncover and place under the broiler for 5 minutes, or until the cheese browns lightly.

Brown Rice Pilaf

Major Phase: Metal
Minor Phases: Earth and Water

YIELD: 6 to 8 servings

Serve this with Coriander Chutney (page 282), Red Lentil–Lemon Soup (page 103), and Green Salad with Miso Coriander Dressing (page 203) for a flavorful lunch or light dinner.

1½ tablespoons unsalted butter
2 cups long-grain brown rice
⅓ cup shredded unsweetened coconut
½ teaspoon sea salt
3 strands saffron
3¾ cups boiling water
½ cinnamon stick
½ cup currants
⅔ cup chopped pistachios

1. In a medium-size heavy saucepan with a tight-fitting lid, heat the butter. Add the rice, coconut, salt, and saffron. Cook over medium heat, stirring, for 5 minutes.
2. Add the boiling water and the cinnamon stick. Simmer over low heat, covered, for 15 minutes. Uncover and add the currants but do not stir them in. Replace cover and cook until the water is absorbed and the rice is tender, another 20 to 30 minutes. Turn off the heat and let rice sit undisturbed for 10 minutes.
3. Add the pistachios, then mix well with a fork. Serve immediately.

Orange Millet Pilaf

Major Phase: Earth

YIELD: 6 to 8 servings

The combination of orange and millet flavors is just delightful. Try it with a topping of spicy peanut sauce. Collard-Miso Soup (page 78) would be a good accompaniment. Apple-Cranberry Pie (page 245) makes a smashing finale.

3 oranges, plus their juice
2 to 3 cups water or Light Vegetable Stock (page 72)
2½ cups millet
½ teaspoon sea salt
2 tablespoons unsalted butter or unrefined sesame oil
Freshly ground nutmeg to taste
½ cup walnuts (optional)

1. Grate the rind of the oranges and set aside. Juice the oranges, measure, and add enough water or stock to make 4 cups plus 2 tablespoons liquid; set aside.
2. Wash and drain the millet. In a 3- to 4-quart heavy stainless-steel pot,* dry-roast the millet over high heat, stirring continuously, for about 10 minutes, or until fragrant.
3. Add the liquid to the saucepan along with the salt. Bring to a boil, reduce heat, and simmer for 30 minutes, covered.
4. While the millet is cooking, heat the butter or oil in a small skillet, add the grated orange rind, nutmeg, and walnuts. Stir once and remove from heat.
5. Fold into the cooked millet. Serve immediately.

---

* If you dry-roast in an enameled pot, you run the risk of cracking the enamel.

Quinoa and Millet Pilaf

Major Phases: Fire and Earth

Yield: 6 to 8 servings

*H*ere's *a really nice way to use quinoa (pronounced* kee-noh-ah)*, a centuries-old, newly popular, highly nutritious, and fairly expensive grain. This tastes delicious with Clear Mushroom Sauce with Shallots (page 287).*

> 2 tablespoons extra-virgin olive oil
> 1 medium Spanish onion
> 1 large carrot
> 1 teaspoon ground cumin
> 1 cup millet
> 1 cup quinoa
> 5 cups water
> ½ teaspoon sea salt

1. Chop the onion finely; wash and dice the carrot. In a 3- to 4-quart saucepan, heat the oil over medium heat. Add the onion and sauté for 3 to 4 minutes or until translucent; Add the carrot and sauté for 3 to 4 minutes more.
2. Add the cumin, stir for another minute, then add the millet and sauté for 5 minutes.
3. Add the quinoa, sauté for 2 to 3 minutes more.
4. Add the water and salt, bring to a boil, reduce heat, and simmer, covered, for 35 to 40 minutes, or until the water is absorbed. Fluff before serving.

Aromatic Spiced Rice
(India)

Major Phase: Metal
Minor Phase: Earth

YIELD: 6 servings

*T*his delicious Indian brown rice dish uses a sweet curry powder, the unbeatable garam masala—made from scratch—that will ruin your taste for commercial curry powders forever.

2 cups brown Basmati rice
3 cups Light Vegetable Stock (page 72)
½ teaspoon sea salt (optional)
2 teaspoons Garam Masala (page 282)
⅓ cup shelled pistachio nuts
1 tablespoon unsalted butter, softened

1. In a heavy 3- to 4-quart saucepan, combine the rice, stock, salt, and garam masala. Stir once or twice to distribute the spice powder.
2. Bring to a boil over medium heat. Reduce heat as much as possible or place on Flame-Tamer. Cover the pot securely and allow the rice to cook undisturbed until the water is absorbed and the rice tender, about 50 to 55 minutes. Remove from heat and let stand, still covered, for a few minutes.
3. While the rice is cooking, chop the pistachios and toast in a 300°F oven or toaster oven for 8 to 10 minutes. Add about ¾ of the pistachios along with the butter to the standing rice, stirring gently with a fork to blend. Turn out onto a serving dish and top with the remaining nuts.

Curried Basmati Rice

Major Phase: Earth
Minor Phase: Metal

YIELD: 6 to 8 servings

         2 cloves garlic
         1 medium onion
         1 tablespoon extra-virgin olive oil
         1 tablespoon unsalted butter
     1 ¼ teaspoons curry powder
         1 cup shelled fresh peas
       ¾ teaspoon sea salt
         3 cups water
         2 cups brown Basmati rice

1. Mince the garlic. Chop the onion finely.
2. Heat the oil and butter in a 4-quart casserole, add the garlic and onion, and sauté over medium heat for 2 minutes.
3. Add the curry powder and sauté briefly. Add the salt and water and bring to a boil. Add the rice, reduce heat, cover, and simmer for 30 minutes; add the peas, but do not mix into the rice. Replace the cover and continue cooking another 15 to 20 minutes, or until the rice is tender. Fluff with a fork, mixing in the peas, before serving.

Asparagus Risotto

Major Phase: Metal
Minor Phase: Fire

YIELD: 6 to 8 servings

This classic Italian rice-cooking technique lends itself very well to whole-grain brown rice: the dish comes out creamy but still textured and pleasant to the bite. It has become one of my favorite methods of cooking rice. This flavorful version uses fresh asparagus and is great in the spring.

  5 to 6 cups Light Vegetable Stock (page 72)
        2 cloves garlic
        3 shallots
        2 tablespoons extra-virgin olive oil or 1 tablespoon oil and
          1 tablespoon unsalted butter
        2 cups short-grain brown rice
        2 pinches saffron threads, soaked in ½ cup vegetable stock
        ½ teaspoon sea salt
        1 bunch asparagus
        1 tablespoon umeboshi vinegar
        1 tablespoon mirin (sweet rice wine) or dry sherry

1. Warm the vegetable stock and keep warm over low heat. Mince the garlic and shallots.
2. In a heavy 3- to 4-quart saucepan or casserole, heat the oil or oil and butter. Sauté the garlic and shallots over medium heat until translucent. Add the rice and stir to coat grains with the oil. Keep the pot uncovered throughout the entire cooking time.
3. Add the warm vegetable stock a ladleful at a time, stirring continuously. Add more, stirring, as the stock is absorbed. At no time should the stock be allowed to cover the rice more than ¼ inch. Continue the ladling procedure, stirring every 5 to 7 minutes, or until the rice is creamy and cooked, but not totally soft or mushy. Be careful to not let the rice stick to the bottom of the pan. This should take about 1 hour and 15 minutes. The rice will triple in volume.
4. Add the soaked saffron and the salt toward the middle of the cooking time.
5. While the rice is cooking, wash the asparagus. Snap off and discard the tough ends. Cut off the tips and reserve. Cut the tender stems into ¾-inch rounds.
6. Add the umeboshi vinegar, mirin or sherry, and asparagus rounds 20 minutes before end of cooking, and the tips 10 minutes before end. Serve hot.

Noodles with Sesame Sauce

Phases: Water and Wood

YIELD: 6 servings

A popular dish in many Chinese restaurants—where the "sesame" sauce is usually made with peanut butter. Here, then, is the real thing. It harmonizes beautifully with the Stir Fried Bok Choy with Marinated Tofu (page 169).

- 1 package (8 ounces) soba (buckwheat pasta) or udon (Japanese wholewheat pasta)
- 2 quarts boiling water
- ½ teaspoon sea salt

Sauce

- 2 cloves garlic
- ½ cup tahini
- 3 tablespoons shoyu or tamari
- 2 teaspoons maple syrup
- 1 tablespoon brown rice or apple cider vinegar
- ½ cup prepared bancha or kukicha tea* or Chinese tea or plain tea
- 1 teaspoon chili oil, or to taste (optional)
- 3 scallions

1. In a large pot, cook the pasta in the boiling water with salt for 8 to 10 minutes. Drain, and quickly rinse with cold water. Return the pasta to the empty pot, and cover—this will keep the noodles warm about 10 minutes.
2. While the pasta is cooking, prepare the sauce. Mince the garlic.
3. To make the sauce, place the tahini, shoyu, maple syrup, garlic, and vinegar in a 2 quart mixing bowl. Blend carefully with a wooden spoon. The mixture will thicken.

---

* Available in Oriental or natural-foods stores.

4. Add the tea several spoonfuls at a time, blending it in well after each addition, until you get a smooth sauce consistency. Add more tea if needed to thin.
5. Add the optional chili oil a few drops at a time, until you reach the spiciness that you like.
6. Sliver the scallions finely. Serve about 3 tablespoons sauce over each portion of noodles, garnished with scallions. This dish can be served warm or cold.

❦ · ❦

Barley Croquettes
with Shiitake Mushroom Sauce

Major Phase: Wood
Minor Phase: Water

YIELD: 24 to 30 croquettes

I customarily fry my croquettes, but if you are trying to limit your fat intake, you might want to try baking them. This recipe provides instructions for both. Either way, these are delicious.

    4 stalks celery
    1 large carrot
    3 cups barley
    6 cups water
    ½ teaspoon sea salt
      Freshly ground black pepper to taste
    1 teaspoon dried basil
    2 bay leaves
    2 cups sesame seeds (optional, for baked croquettes only)
      Cold-pressed sunflower oil for frying or brushing the croquettes
    ½ cup chopped Italian parsley for garnish

1. Wash and dice the celery and carrot and place in a pressure cooker (or a 4-quart sauce pan) along with the barley, water, salt, a few grindings of pepper, basil, and bay leaves. Bring to pressure (or a boil) over high heat, then reduce heat

to low and pressure cook for 40 minutes (or simmer, covered, for 1 hour), or until the barley is tender.

2. Wash the sesame seeds and drain well. In a 1½-quart stainless-steel saucepan, toast them over medium-high heat, stirring constantly, until fragrant and barely smoky, about 15 minutes. Grind well in a mortar or food processor; set aside.

3. Wash and chop the scallions; set aside.

4. Preheat the oven to 375°F.

5. When the barley is finished cooking and the pressure is down, remove the bay leaves. Place half of the grain in a food processor and process until well mixed but not pureed. Combine with the remaining grain in a large bowl and set aside until cool enough to handle.

6. Moisten your fingers with water and form the barley into 2½-inch round croquettes. Fry in 1 inch sunflower oil on both sides until lightly browned. Drain on brown paper (a grocery bag does nicely) or paper towels. Alternatively, brush with oil and roll in the toasted sesame seeds. Place on oiled baking sheets and bake for 1 hour, or until lightly browned. Serve hot with Shiitake Mushroom Sauce (see below), garnished with chopped parsley.

Shiitake Mushroom Sauce

Major Phase: Water

Yield: 2 cups

        1 package (1.75-ounce size) dried shiitake mushrooms
    2½ cups water
        4 large shallots or cloves garlic, peeled and minced
        2 tablespoons shoyu or tamari
    2½ tablespoons kuzu
        1 teaspoon fresh lemon juice
        1 tablespoon whole-grain mustard (optional)

1. Place the mushrooms in a small bowl. Bring 1 cup of the water to a boil, pour it over the mushrooms, and set aside to soak until soft, about 30 minutes.

2. Drain the mushrooms and press out excess liquid, reserving the soaking water. Cut off tough ends of mushroom stems and discard. Slice the mushrooms into thin strips.

3. Place 2 to 3 tablespoons of the soaking water in a small saucepan along with the shallots or garlic and 1 tablespoon of the shoyu. Simmer, stirring, until the shallots are tender, about 3 to 5 minutes, adding more liquid if necessary. Add the mushrooms and simmer for 1 minute more. Add the remaining soaking water, 1¼ cups of the water, the shoyu, and the lemon juice.

4. Dissolve the kuzu in the remaining ¼ cup water. Bring sauce to a simmer, add the kuzu and cook, stirring constantly, until the sauce is thickened and translucent. Add the whole-grain mustard if you wish. Serve hot.

❧ · ❧

Focaccia (Pizza) with Fresh Tomatoes and Rosemary

Major Phase: Wood
Minor Phases: Fire and Metal

YIELD: One 11-inch × 14-inch pizza

The fresh tomatoes give this classic dish an entirely new twist.

Crust

1 package fast-acting yeast
1 cup warm water
1 tablespoon malt or rice syrup
¼ cup extra-virgin olive oil
1 teaspoon sea salt
2½ cups whole wheat flour,
    plus ¼ to ½ cup additional flour for kneading

Topping

4 medium onions
6 tablespoons extra-virgin olive oil
½ teaspoon sea salt, or to taste

    3 large cloves garlic
    1 tablespoon fresh rosemary or 1 teaspoon dried
    3 very large ripe beefsteak tomatoes
18 to 20 Kalamata (Greek) olives, pitted and sliced

1. *To make the crust:* Dissolve the yeast in the warm water along with the sweetener. Let sit for 5 minutes, or until frothy; then stir and add the oil.

2. In a large bowl, combine the salt and flour. Pour the yeast mixture into the flour and mix with a wooden spoon until it forms a ball of dough. If the dough seems too sticky, add a bit more flour. Knead until smooth and elastic, about 2 to 3 minutes. Return the dough to the bowl and set in a warm place, covered, to rise until doubled in size, about 40 to 50 minutes.

3. Warm the oven to 175°F. Punch down the dough, remove from bowl, and roll out to make a round or rectangular pizza, about ½ inch thick. Place on a baking stone or greased cookie sheet; shape a raised border all around it. Set in the warm oven to rise for 15 minutes.

4. Raise the oven temperature to 325° and bake for 15 minutes, or until the dough sounds hollow when you tap it with a spoon. Increase oven temperature to 375°. While the dough bakes, make the topping.

5. *To make the topping:* Slice the onions in half lengthwise, then again lengthwise into very thin half-moons. You should have about 2½ cups. In a large skillet, heat 2 tablespoons of the oil and sauté the onions over medium-low heat for 5 minutes, or until wilted and translucent. Sprinkle with the sea salt; set aside.

6. Mince the garlic. In a small bowl, combine the garlic with 3 tablespoons of the oil and the rosemary.

7. Slice the tomatoes crosswise into thin disks. Brush the prebaked pizza dough with the remaining 1 tablespoon oil. Top with the tomatoes, then the sautéed onions and the olives. Pour or spoon the rest of the rosemary/garlic mixture on top. Bake at 375° for 20 minutes and serve hot. (Leftovers can be reheated in the oven.)

San Franciscan Pizza

Major Phase: Wood

YIELD: One 11-inch × 14-inch pizza

A "sandwich-pizza" that is delicious as a main dish for lunch with a salad.

Crust

2½ cups warm water
1 teaspoon maple syrup
1 tablespoon dry yeast (1 package)
2 tablespoons extra-virgin olive oil
2 teaspoons sea salt
4½ to 6 cups whole wheat flour
6 tablespoons sesame seeds

Filling

2 medium Bermuda onions
1 clove garlic
1 to 2 tablespoons extra-virgin olive oil
12 to 15 sun-dried tomatoes
1 cup fresh basil leaves (tightly packed)

1. *To prepare the crust:* Run a large bowl under hot tap water to warm it. Empty the bowl and add 2½ cups warm—*not hot*—water. Stir in the maple syrup and the yeast. When the yeast bubbles to the surface, after 4 to 6 minutes, stir in the oil and salt.

2. Stir in the flour, a cup at a time, and after 4½ cups, add only a little at a time, mixing it in by hand. Add just enough flour to get a workable ball of dough that's not sticky. Knead until you get a smooth, elastic dough; set aside.

3. Wash and dry the bowl. Oil the inside lightly, then return the dough to the bowl and roll until the dough is coated with oil. Cover the bowl and place in a warm, draft-free place to rise for 1½ to 2 hours, or until doubled in size.

4. *To make the filling:* Slice the onions finely into half-moons. Smash the garlic with

the side of a heavy knife and remove the skin. Heat the oil in a large skillet over medium heat. Add the garlic. When the garlic begins to brown, add the onions and sauté for 3 to 4 minutes, or until the onions are soft. Slice the tomatoes into thin strips and add to the onions. Chop or tear the basil coarsely. Add to the pan and sauté a few minutes longer. Discard the garlic. Turn off heat and let sit while you return to the crust.

5. When the dough has risen, punch it down and divide it in half. Lightly oil a shallow 11-inch × 14-inch baking pan and sprinkle it with 3 tablespoons of the sesame seeds. Using a rolling pin, roll out each half of the dough into a rectangle the size of the baking pan.

6. Preheat the oven to 425°F. Place 1 sheet of dough in the pan, stretching it as necessary to fit.

7. Spread the topping evenly over the dough, reserving ¼ cup.

9. Carefully place the second sheet of dough on top of the first, pressing the edges together with your fingers to seal.

10. Brush the dough with oil and sprinkle the remaining sesame seeds on top. Scatter the remaining filling on top. Set aside to rest for about 10 minutes before placing in the oven.

11. Bake for about 30 minutes, or until golden and crisp.

Lissa's Homemade Black Pepper Pasta with Scallion-Butter Sauce

Phase: Wood

Yield: About 1 pound pasta

Made with fresh, wholesome ingredients, homemade pasta has a depth of flavor and a richness that is generally lacking in the commercial kind. The dough may be rolled out by hand, following the traditional method, or on a machine, which is a wonderful labor-saving device. Both produce fine results, but sauce seems to cling better to hand-rolled pasta. Try this with the Bean Soup with Arugula (page 97) and the Festive Salad (page 205).

1½ cups durum, semolina, or whole wheat flour
(or a mixture of whole wheat with either)
½ teaspoon sea salt
2 to 3 teaspoons freshly ground black pepper
2 large eggs, preferably organic or free-range
2 tablespoons extra-virgin olive oil

1. In a 4-quart bowl, mix together the flour, salt, and black pepper. Make a well in the center. Break 1 of the eggs into a small cup, then pour it into the center of the well; repeat with the second egg. Pour in the oil.

2. Using a fork, gently stir up the eggs, gradually incorporating small amounts of flour from the edges of the well. Continue this process, turning the bowl as necessary until the dough is too stiff to stir with the fork. Using your fingertips, blend in the rest of the flour. The dough should feel pliable but not sticky. (You may find that you have some flour left over, depending on the age of the flour and weather conditions.)

3. Gather the dough into a ball and knead with the heel of your hand for 7 to 10 minutes, or until smooth and elastic. Allow it to rest, covered with an inverted bowl or pot, for 20 to 30 minutes. If it feels sticky, cover it with a dry towel instead. The towel will absorb some of the moisture.

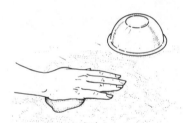

4a. *To roll out dough by hand:* Flatten the dough with a rolling pin. Sprinkle some flour on the board and on both sides of the dough.

Using a long rolling pin, working from the center of the dough outward, roll out to a thickness of about ⅛ inch. Take care not to roll it too thin at the edges. Allow to rest on the board and dry for about 10 to 15 minutes.

Then fold the dough into a flat roll about 2½ to 3 inches wide and,

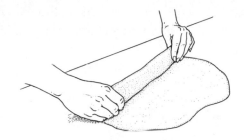

Using a sharp knife, slice the roll crosswise into strips of the desired width.

Unroll and use immediately, or fold into nests and allow to dry for storage.

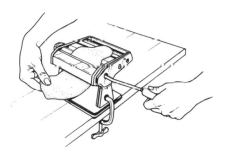

4b. *To roll out dough with a pasta machine:* Divide the kneaded dough into 4 portions. Cover 3 of them with an inverted bowl and flatten the fourth one with the heel of your hand.
Starting with the roller in the machine at the largest setting, run the dough through the rollers. Flour the dough slightly. Change the setting of the rollers one notch

and run the dough through again. Repeat procedure twice more, continuing to close rollers tighter to make a thin dough, about ⅛ inch.

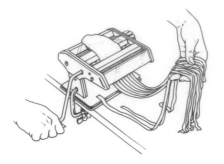 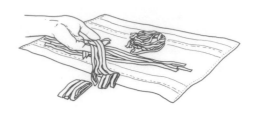

When done, flour the dough sheet lightly and set aside. Repeat with the rest of the dough. Let the floured sheets sit for 5 to 10 minutes, then run them through the desired cutter.

5. *To cook homemade pasta:* In a 6- to 8-quart stockpot, bring 3 to 4 quarts water with 1 tablespoon sea salt to a boil over high heat. Add the pasta; timing from the time the water starts boiling again, cook the pasta for about 1 to 2 minutes (the more whole wheat in the pasta, the longer it should cook). Remove a strand and sample: the pasta should have a slightly chewy texture (*al dente*), and not be overly soft all the way through. When done, drain well in a colander, quickly rinse with cold water, and dump back into the pot. It may be kept warm like that for 5 to 10 minutes if necessary.

6. Serve with Scallion-Butter Sauce (see below).

Scallion-Butter Sauce for Pasta

Major Phase: Fire

YIELD: ⅓ cup

6 scallions
4 tablespoons sweet butter, softened
1 tablespoon vegetable seasoning salt or 1 tablespoon white miso

1 fresh or roasted sweet red pepper (see page 87), cut into strips for garnish

2 tablespoons chopped parsley for garnish

1. In a blender or food processor, combine the scallions, butter, and salt and process until smooth. Scrape into a bowl.
2. To serve, place a heaping teaspoonful onto each serving of hot, cooked pasta. Decorate with red pepper strips and chopped parsley.

❦ · ❧

Pasta Primavera With Pesto

Major Phase: Wood

YIELD: 8 to 10 servings

This is my version of two classic pasta dishes—pesto and primavera. For an extra-special treat, try it with fresh homemade pasta—the results are positively ambrosial.

     1 cup pignolias
     5 medium cloves garlic
2 to 3 bunches basil (about 5 cups packed)
     2 tablespoons red barley miso
¾ to 1 cup extra-virgin olive oil
     ½ teaspoon sea salt
     1 pound zucchini
     1 bunch broccoli (1 to 1¼ pounds)
     1 pound fresh homemade pasta (see page 122), or udon noodles

1. Chop the pignolias. Mince the garlic. Chop the basil coarsely, and place it in a large suribachi or mortar with the miso and the pignolias. Crush thoroughly.*
2. Add the oil slowly, stirring, to form a thick paste.

---

* Making pesto by hand gives a slightly richer, more aromatic flavor. In the interest of time and/or labor, you may, of course, use a blender or food processor.

3. Bring a 4- to 6-quart pot of water to a boil. Add the salt.

4. Wash and dice the zucchini. Cut the broccoli florets off the stalks and reserve stalks for another use; you should have about 2 cups florets.

5. Drop the broccoli florets into the boiling water for 1 minute, then fish them out with a slotted spoon; set aside. Repeat with the zucchini. Finally drop in the pasta or noodles and cook until done. Fresh pasta cooks in 5 to 8 minutes, so test after 5 minutes. Udon needs 10 to 15 minutes.

6. Drain the pasta. Place in a serving dish and toss with pesto and vegetables. Serve immediately.

Mediterranean Pasta Garni

Major Phase: Wood
Minor Phases: Water and Fire

YIELD: 8 servings

     2 cloves garlic
     4 whole scallions
     2 sweet red peppers, seeded
    24 brine- or oil-cured black olives*
     6 tablespoons extra-virgin olive oil
    ½ teaspoon plus 1 pinch sea salt
     2 sheets nori seaweed for garnish
     2 quarts water
     1 pound fresh homemade pasta (see page 122), or udon noodles

1. Mince the garlic. Thinly slice the scallions and red peppers. Pit the olives and cut lengthwise into slices.

2. In a skillet, heat the oil and sauté the garlic over medium heat for 1 minute. Add the scallions and sauté for 1 minute, then add the red peppers and olives

---

* Avoid using canned black olives; they have no taste.

and cook, uncovered, for 2 minutes. Add the pinch of salt and continue cooking for 4 minutes more; set aside.

3. Toast the nori by placing it in a toaster oven at the lowest setting or waving it over a high flame until it shrinks a bit and turns green. Cut into thin slivers with a scissors or sharp knife; set aside.

4. In a large pot, bring the water to a boil with the remaining salt. Add the pasta or noodles and cook, uncovered, at a rolling boil, for 5 to 8 minutes for fresh pasta, 10 to 15 minutes for udon.

5. When the noodles are done, drain and rinse quickly under cold running water. Return to the pot and toss with the olive-and-pepper mixture. Serve immediately. Garnish with the nori slivers.

Rice-Spinach Timbales with Mushroom Sauce

Major Phase: Metal
Minor Phase: Wood

YIELD: 12 timbales or 6 servings

Here is an elegant and simple way to serve brown rice—excellent for company! It goes especially well with Red Lentil Pâté (page 144) and Crunchy Fennel Salad with Lemon Dressing (page 199).

Timbales

2 cups short-grain brown rice
1 cup brown Basmati rice, wild rice, or "Wehani" rice
5 cups water
½ teaspoon plus 1 pinch sea salt
1 pound spinach
    Pinch freshly ground nutmeg
1 tablespoon shoyu or tamari or to taste

Mushroom Sauce

    2 small onions
    ¾ pound fresh mushrooms
    2 tablespoons unsalted butter or unrefined sesame oil
    1 tablespoon extra-virgin olive oil
    ¼ cup whole wheat pastry flour
    2 cups Light Vegetable Stock (page 72),
        or water heated
        Sea salt to taste
    3 grindings black pepper

1. *To make the timbales:* Wash the rice and combine with the water and salt in a 4-quart pot; cook, covered, over medium heat until the water is absorbed and the rice is tender, about 55 minutes.

2. Wash the spinach (page 41). Place in a 6- to 8-quart pot and cook, covered, in only the water clinging to the leaves for 4 to 5 minutes, or until wilted. Drain. When cool enough to handle, squeeze out the excess moisture and chop. (If the rice is very dry, do not squeeze spinach too much.)

3. Season the spinach with the nutmeg and the pinch of salt. In a large bowl, combine the spinach and the rice and add a bit of shoyu to taste. Keep in warming oven while you prepare the sauce.

4. *To make the mushroom sauce:* Mince the onions. Wipe the mushrooms and chop them finely.

5. In a 3-quart heavy saucepan, heat the butter or sesame oil and the olive oil. Add the onions and sauté over medium heat, stirring, until translucent, about 4 to 5 minutes.

6. Add the flour and sauté, stirring, until flour becomes fragrant, about 5 to 7 minutes. Remove from heat.

7. Whisk in the hot stock, stirring continuously until the sauce has thickened. Return to heat.

8. Add the chopped mushrooms, salt, and pepper. Cook, covered, over low heat until all the flavors are blended, about 15 minutes. Keep hot until time to serve.

9. Using a small paper cup or ice-cream scoop (about ½-cup capacity) as a mold, shape the spinach-rice mixture into timbales.

10. Serve 2 timbales per guest with mushroom sauce.

Stuffed Cabbage Rolls

Major Phase: Metal
Minor Phase: Wood

YIELD: 8 to 10 servings

A salute to Eastern Europe! This dish was one of my earliest efforts (1966) to adapt traditional dishes made with white flour or polished grain to whole-grain cookery. I still love it for the rich, earthy flavor imparted by the brown rice.

> 1 tablespoon unrefined sesame oil
> 1½ teaspoons cumin seeds or caraway seeds
> 3 cups short-grain brown rice
> 2 quarts cold water
> ¾ teaspoon sea salt, or to taste
> 1 head green cabbage
> ⅔ cup raw or toasted sunflower seeds

Béchamel Sauce

> 6 tablespoons cold-pressed safflower oil or unsalted butter
> ½ cup whole wheat flour*
> Cabbage-cooking water
> 1 teaspoon sea salt, or to taste
> 1 cup whole wheat bread crumbs
> 2 tablespoons extra-virgin olive oil or unsalted butter

1. In a 4-quart pot, heat the oil. Add the cumin or caraway seeds and the rice and sauté for 10 to 15 minutes, or until the grains start to look opaque and toasted and the cumin or caraway begin to give off its scent.

---

* Whole wheat pastry flour may also be used in this recipe.

2. Add 5 cups of the water and the salt. Bring to a boil, cover, reduce heat, and simmer for 50 to 60 minutes, or until rice is soft.

3. With a pointed paring knife, core the cabbage by cutting a cone into the bottom. Discard the core.

4. Place the cabbage on its bottom with the remaining 3 cups water in a 3- to 4-quart pot and steam for 10 to 15 minutes. Remove cabbage from the pot, reserving the cooking water, and allow to cool.

5. *To prepare the sauce:* Heat the safflower oil or butter in a saucepan, add the flour, and cook, over medium-high heat, stirring until fragrant and lightly browned, about 8 to 10 minutes. Remove from heat and rapidly whisk in 2 cups of the hot cabbage-cooking water. (The mixture will thicken rapidly, and by working fast enough, you will avoid lumps in the sauce.) Return to the heat, stir, season with the salt to taste, and simmer, covered, for 10 to 15 minutes, stirring occasionally. Keep warm over very low heat while you stuff the cabbage leaves, otherwise the sauce will set.

6. Preheat the oven to 350°F. Oil a shallow baking pan.

7. Very gently peel the outside leaves off the cooled cabbage. If the inside is still raw and brittle, steam for another 6 to 8 minutes.

8. Mix the sunflower seeds and ⅔ cup of the béchamel into the rice. Place 2 to 3 tablespoons of the rice mixture onto the bottom half of each cabbage leaf, roll up, and tuck under the sides, to make a thick roll. Place, seam side down, in the baking pan. Repeat with the remaining filling. You should have at least 16 to 18 rolls. Pour the rest of the warm béchamel over the rolls, making sure to cover each one. Sprinkle the bread crumbs over everything, and if you wish, a bit of olive oil or pieces of butter. Bake for 25 to 30 minutes, or until the bread crumbs are lightly browned. Serve hot.

Locro (Argentine Vegetable Stew)

Major Phase: Mixed

Yield: 6 to 8 servings

This is an authentic Argentine recipe—yes, from the land of twice-a-day steak! One of the great hearty stews of all time; especially popular are the slices of corn on the cob it contains—everyone wants a few to eat with their fingers. The sofrito is an excellent topping for other types of grains as well. Stored in an airtight container in the refrigerator, leftovers will stay fresh for 2 to 3 days.

½ cup dried navy beans, soaked
¼ cup whole wheat berries
¼ cup barley
3 cups water
1 large piece Calabaza squash or 1 small butternut squash (about 1 pound)
½ pound boiling potatoes
1 large carrot
1 small yam or sweet potato
2 ears corn
2 bay leaves
½ teaspoon sea salt
3 whole scallions, chopped

1. Drain the beans. In a 4-quart pot, combine the beans with the wheat berries, barley, and 2 cups of the water. Bring to a boil, reduce heat, and simmer, covered, for 15 to 20 minutes.
2. Meanwhile, cut the squash, potatoes, carrot, and yam or sweet potato into medium chunks. (They should not be too small.) Cut the corn into ½- to ¾-inch slices. Combine all the vegetables with the beans and grain. Add the remaining 1 cup water, the bay leaves, and the salt. Bring to a simmer. Cook for 1 hour, covered, over low heat. Stir occasionally, and add a bit more water

if needed. The vegetables should be soft; the squash will disintegrate, making a thick stew. Serve hot, topped with Sofrito Topping (see below).

Sofrito Topping

Phase: Fire

Yield: About 1⅓ cups

2 sweet red peppers
3 ripe tomatoes
4 teaspoons extra-virgin olive oil
1 tablespoon paprika
3 whole scallions
¼ teaspoon sea salt

1. Finely chop the peppers and tomatoes, discarding seeds.
2. In a large skillet, heat the oil. Add the peppers, tomatoes, sea salt, and paprika. Stir well and cook, uncovered, over medium heat for 30 minutes, stirring often. Serve hot.

❧ • ❧

Jenny's Holiday Bread Crumb Stuffing

Phase: Wood

Yield: 2 loaves or 12 to 14 cups, packed

Jenny decided that she was tired of never getting enough stuffing during holiday feasts, so here is her simple solution: stuffing loaf as an entrée! This may also be used as a stuffing for squash, fish, or fowl.

3 large yellow onions
6 tablespoons unsalted butter
½ tablespoon dried basil
½ tablespoon dried thyme
½ tablespoon dried oregano

½ pound fresh white mushrooms
¼ teaspoon sea salt
Freshly ground black pepper
12 slices fresh whole wheat bread
3 medium apples
1 cup walnuts
½ cup warm water (optional)

1. Preheat the oven to 350°F.
2. Peel the onions and chop them finely. In a large skillet, heat the butter over medium-high heat. Add the onions. Measure out the basil, thyme, and oregano. Rub the herbs between the palms of your hands to crush and add to the onions. Meanwhile, slice the mushrooms thinly and add to the pan with the salt and pepper. Continue sautéing until the onions are soft and the mushrooms have given off their liquid, about 5 to 6 minutes. Remove from heat and set aside.
3. Cut the bread into ½-inch cubes. (You should have about 6 cups.) Dice the apples and chop the walnuts into medium-size pieces. In a large bowl, mix together the bread cubes, apples, and walnuts with your hands. Add the onion mixture, blending well. Add the water if a very moist stuffing is desired.
4. Lightly grease two 9-inch loaf pans or a 4-quart covered casserole and pack in the stuffing. Cover the pans or casserole (if you are using loaf pans, cover them tightly with foil). Bake for 30 minutes, then remove the cover and continue baking for 15 minutes, or until the top is nicely browned. Serve hot.

Jalapeño Corn Bread

Phase: Water (blue cornmeal) or
Fire (yellow cornmeal)

Yield: One 9-inch × 9-inch square
or 12 muffins

We made this recipe originally with yellow cornmeal, but in later tests we found the blue just wonderful, despite its less-than-glorious grayish color. Blue corn has a delicate corn flavor and never goes bitter.

2½ teaspoons aluminum-free baking powder*
¼ teaspoon sea salt
2 cups blue cornmeal**
2 ears corn
1 egg
3 tablespoons melted butter or cold-pressed sunflower oil
1 cup soymilk
1 tablespoon maple syrup
1 fresh jalapeño pepper, or to taste, depending on spiciness

1. Preheat the oven to 425°F. Oil or butter a 9-inch × 9-inch baking pan or a muffin pan.
2. In a large bowl, mix together the baking powder, sea salt, and cornmeal. Blend thoroughly.
3. Using a sharp knife, slice the corn kernels off the cobs and into a bowl; then turn the knife around and scrape off the remaining pulp with the back of the blade; set aside.
4. In another bowl, beat the egg until fluffy, then beat in the butter or oil, the soymilk, and the maple syrup. Seed and mince the jalapeño. Taste a small piece to determine hotness and add as much as is to your liking.
5. Pour the liquid ingredients into the cornmeal mixture and combine with a few rapid strokes. Do not overbeat, or the cornbread will be dry. Pour into the prepared pan and bake for 20 to 25 minutes, or until it springs back when lightly pressed with a finger, or a cake tester inserted into the middle comes out clean.

---

* Available in natural-foods stores.
** If unavailable, substitute yellow cornmeal, as freshly ground as possible.

❧ Beans and Legumes ❧

Power and joy emerge from a sense of well-being, from being nourished without being overloaded, from feeling satisfied yet light, and beans help create that condition. What's more, the latest research shows that they are good for you: One half to one cup of beans daily can lower your cholesterol and blood pressure, control your blood sugar, and regulate your intestinal tract. For meatless meals, they are an indispensable staple; no long-term vegetarian regime is complete without them. And as for their digestibility, there are a number of techniques that will improve it. Among these are discarding the soaking water; long, slow cooking; the use of aromatic herbs and spices, such as basil, ginger, cumin, caraway, and the various curry ingredients; and finally, getting used to eating beans in small but steady amounts.

Baked Beans
with Miso and Apple Butter

Major Phase: Water
Minor Phase: Earth

<small>YIELD:</small> 6 to 8 servings

I love this recipe! Miso and apple butter is a wonderfully harmonious combination. Serve it with plain brown rice or polenta and a leafy green salad.

2 cups dried kidney beans, soaked
6 cups water
1½ tablespoons mellow barley miso or mugi miso
¼ cup unsweetened and unspiced apple butter
1½ teaspoons whole-grain mustard, such as Pommery
1 tablespoon grated onion
⅔ tablespoon brown rice vinegar

1. Drain the beans and place in a 4-quart pot. Add the 6 cups water and cook, covered, over low heat until tender, about 40 to 45 minutes. Drain, reserving 1 cup of the cooking liquid.
2. Preheat the oven to 350°F. Oil a heavy 3-quart casserole or bean pot.
3. In a medium bowl, combine the reserved bean-cooking liquid and the miso, apple butter, mustard, onion, and brown rice vinegar.
4. Place the cooked beans in the pot, add the miso-apple butter mixture and stir to combine. Cover and bake for 1½ hours. Serve hot.

Black Bean Feijoada

Major Phase: Water

YIELD: 6 to 8 servings

*H*ere is a meatless adaptation of a popular Brazilian dish, created by Diane after her trip to that country. The beans cook to a thick sauce that is served over rice. Pass around a bottle of hot sauce if you like.

 2 cups dried black turtle beans, soaked
 2 tablespoons extra-virgin olive oil
 2 medium yellow onions
 2 tablespoons fresh grated ginger root
 ½ tablespoon cayenne pepper
 ½ teaspoon ground cumin
 6 cups water
 3 tablespoons umeboshi vinegar
   or 2 tablespoons brown rice or apple cider vinegar
 1 teaspoon sea salt, or to taste
 3 sweet red peppers
 4 cups cooked brown rice (page 38)

1. Drain the beans. Chop the onions. In a 4- to 6-quart soup pot, heat the oil. Add the onions and sauté over medium heat until translucent, about 3 to 4 minutes. Stir in the ginger, cayenne, and cumin, then add the drained beans and the 6 cups water. Bring to a boil, cover, reduce heat, and simmer for 1 to 1½ hours, or until beans are quite soft.
2. Add the vinegar and salt and cook for 10 minutes more. You should have a thick stew.
3. While the beans are cooking, roast the red peppers over a gas burner or put them under the broiler until they are charred black. Place in a paper bag or covered pot and allow to "sweat" for 10 minutes, then wash off charred peel under cold running water. Seed and slice the peppers into thin strips.
5. Serve the feijoada over the rice, garnished with the red pepper strips.

Black Bean Log
with Fresh Coriander

Major Phase: Water
Minor Phase: Wood

YIELD: 12 servings

This dish works very well for a vegetarian buffet brunch with corn fritters or Mamaliga (page 108) and Pico de Gallo Salad (page 207). It looks very dramatic on a serving plate; you can loosen your artistic impulses and garnish it prettily, with lettuce leaves slivered scallions, and cherry tomatoes for example.

3 cups dried black turtle beans, soaked
10 cups water
1 small onion
1 small carrot
1 bay leaf
2 tablespoons extra-virgin olive oil
2 cups minced onions
1 teaspoon sea salt, or to taste
1 tablespoon umeboshi vinegar
½ to 1 teaspoon hot sauce, to taste
⅔ cup chopped fresh coriander

1. Drain the beans and place them along with the 10 cups water, the onion, carrot, and bay leaf in a 4- to 6-quart saucepan. Bring to a boil, reduce heat, and simmer, covered, for 1 to 1¼ hours, or until the beans are very soft. Remove the onion, carrot, and bay leaf. Drain the beans, and puree in a food processor.
2. Meanwhile, heat the oil in a 10-inch skillet. Add the minced onions and sauté until very soft, about 5 to 6 minutes.
3. Add the bean puree to the onion mixture and sauté over low heat for 7 to 10 minutes to dry it out a bit. Add the salt, vinegar, and hot sauce. Taste and adjust the seasonings. Add ½ cup of the chopped coriander and stir thor-

oughly. Shaking the skillet over the heat, push the beans into a roll shape with a spatula. When the beans hold their shape, gently flip the roll over into a platter. Pat it once or twice to smooth and even it out. Cool. Slice into ½-inch slices. Serve at room temperature, garnished with the remaining coriander.

❧ • ❧

Black-eyed Peas
with Wild Mushrooms

Major Phase: Water
Minor Phase: Metal

YIELD: 6 to 8 servings

This unusual dish harmonizes beautifully with the Asparagus Risotto (page 113) and the Green Salad with Miso-Coriander dressing (page 203).

            2 cups dried black-eyed peas, soaked
            5 cups water
               Sea salt to taste
            2 cloves garlic
         1½ -inch slice ginger root
            3 medium onions
           ¼ pound fresh wild mushrooms (chanterelles,
               oyster mushrooms, or shiitake)
         1½ tablespoons extra-virgin olive oil and
               1½ tablespoons unsalted butter
               or 3 tablespoons extra-virgin olive oil
         1½ tablespoons dried thyme
    3 to 4 whole scallions

1. Drain the beans and place them with the 5 cups water in a 3-quart saucepan. Simmer, covered, with ½ teaspoon of the salt for 45 minutes or until soft but not broken. Drain and set aside.

2. Mince the garlic and ginger. Chop the onions. Slice the mushrooms; set aside. Heat the oil and butter in a heavy skillet. Add the onions and sauté over medium heat until translucent, about 3 to 4 minutes. Add the garlic and ginger. Crumble the thyme by rubbing it between the palms of your hands and add. Sauté for a few minutes more.

3. Add the sliced mushrooms and sauté for 5 minutes more. Slice the scallions on the diagonal into very thin slivers.

4. Add the drained beans with a slotted spoon and season with sea salt to taste. Stir gently. Continue to cook over low heat, uncovered, stirring occasionally for 15 minutes. Take care not to mash the beans. Serve immediately, garnished with slivered scallions.

Falafel with Tahini Sauce

Major Phase: Earth
Minor Phase: Wood

Yield: 6 to 8 servings

If you've ever made falafel with cooked chick-peas or a mix and wondered why they came out oily or gummy, get ready for the real thing! These are delicious, crisp, (croquant, as they say in French), and absolutely nonoily. They take a while to prepare, but they're quite easy to make. The secret of achieving perfectly crisp results is that the chick-peas are soaked but not cooked beforehand.

　　2 cups dried chick-peas
　　6 cloves garlic
　⅓ cup chopped parsley
　⅔ teaspoon sea salt, or to taste
　　2 cups cold-pressed sunflower oil for frying

1. Soak the chick-peas in 2 quarts cold water for 8 to 10 hours. Drain, reserving 1 cup of the soaking water.
2. Grind the soaked chick-peas in a meat grinder or food processor and place in a large bowl. Peel the garlic cloves and squeeze them through a garlic press over the chick-peas and stir to mix thoroughly. Add the parsley and salt to taste. At this point, the mixture should hold a shape if you take some in your hand and squeeze it. If it is too dry, add some of the reserved bean-soaking water.
3. Heat the oil in a wok to 350°F. The oil should move but not smoke; a piece of bread dropped in should come to the surface immediately.
4. While the oil is heating, make the falafel balls: Working with lightly moistened hands, roll the chick-pea mixture into balls 1½ or 2 inches in diameter, packing them tightly so that they hold their shape in the oil. Place on a large platter or tray.
5. When the oil is hot enough, gently lower the falafel balls into it by letting them roll down the sides of the wok. Only add as many as will float comfortably in a single layer. Do not disturb until they set, about 3 to 4 minutes, to avoid crumbling. Fry for a total of about 10 minutes, or until browned all over, turning often. They should be about the same color as unblanched almonds. Remove with a wire-mesh spatula and drain on a brown paper bag or paper towels. Remove the crumbs from the oil before adding another batch. Repeat until all the falafel are done (you will probably have to do two batches). Keep warm in a 200° oven until ready to serve. Serve with Tahini Sauce (see below) as a dip.

Tahini Sauce

Major Phases: Fire and Wood

Yield: About 2 cups

1 cup tahini
⅔ cup water
2 tablespoons fresh lemon juice
½ teaspoon sea salt

1. Place the tahini in a bowl. Add the water, ⅓ cup at a time, blending thoroughly with a wooden spoon after each addition.
2. Mix in the lemon juice and salt and serve.

Lentil Puree

Major Phase: Wood

Yield: 6 to 8 servings

Served hot, this tasty puree makes a good protein side dish. Served cold, with perhaps a few extra tablespoons of stock or water to thin it a bit, it makes a fabulous dip with crackers. Add some freshly ground pepper or hot sauce if you like; for the gourmet touch, use the butter.

> 2 cups dried lentils
> 1 quart Rich Vegetable Stock (page 73) or water
> 1 large bay leaf
>   Sea salt to taste
> 1 tablespoon sweet butter (optional)
> 1 teaspoon umeboshi vinegar

1. Wash and pick over the lentils. In a 3- or 4-quart saucepan, combine the lentils, stock or water, and bay leaf. Bring to a boil, reduce heat, and cook, covered, over low heat for 1 hour, or until the lentils are soft and the liquid is absorbed.
2. Remove the bay leaf. Mash the lentils with a fork until you get a thick puree. Add the sea salt, vinegar, and the butter if you wish. Serve either hot or cold.

Saffron Beans with Tomato

Major Phase: Metal
Minor Phase: Fire

Yield: 6 to 8 servings

*S*affron *gives both color and unique flavor to this dish, and it aids in the digestibility of starches. Serve this with grain as a main dish or as a side dish, by itself.*

6¼ cups water or Light Vegetable Stock (page 72)
   Large pinch saffron strands
2 cups dried navy pea beans or great northern beans, soaked
1 bay leaf
½ teaspoon sea salt, or to taste
2 ripe medium tomatoes
2 medium onions
2 cloves garlic
2 tablespoons extra-virgin olive oil
½ cup finely chopped parsley for garnish
   Freshly ground black pepper to taste

1. Heat ¼ cup of the water or stock. Place the saffron in a small bowl, add the hot liquid and soak for 5 minutes.
2. Drain the beans and place them in a 3- to 4-quart pot with the remaining 6 cups water or stock. Bring to a boil, skimming foam from the surface if necessary, and add the bay leaf and soaked saffron. Reduce heat, cover, and cook for 30 to 40 minutes, or until the beans are tender but not mushy. Add the salt and cook for 5 minutes more.
3. Meanwhile, prepare the vegetables: Peel, seed, and chop the tomatoes coarsely; set aside. Peel the onions and garlic and chop coarsely.
4. In a large skillet, heat the oil. Add the onions and garlic and sauté gently for 5 minutes. Add the tomatoes and sauté for 5 minutes more.
5. Meanwhile, drain the beans, reserving the cooking liquid. Add the beans to the skillet with just enough bean-cooking liquid to keep them from sticking to the bottom of the pan. Continue to cook until the vegetables are soft, about 10 minutes.

6. Taste and adjust the seasoning. Cook for 5 minutes longer to blend flavors. More liquid may be added to make a soupier dish. Serve immediately, garnished with chopped parsley, and pass the pepper mill.

Red Lentil Pâté

Major Phase: Fire

YIELD: 10 to 12 servings

This pâté is a staple in my French vegetarian cooking class, where it never fails to win raves. It may be sliced and served as an appetizer, or spread on crackers as a pâté, or served with a grain such as the Orange-Millet Pilaf (page 110) for a protein-rich entrée.

2 cups red lentils

3½ cups water or Light Vegetable Stock (page 72)

2 medium onions

3 cloves garlic

2 tablespoons unrefined sesame or extra-virgin olive oil

1 teaspoon each dried basil, oregano, and thyme

¼ cup whole wheat bread crumbs

1 teaspoon sea salt, or to taste

1 large handful parsley

½ teaspoon freshly ground black pepper, or to taste

1 teaspoon umeboshi vinegar

1. Wash lentils quickly (see page 39), drain, and place the lentils in a 3- to 4-quart saucepan. Add the water or stock, bring to a boil, reduce heat to medium, and simmer, covered, for 20 minutes.
2. Chop the onions and the garlic very finely.
3. In a large skillet, heat the oil. Add the garlic, onions, and herbs and sauté over medium heat, stirring constantly, for about 10 minutes, or until the onions and garlic are browned and fragrant.

4. Oil a 9-inch shallow baking pan or loaf pan and sprinkle with half the bread crumbs, completely coating the inside of the pan. Preheat the oven to 375°F. Chop the parsley finely.

5. When the lentils are done, stir them thoroughly to mash, add the onion mixture, bread crumbs, and parsley. Season to taste with sea salt, umeboshi vinegar, and pepper.

6. Pour the lentil mixture into the prepared pan and bake for about 20 to 30 minutes, or until set. Allow to cool to room temperature before slicing.

❦ • ❦

Red Lentil Pâté en Croute (In the Crust)

Major Phase: Fire
Minor Phase: Wood

YIELD: 10 to 12 servings

Red Lentil Pâté is delicious and very elegant when baked in a crust.

    1 cup boiling water
    ⅔ cup cold-pressed safflower oil
    ½ teaspoon sea salt
    3 cups whole wheat flour
    1 egg, beaten; or a mixture of 2 tablespoons oil and 2 tablespoons water
    1 recipe Red Lentil Pâté, unbaked (page 144)
      Parsley sprigs for garnish

1. In a large bowl, combine the oil, water, and salt and beat briskly with a wire whip until the mixture turns milky.

2. Add all the flour at once, mixing first with the whip and then with a wooden spoon. In a minute or so you'll have a nice dough pulling away from the sides of the bowl. Squeeze the dough and knead it lightly, then let it rest, covered, in the refrigerator for about 30 minutes.

3. Preheat the oven to 350°F. Oil a 9-inch loaf pan.

4. Remove the dough from the refrigerator. Separate one-third of the dough and set aside. Place the remaining two-thirds dough between two layers of wax paper and roll it out to a rectangle large enough to fit the loaf pan, about ¼ inch thick. Peel off the top paper and gently flip the dough over into the loaf pan. Fit the dough carefully into the corners and sides of the pan, trim the edges, and prebake for 8 minutes. Remove from the oven. Raise oven temperature to 375°F.

5. Roll out the reserved crust between two sheets of wax paper but do not remove the wax paper until ready to use; set aside.

6. Pour the pâté filling into the prebaked crust. Peel the wax paper off the reserved crust and flip over onto the pan; trim, fold edges over, and pinch to seal. If you wish, cut out decorations from the leftover dough and affix them to the crust by moistening them. Poke some holes in the top crust, brush with the beaten egg or the oil-water mixture, and bake for about 45 minutes, or until the crust is lightly browned and sounds hollow when you tap it with a spoon. Allow to cool to room temperature. Remove from pan. Slice into pieces 1 to 1½ inches thick and serve, garnished with parsley sprigs.

Lentil Croquettes

Major Phase: Wood

YIELD: 6 to 8 servings as entrée
10 to 12 servings as an appetizer

My mother used to make these when I was growing up, and I always considered them a treat. This is not an easy recipe, as you'll see; but if you have the time, and if you're up for the challenge, the results are absolutely worth it. Make sure to season the croquettes to your taste and to cover them completely with the bread crumbs to create a crisp shell. Try serving them with the Curried Apple-Squash Bisque (page 93) and a chicory salad for a special lunch.

                    2 cups lentils
                    3 cups water
                    1 bay leaf
                    1 recipe Béchamel Sauce (see below)
                    1 small onion
                      A handful of parsley
                    1 teaspoon sea salt
                    1 tablespoon umeboshi vinegar
                    1 teaspoon hot sauce or Tabasco
                    2 teaspoon vegetable seasoning salt
                    2 cups whole wheat pastry flour
                    4 eggs
                    3 tablespoons water
                    3 cups fine dry whole wheat bread crumbs
          2½ to 3 cups cold-pressed sunflower oil for deep frying
                    2 tablespoons wasabi powder, dissolved in ⅓ cup water

1. Wash and pick over the lentils. In a 3-quart pot, combine the lentils, water, and the bay leaf. Bring to a boil, cover, reduce heat, and simmer for 1 hour, or until the lentils are soft.

2. Meanwhile, prepare the Béchamel Sauce according to the recipe below.

3. Grate the onion. Chop the parsley. When the lentils are done, puree them in a food mill or food processor and place in a large mixing bowl. Add the onion, parsley, sea salt, and Béchamel, stirring to mix well; then add the umeboshi vinegar, hot sauce or Tabasco, and vegetable seasoning salt. Blend thoroughly.

4. Spread the lentil mixture on a cookie sheet, to a thickness of about ½ inch. Place in a freezer or refrigerator for 20 to 30 minutes, or until cool and firm.

5. Place the flour, eggs, and bread crumbs individually in three soup or dinner plates. Beat the eggs with the 3 tablespoons water until frothy.

6. Heat the oil in a wok or a large skillet to 350°F; the oil should move but not smoke; a piece of bread dropped in should rise to the surface immediately.

7. Working quickly with moistened hands, take a heaping tablespoonful of the chilled lentil mixture and shape into flat burgers or short, fat cigars. The mixture will be very soft, so don't squeeze too hard. Drop the first 6 or 8 croquettes in the bowl with the flour and gently roll each croquette until it is covered with flour.

8. Then place each one in the egg; roll in the egg. Then place in the bread crumbs and roll to cover thoroughly. Lower the croquettes gently into the hot oil and fry on both sides, turning often, until medium brown and crusty, about 6 to 8 minutes. Drain on a brown paper bag or paper towels. Repeat until all the croquettes are done.

9. Serve the wasabi/water mixture as a dip with the hot croquettes.

Béchamel Sauce

Major Phase: Wood

Yield: 1¼ cups

4 tablespoons cold-pressed sunflower oil
9 tablespoons whole wheat flour
1½ cup boiling water
½ teaspoon sea salt, or to taste

1. In a heavy 1-quart saucepan, heat the oil over medium heat and add the flour, stirring until toasted and aromatic, about 5 to 6 minutes.

2. Remove from heat. Place the pot on a heat-resistant, nonslip surface. Pour the water into the flour slowly, whisking continuously and briskly and scraping up all the bits of toasted flour from the bottom and sides of the pan. The sauce will begin to thicken immediately. Add the salt.

3. Return the pan to the heat, cover, and cook over low heat for another 10 to 15 minutes, stirring occasionally. Keep hot over a warming plate or Flame-Tamer until ready to use, to avoid filming over or hardening.

Refried Beans

Phase: Water

Y<small>IELD</small>: 6 to 8 servings

*H*ere is our version of the classic Mexican dish. Incidentally, the word refried derives from the Spanish word refrito, which doesn't mean "fried twice," but "fried well" or "fried long enough." In any event, this version uses very little oil. In calling these beans "refried," we are merely following tradition. Refried beans are good with cornmeal dishes like Mamaliga (page 108), or rice dishes like the Spinach Rice-Timbales (page 127). Add greens or salad and maybe Almond Flan with Raspberry Sauce (page 264), and you're set.

3 cups dried pinto beans, soaked
6 cups water
1 bay leaf
1 carrot
1 teaspoon sea salt
3 medium onions
3 tablespoons extra-virgin olive oil
1 heaping teaspoon dried oregano
1 heaping teaspoon dried basil
1 tablespoon ground cumin
Tabasco or hot sauce to taste (optional)

1. Drain the beans. Place them in a 4-quart pot. Add the 6 cups water or enough to cover by 1 inch. Add the bay leaf and carrot. Bring to a boil, reduce heat, and simmer, covered, for 45 minutes, or until the beans are soft. Add the salt and cook for 10 minutes more, then remove the carrot and bay leaf. Drain the beans, reserving the cooking liquid.
2. Chop the onions; you should have about 2 cups. In a large skillet, heat the oil, add the onions and sauté over medium heat for about 6 to 8 minutes, or until soft. Add the oregano, basil, and cumin.
3. Continue to sauté for 5 minutes more, adding about ¼ cup of the bean liquid so that the onions do not burn. When the onions are sweet and soft, add the

beans and mash to a thick paste. Cook over low heat, uncovered, for about 5 to 8 minutes, adding bean liquid as necessary to keep the beans from drying out and burning. If you wish, season with Tabasco or hot sauce to taste. Serve hot.

White Bean Chili

Major Phase: Metal
Minor Phase: Fire

YIELD: 6 to 8 servings

Here is a slightly different chili, made with white beans and somewhat milder than the conventional version. It is delicious over cooked kasha, millet, or polenta, or simply with corn chips on the side. It will keep in the refrigerator for 4 or 5 days.

2 cups dried navy beans, soaked
6 cups water
2 bay leaves
2 medium onions
1 pound ripe tomatoes
3 large cloves garlic
2 tablespoons extra-virgin olive oil
1 tablespoon sweet paprika
1 to 2 teaspoons chili powder, or to taste
1 teaspoon ground cumin
1 teaspoon sea salt, or to taste
2 tablespoons chopped fresh coriander for garnish

1. Drain the beans. Place in a 4-quart pot. Add the 6 cups water or enough to cover the beans by 1 inch. Add the bay leaves. Bring to a boil, reduce heat, cover, and simmer for 40 minutes.

2. Mince the onions and garlic. Peel the tomatoes by dropping them in boiling water for 10 seconds, then slipping off the peel. Cut the tomatoes in half crosswise and gently squeeze out the seeds; chop coarsely.

3. In a 4-quart casserole, heat the oil, then sauté the onions and garlic over medium heat for 1 to 2 minutes; stir in the paprika, chili powder, and cumin and sauté briefly, or until fragrant. Add the tomatoes. Fish the beans out of their pot with a slotted spoon and add to the tomato-onion mixture, stirring to blend. Add the salt and 1 to 1½ cups of the bean-cooking liquid, just enough to bring the liquid level 1 inch below the level of the beans. Simmer for 1 hour, or until the beans are soft and the flavors well blended. Serve immediately, garnished with chopped coriander.

White Bean Vegetable Terrine

Major Phase: Metal
Minor Phase: Wood

Yield: 10 to 12 servings

Here's a complex, interesting dish—worth every moment you spend making it! Delicious, unusual, and beautiful, you'll impress everyone with its delicate blend of flavors when it's part of your party meal. Serve it sliced on a "bed" of fresh tomato sauce, as an appetizer or side dish. My thanks to John B. for this great recipe.

<pre>
        1 pound dry white beans,* soaked
      ½ cup coarsely chopped onions
      ½ tablespoon chopped garlic
      ½ cup plus 1 tablespoon extra-virgin olive oil
      ¼ cup dry white vermouth or sake
      ¼ teaspoon ground thyme
        3 small bay leaves, pulverized
      ¼ teaspoon ground coriander seeds
        2 sprigs parsley
      ¾ pound thin carrots
      ½ pound green beans
        2 sweet red peppers
          Sea salt to taste
      ⅓ cup fresh lemon juice
        2 tablespoons kuzu or arrowroot
          Freshly ground white pepper to taste
10 to 12 large grape leaves
</pre>

1. Drain the beans.
2. Heat 1 tablespoon of the oil in a 4-quart saucepan and sauté the onions and garlic over medium heat until transparent, about 2 to 3 minutes. Add the beans and enough fresh water to cover by 2 inches. Add the vermouth or sake, thyme, bay leaves, coriander seeds, and parsley. Bring to a boil, reduce heat, and simmer until very soft, about 1 hour.
3. In another pot, simmer the whole carrots in water until tender, about 25 minutes. Remove the carrots and set aside, reserving the cooking water.
4. Trim the green beans. Slice the tops and bottoms off the peppers and cut each one into four *flat* pieces. Cook the green beans in the carrot water until about half done, 3 to 4 minutes, then add the peppers and cook for 10 minutes more.
5. Ten minutes before the end of the cooking time, salt the beans. When the beans are finished cooking, puree in a food processor. With the machine running, add the remaining ½ cup oil and the lemon juice. Return to the pot.
6. Mix the kuzu or arrowroot with a few tablespoons of the cooled bean liquid

---

* Navy, pea beans, Puerto Rican white beans, etc.—any small white bean except lima beans.

and add to the bean puree. Cook until mixture "boils" and becomes very thick.

7. Oil a 9-inch × 5-inch loaf pan and line with the grape leaves, overlapping them over the bottom of the pan. The shiny side of the leaf should be down, the veiny side up. About ½ of each leaf should hang over the sides of the pan. (Rinse leaves before using if you don't want their salty flavor.) Cover the bottom of the pan with a thin layer of bean puree, then carefully arrange a layer of carrots end to end on top. Add more puree, then the green beans; more puree, then the red pepper. Layer the vegetables so that they evenly cover the length of the pan, cutting them to size if necessary to fill in space. Finish with a layer of puree. Fold the grape leaves over the top. (This will become the bottom of the terrine.) Press down with a smaller loaf pan to pack evenly. Chill for at least 4 hours before serving. Unmold onto a serving platter.

8. Cut into ¾- to 1-inch slices. To serve, place a thin layer of uncooked Tomato Sauce (see below) on a plate, then cover with a slice of terrine.

Uncooked Tomato Sauce

Major Phase: Fire

YIELD: ABOUT 1½ CUPS

  1 pound ripe tomatoes
  1 rounded teaspoon white or yellow miso
  1 tablespoon balsamic or apple cider vinegar
  ¼ cup extra-virgin olive oil
  ¼ teaspoon freshly ground pepper, or to taste
  1 tablespoon chopped fresh tarragon, or 1 teaspoon dried
  2 tablespoons chopped parsley

1. Peel, seed, and chop the tomatoes. Place them in a colander and let them drain for about 10 minutes.

2. Place all the ingredients in the container of a blender or a food processor, and puree until smooth. (If you have no fresh tarragon, soak the dried tarragon in the vinegar for 5 minutes before adding.)

Vegetable-Tofu Sauté

Major Phase: Metal
Minor Phase: Wood

YIELD: 6 servings

A lovely summer dish, this goes well with Quinoa and Millet Pilaf (page 111) and perhaps the cold Cantaloupe Soup (page 104) for dessert.

  1 pound firm tofu
  1 pound mushrooms
  ½ bunch watercress
  1 medium carrot
  ½ small daikon (Japanese white radish), about 2½ inches long
  1 cup cold water
  1 egg white
  ¼ cup plus 1 teaspoon shoyu or tamari
  1 tablespoon sake or mirin (sweet rice wine)
  ¼ teaspoon sea salt
  6 tablespoons arrowroot
  2 teaspoons brown rice or apple cider vinegar
  2 tablespoons unrefined sesame or cold-pressed sunflower oil
  1 tablespoon chopped parsley for garnish

1. Drain the tofu. Cut it horizontally into three ⅜-inch layers; then make one cut lengthwise down the middle, to make 6 rectangles. Press with dry paper towels to remove excess moisture; repeat several times, until the tofu feels cool but dry to the touch. Set aside while you prepare the vegetables.
2. Wipe the mushrooms and cut them into thin slivers. Pull the leaves off the watercress, discarding stems. Set aside.
3. Scrub the carrots, then cut into very thin matchsticks by cutting into 1/16-inch diagonal slices, then again into 1/16-inch strips.
4. Peel the daikon and cut into matchsticks. Soak for 5 minutes in the water; drain.
5. In a medium bowl, mix the mushrooms, carrots, daikon, watercress, egg white, 1 teaspoon of the shoyu, the sake or mirin and the salt. Sprinkle on 4 tablespoons of the arrowroot and mix well.

6. Lay the tofu slices on a flat work surface. Using a strainer, sprinkle the remaining 2 tablespoons arrowroot evenly over the tofu. Spread a ½-inch layer of the vegetable mixture evenly over the tofu slices. Press lightly.

7. Mix the remaining ¼ cup shoyu and vinegar in bowl; set aside.

8. In 12-inch skillet over high heat, heat 1 tablespoon of the oil. Using two spatulas, add half the tofu slices, vegetable side down, and sauté for 6 to 8 minutes, or until lightly browned. Carefully turn the slices over, using both spatulas. Add the remaining tablespoon of oil to the pan and sauté tofu for 4 to 5 minutes more, or until light brown. Remove to a warm plate and repeat with the remaining tofu slices.

9. Sprinkle ½ teaspoon parsley over each tofu slice, then sprinkle with the shoyu vinegar sauce. Serve immediately.

❧ • ❧

Tofu Mushroom Stroganoff with Bulgur

Major Phase: Metal
Minor Phase: Wood

YIELD: 6 servings

3½	cups water
¾	teaspoon sea salt, or to taste
1½	cup bulgur
1	pound green beans
2	medium yellow onions
2	tablespoons cold-pressed soy or sunflower oil
1	red pepper
¾	pound button mushrooms
3	tablespoons whole wheat flour
3	tablespoons shoyu or tamari
	Freshly ground pepper to taste
1½	tablespoons chopped fresh dill

Tofu Sour Cream

1 pound soft tofu
3 tablespoons cold-pressed soy or sunflower oil
2½ tablespoons fresh lemon juice
(about 1 large lemon)
2 scallions, white part only
¾ tablespoon umeboshi vinegar
¼ teaspoon sea salt

1. In a 2- or 3-quart saucepan, bring 2¼ cups of the water to a boil with ½ teaspoon of the salt, add the bulgur, return to a boil, and remove from the heat. Cover and let stand 45 minutes.
2. Wash and trim the green beans, and snap them into 2-inch pieces. Steam in a small saucepan with ½ cup water for 5 minutes. Drain and set aside, reserving the cooking liquid.
2. Chop the onions. In a 3-quart saucepan, heat 2 tablespoons of the oil and sauté the onions until soft, about 3 to 4 minutes. Seed and chop the pepper and add, sautéing another 3 to 4 minute. Slice the mushrooms, and add with the remaining ¼ teaspoon salt, cooking until they release their liquid. Add the flour, stir, and continue cooking for 2 to 3 minutes longer, until the flower has absorbed all the liquid.
3. Add the remaining ¾ cup water, a little at a time, stirring constantly to blend well. Simmer 15 minutes, covered, add shoyu and pepper, and cook 5 minutes.
4. *To make the tofu sour cream:* combine the tofu, oil, lemon juice, salt, scallions, and vinegar in a blender or a food processor. Process until smooth.
5. Stir the tofu sour cream into the onion mixture, then add the green beans and the chopped dill. Remove from heat, adjust seasonings, and serve immediately over the fluffed bulghur.

Broccoli-Tofu Quiche
with Wild Mushrooms

Major Phase: Wood
Minor Phase: Metal

YIELD: 8 to 12 servings

As *a rule, I dislike "mock" dishes—healthful imitations of unhealthy foods. Here, however, is one exception. Imitation quiche (Look, Ma, no eggs!) or not, this pie is really tasty. There is good protein complementarity, too, between the tofu and the crust. Try it for brunch with Crunchy Fennel Salad (page 199).*

Crust

2 cups whole wheat pastry flour, or barley or brown rice flour,
  or a combination of these
⅓ cup cold-pressed safflower oil
⅓ cup water
¼ teaspoon sea salt

Filling

4 cloves garlic
6 ounces fresh wild mushrooms, such as shiitake,
  porcini, chanterelles, or any others
6 ounces fresh white button mushrooms
1 tablespoon extra-virgin olive oil
1 teaspoon dried basil
1 teaspoon dried marjoram
1 cup very small broccoli florets
1½ pounds soft tofu
2 tablespoons umeboshi vinegar
2 tablespoons cold-pressed sunflower oil
½ teaspoon sea salt, or to taste
  Freshly ground black pepper to taste

1. Preheat the oven to 350°F.
2. *To prepare the crust:* Place the flour in a large mixing bowl.
3. In a smaller bowl, mix together the oil, water, and salt; add to the flour and blend well. The mixture will be crumbly.
4. Press the crust into a 9-inch pie plate, making sure the thickness is uniform all around, especially where the bottom meets the side. Smooth out the edges to make an even rim.
5. Bake in the preheated oven for 10 minutes, or until the crust sounds hollow when you tap it with a spoon.
6. *To prepare the filling:* Mince the garlic. Wipe the mushrooms and slice them thinly, discarding the tough stems.
7. In a large skillet, heat the oil over medium heat. Sauté the garlic for 15 seconds, then add the mushrooms and sauté over low heat, stirring, for 3 to 4 minutes. Sprinkle on the basil and marjoram and sauté for 2 minutes more. Remove from the heat.
8. In a medium pot, bring 1 quart of water to a boil and blanch the broccoli for 15 seconds, or just until it turns bright green. Remove with a slotted spoon or fine-mesh spatula and plunge briefly into a bowl of cold water to stop the cooking. Drain and set aside.
9. Place the tofu, vinegar, and oil in a blender or food processor and blend until very smooth and creamy. Add salt and freshly ground black pepper to taste.
10. *To assemble the quiche:* Spread the mushroom mixture over the bottom of the prebaked piecrust, top with the broccoli florets, then top with the creamed tofu, making sure it completely covers the vegetables. Bake for 30 minutes, or until the tofu ridges take on a faintly beige hue. Good hot or cold.

Open Herbed Tofu Sandwiches

Major Phase: Metal
Minor Phase: Wood

Yield: 4 sandwiches

*T*hese make a delicious summer brunch.

1 pound soft tofu
  2 tablespoons tahini
  1 teaspoon dried oregano
  1 teaspoon dried basil
  1 tablespoon fresh chopped dill
  ½ teaspoon dried marjoram
  1 tablespoon chopped parsley
  1 tablespoon umeboshi paste
  4 slices sourdough whole wheat bread
    Salad dressing of your choice (or see recipe below)
  ⅓ cup alfalfa sprouts

1. In a large bowl, mash the tofu with a fork until you get a thick paste. Add the tahini, oregano, basil, dill, marjoram, parsley, and umeboshi paste. Mix well.
2. Spread on the bread and top with alfalfa sprouts. Cut each slice in half if desired.
3. Put a few drops of your favorite salad dressing on top of the sprouts or use the one below.

Dressing

Phase: Wood

Yield: ½ cup

  3 tablespoons extra-virgin olive oil
  3 tablespoons umeboshi vinegar
  1 tablespoon water
  1 tablespoon fresh lemon juice

1. Place all the ingredients in a small bowl or a jar with a lid and stir or shake to mix well.

Tempeh with Shallots
and White Wine

Major Phase: Metal
Minor Phase: Water

Yield: 4 to 6 servings

The wine and the shallots give this dish an authentically French touch. It works equally well when made with cubed fresh swordfish instead of tempeh. Swordfish does not need to be marinated. You can serve this with Orange Millet Pilaf (page 110) and a cool leafy green salad.

One 8-ounce package tempeh
4 cloves garlic
1¾ cups water
¼ cup shoyu or tamari
2 to 3 slices fresh ginger root
3 shallots
3 tablespoons cold-pressed sunflower oil or unsalted butter
2 tablespoons water
1 teaspoon fresh lemon juice
⅓ cup dry white wine
1 tablespoon chopped parsley or scallions for garnish

1. Slice the tempeh horizontally through the middle into 2 layers, then cut each layer into 1-inch strips, and across into 1-inch cubes.
2. Smash the garlic with the flat side of your knife; peel. In a medium saucepan, combine the water, shoyu, 2 of the garlic gloves, and the ginger. Add the tempeh cubes. Bring to a boil, reduce heat, cover, and simmer for 10 minutes. Remove the tempeh with a slotted spoon and drain in a colander, reserving the cooking liquid. Discard the garlic and ginger.
3. Peel the shallots and mince them along with the remaining cloves of garlic.
4. In a large skillet, heat the oil or butter. Sauté the garlic and shallots over medium heat for 3 to 4 minutes, or until translucent.

5. Add the tempeh cubes and sauté over a high heat until the tempeh browns slightly, scraping it up with a spatula.

6. Add 2 tablespoons of the tempeh-cooking liquid, 2 tablespoons water, the lemon juice, and the wine. Stir well; scrape any browned bits that have stuck to the bottom of the pan and cook over medium heat until the liquids have reduced to half and thickened somewhat. Serve immediately, garnished with chopped parsley or scallions.

Tempeh in Sweet and Sour Sauce

Major Phase: Metal
Minor Phases: Wood and Earth

YIELD: 4 to 6 servings

*H*ere's a meatless dish with an Oriental flavor. It is most often served over a bed of grain, (the Quinoa and Millet Pilaf, page 111, is especially nice), but you can also wrap a ladleful in a lettuce leaf and eat it out of hand.

One 8-ounce package tempeh
2 to 3 cloves garlic
1¾ cups water
¼ cup shoyu or tamari
Two 1½ -inch slices fresh ginger root
1 tablespoon cold-pressed safflower oil for frying

Sweet and Sour Sauce

1 cup unfiltered apple juice
½ cup reserved tempeh-cooking broth (with garlic cloves)
2 tablespoons umeboshi vinegar;
    or 2 tablespoons lemon juice, mixed
    with ½ teaspoon sea salt
2 tablespoons brown rice vinegar
¼ cup rice syrup
1 tablespoon whole-grain mustard
3 tablespoons kuzu
    Grated rind from ½ orange

1. *To season the tempeh:* Cut the tempeh into ⅔-inch cubes. Smash garlic with the flat side of your knife; peel.
2. Place tempeh and garlic in a saucepan with the water, shoyu, and ginger. Bring to a boil, reduce heat, cover, and simmer for 10 minutes. Drain, reserving the cooking liquid with the garlic. Discard the ginger.
3. In a skillet, heat the oil and sauté the tempeh over high heat briefly, or until lightly browned. Set aside in a serving bowl.
4. *To make the sauce:* In a medium saucepan, combine ½ cup of the apple juice with the tempeh broth, vinegars, syrup, and mustard. Place over high heat.
5. In a small bowl, dissolve the kuzu in the remaining apple juice. Add to the saucepan, stirring until the mixture has thickened and comes to a boil, about 2 to 3 minutes. Add the orange rind and cook for 1 minute more. Pour over the tempeh immediately and mix. Serve hot over grain.

Tempeh with Creamy Horseradish Sauce

Major Phase: Metal
Minor Phase: Water

YIELD: 4 servings

There is really no substitute for fresh horseradish root in this dish. Serve it over millet or rice, perhaps with the Cream of Squash and Parsnips Soup with Dill (page 92) and the Four-Greens and Walnut Sauté (page 179).

⅔ cup freshly grated horseradish
2 tablespoons umeboshi vinegar; or 2 tablespoons brown rice vinegar, mixed with ⅓ teaspoon sea salt
3 teaspoons kuzu or arrowroot
2 cups cold water or Light Vegetable Stock (page 72)
3 tablespoons tahini
Sea salt to taste (optional)
1 recipe seasoned tempeh (from Tempeh in Sweet and Sour Sauce, page 161)
2 cups cooked millet

1. Mix the horseradish with the vinegar; set aside.
2. In a 1½-quart saucepan, dissolve the kuzu or arrowroot in the water or stock. Cook over high heat, stirring continuously, until thick, about 4 to 5 minutes.
3. With a wooden spoon, stir in the tahini, then add the horseradish-vinegar mixture. Add salt to taste if needed. Serve over seasoned tempeh and millet.

❧ Vegetables ❧

There was a time when it was customary to cook fresh vegetables by boiling them into oblivion— two, four, even twelve hours (the latter for beets). Needless to say, vegetables were not very popular, or even very healthy for that matter, since the over-long cooking depleted them of most of their nutrients. Then canning and freezing came on the scene—or embalming and cryogenics, respectively. We have treated plants with too much disrespect. They are, after all, our link with the cosmos. Green plants keep us breathing, roots give us their grounding, stalks and pods their strength, fruits their cheerfulness. Respect is in order—as is proper cooking technique.

Mushroom-Stuffed Artichokes

Major Phase: Wood

<small>YIELD:</small> 6 servings

*T*hese are absolutely delicious! Something out of the ordinary to do with artichokes. Serve them at room temperature, or, in really hot weather, chilled, as an appetizer or side dish.

6 artichokes

Juice of ½ lemon

9 ounces mushrooms, finely chopped

1 small onion

2 cloves garlic

2 tablespoons chopped parsley

½ cup whole wheat bread crumbs

½ tablespoon dried oregano

½ tablespoon paprika

½ teaspoon dried sage

2½ tablespoons extra-virgin olive oil

½ teaspoon sea salt

Freshly ground pepper to taste

1. Wash the artichokes by holding each one by the stem and push it up and down in a large bowl of cold water; drain. Slice ¼-inch off the tips. Trim the pointy tips of the leaves with scissors. Cut the stems short and to equal lengths. Pull off and discard any tough bottom leaves. Dip the cut surface of the stems in the lemon juice to prevent discoloration. (If the artichokes are very fresh, the stem pieces may also be eaten. Peel them, then dice and soak in lemon juice and water.)

2. Choose a pan large enough to hold all of the artichokes in a single layer. Place the artichokes, tops down, on a trivet or steaming basket. Add 1 to 2 inches water, bring to a boil, and steam the artichokes for 15 to 20 minutes, or until halfway tender. Remove with tongs. Reserve the steaming water.

3. Preheat the oven to 350°F. Finely chop the mushrooms, mince the onion and garlic. In a large bowl, combine the mushrooms, onion, garlic, parsley, bread crumbs, oregano, paprika, sage, and 2 tablespoons of the olive oil. Toss, seasoning with the salt and pepper.

4. When the artichokes are cool enough to handle, open each one from the center to force the leaves open and apart. With a teaspoon, scoop out and discard the choke and spiney inner leaves. Fill each cavity with a large spoonful of the mushroom mixture. Return the stuffed artichokes to the casserole, placing them, tops up, on the trivet or steaming basket over ½ inch of boiling artichoke or plain water. Add the diced stem pieces. Sprinkle the remaining ½ tablespoon olive oil over all. Cover, transfer to the oven, and bake for 30 minutes, or until the leaves are tender and can be easily pulled from artichoke. Serve hot, with a few of the stem pieces on the side.

Arame or Hiziki
with Ginger and Garlic

Major Phase: Water
Minor Phase: Metal

Yield: 4 to 6 servings

Sea vegetables are full of health-giving minerals, but for most Westerners their briny sea taste takes some getting used to. This combination is one of my favorites and is also one that even first-timers seem to like.

> ½ cup arame or hiziki seaweed
> 2 cups water
> 2 cloves garlic
> ½ -inch piece fresh ginger root
> 1 tablespoon light unrefined sesame oil
> 1 tablespoon shoyu or tamari, or to taste

1. Soak the arame or hiziki in the water for 5 to 10 minutes. Mince the garlic. Peel and mince the ginger.
2. Drain the soaked seaweed.*
3. Heat the oil in a cast-iron skillet. Sauté the ginger and garlic over low heat briefly. Add the drained seaweed, raise heat to medium, and sauté, stirring, for 5 minutes. Add the shoyu and cook for 3 minutes more. Serve immediately, about two tablespoons per person as a small side dish.

Gail's Hiziki with Snow Peas, Ginger, and Radish

Major Phase: Water
Minor Phases: Metal and Wood

YIELD: 6 to 8 servings

The secret of this dish lies in barely heating the snow peas, as they take literally just a minute to cook. They should retain their bright green color.

½ cup hiziki seaweed
2 cups water
3 large red radishes
¼ pound snow peas
½ -inch piece ginger root
2 tablespoons toasted sesame oil
1 tablespoon shoyu or tamari
Umeboshi vinegar to taste or lemon wedges (optional)

1. Soak the hiziki in the water for 10 minutes.
2. Meanwhile wash and trim the radishes, then slice them thinly. String the snow

---

* Seaweed soaking water may be used to water your house and garden plants.

peas and trim the stem ends. Peel the ginger root, slice thinly, then cut slices into thin matchsticks.

3. Drain the hiziki, pressing out the excess moisture.
4. Heat the sesame oil in a wok over high heat. Add the ginger and sauté, stirring, for 1 to 2 minutes. Add the hiziki, stir once or twice, and cook for 2 to 3 minutes. Add the shoyu, cover, lower the heat to medium, and cook for 5 minutes more. Add the snow peas and radishes, toss well, and cook very briefly—about 30 seconds—just until the snow peas are bright green.
5. Sprinkle with the umeboshi vinegar, or serve with lemon wedges if desired. Serve immediately.

Stir-fried Bok Choy with Marinated Tofu

Major Phase: Metal
Minor Phase: Fire

YIELD: 4 to 6 servings

Stir-frying requires a bit of preparation time but is very simple once you get to heating the wok. This is one of the easiest dishes, and very popular in my classes as well as at home with my children. My thanks to Karen Lee, noted teacher and author, for teaching me the basics of stir-frying.

½ pound soft tofu
¾ cups water
2 tablespoons shoyu or tamari
½ teaspoon five-spice powder*
1 large head bok choy
2 cloves garlic
4 thin slices fresh ginger root
3 whole scallions
1 tablespoon kuzu or arrowroot
1 teaspoon unrefined sesame oil
½ teaspoon toasted sesame oil

1. Drain the tofu and pat it dry with a paper towel. Slice into ½-inch slices; pat dry again. Place the water, shoyu, and five-spice powder in a bowl and add the tofu slices. Marinate for at least 30 minutes, preferably longer, up to 24 hours.
2. Preheat the oven to 375°F. Oil a cookie sheet.
3. Remove the tofu from the marinade. Reserve the marinade. Place the tofu on the cookie sheet and bake for 20 minutes, or until browned, then turn and bake for another 10 minutes. Remove from the oven and set aside until cool enough to handle.
4. Cut the tofu into ½-inch cubes.
5. Slice 1 inch off the lower end of the bok choy and discard. Separate and wash the leaves. Slice the whites and the greens into bite-size pieces; set aside in separate bowls.
6. Peel and mince the garlic and ginger; slice the scallions finely. Set aside in separate bowls.
7. Dissolve the kuzu or arrowroot in ¼ cup of the tofu marinade; set aside.
8. In a wok or 4-quart pot, heat the light sesame oil over medium-high heat. Add the garlic, ginger, and scallions and sauté, stirring, for about 1 minute. Add the white parts of the bok choy, stir, cook briefly, then reduce heat to low, cover, and steam for 5 minutes.
9. Uncover and add the bok choy leaves, stirring continuously until the leaves are wilted. The bok choy will have released quite a bit of water. Push the vegetable

* Obtainable in Oriental groceries or natural-foods stores.

to the side. Restir the kuzu or arrowroot mixture and gradually pour it into the bok choy liquid over medium heat, stirring continuously until thickened. (You may not need to use all the starch mixture to get the sauce consistency you want. On the other hand, if the mixture gets too thick, thin with a bit of water or additional tofu marinade liquid.) Stir the bok choy into the sauce until well blended, then stir in the tofu.

10. Sprinkle on the dark sesame oil, stir once more, and serve immediately.

Broccoli Rabe with Garlic

Major Phase: Fire

Yield: 4 to 6 servings

A classic Italian vegetable dish; the lengthy cooking time is necessary to soften the bitterness of the greens.

> 1 large bunch broccoli rabe (about 2 pounds)
> 2 cloves garlic
> 1 tablespoon extra-virgin olive oil
> ½ cup water

1. Soak the broccoli rabe in a basin of cold water, allowing the sand to settle to the bottom; drain. Chop coarsely, discarding discolored leaves and pieces of stem.

2. Peel and mince the garlic. In a large skillet, heat the oil over high heat and sauté the garlic for 15 seconds.

3. Add the chopped broccoli and sauté for 2 to 3 minutes, tossing to coat all pieces with the oil. Reduce heat to low. Add the water, cover, and steam for 20 to 25 minutes. Uncover, stir, and serve. Rabe should be tender, but retain a bright green color.

Puree of Brussels Sprouts

Phase: Fire

Yield: 4 servings

*H*ere is a lovely way to prepare this underused vegetable. Make sure to cook just briefly to retain the color.

 1 small sweet red pepper
 1 pint brussels sprouts (about ⅔ pound)
 2 large cloves garlic
 1 tablespoon cold-pressed sunflower oil or unsalted butter
 2 tablespoons oat flour
 ⅔ cup water
 ¼ teaspoon sea salt, or to taste
  Freshly ground black pepper to taste

1. Roast the red pepper over high heat until the skin is well charred. Place in a brown paper bag or a covered pot to steam for 10 minutes. Remove the skin under cold running water, seed, and slice into long, thin strips; set aside.
2. Trim and cut an X in the stems of the brussels sprouts. Cut the large ones in half. Place in a 3- to 4-quart saucepan, add 1 inch of water, and cook covered, until barely tender, 5 to 7 minutes.
3. Finely shred the sprouts in a food processor, being careful not to overprocess, or the result will be mush. (You may also use a hand grater.)
4. Peel the garlic and squeeze it through a garlic press. In a large skillet or 4-quart pot, heat the oil or butter over medium heat and sauté the garlic for 30 seconds. Add the flour and cook for a minute or two, stirring. Add the water slowly, whisking constantly to avoid lumps, until the mixture boils. Add the salt and pepper and cook, covered, for 5 minutes more over medium heat. Stir in the sprouts and cook for 5 minutes, uncovered, until the sprouts are bright green and the flavors thoroughly blended.
5. Garnish each serving with 3 strips of red pepper. Serve immediately.

Cabbage with Cumin

Major Phase: Metal

YIELD: 4 to 6 servings

This easy-to-make dish is an old Hungarian standby, a classic combination of the seasoning and the vegetable. When I make cabbage as a side dish, this remains the recipe I prefer.

½ small head green cabbage (about 6 inches in diameter)
2 tablespoons unrefined sesame oil or extra-virgin olive oil
1 teaspoon cumin seed
1 teaspoon ground cumin
½ teaspoon sea salt

1. Shred the cabbage very fine (you should have around 3½ to 4 cups).
2. In a 4-quart saucepan, heat the oil and add the cumin seed; then add the cabbage and the ground cumin. Sprinkle the salt over everything. Stir several times to blend the ingredients, cover, and cook over low heat until the cabbage wilts, about 10 to 15 minutes. Stir, and cook for 15 minutes more. Serve hot.

Cauliflower Curry

Major Phase: Metal

YIELD: 6 servings

There is really nothing like making your own curry powder. In India every household has its own version. Once you know the basic ingredients, you can make up your own, too.

Curry Powder

¼ teaspoon ground ginger
¼ teaspoon ground fenugreek
¼ teaspoon ground turmeric
¼ teaspoon ground dill
½ teaspoon ground cumin
¼ teaspoon ground coriander
¼ teaspoon ground paprika or cayenne pepper
¼ teaspoon commercial curry powder
¼ teaspoon sea salt

1 small head cauliflower
1 medium onion
1 tablespoon unrefined sesame oil or unsalted butter
¼ cup water

1. *To make the curry powder:* Mix all the spices together in a small bowl; set aside.
2. Cut the cauliflower into florets; discard the core.
3. Peel and chop the onion. Heat the oil in a cast-iron skillet, add the curry powder and the onion and sauté over medium heat for 4 minutes.
4. Add the cauliflower; stirring well to distribute the spices. Add the water, reduce heat to low, cover, and cook for 20 minutes, or until the cauliflower is tender. Serve immediately.

❧ • ☙

Cauliflower Curry with Coconut

Major Phase: Metal

YIELD: 6 servings

*H*ere's another version of cauliflower curry. The coconut gives this dish a totally different flavor, richer and fuller.

  2 cloves garlic
¼ teaspoon sea salt
¼ cup unsweetened shredded coconut
  2 tablespoons sesame seeds, toasted
  1 tablespoon cumin seeds, toasted
  1 teaspoon black or brown mustard seeds
⅛ teaspoon ground cloves
¼ cup roasted peanuts
½ teaspoon ground turmeric
¼ teaspoon cayenne pepper
½ cup water
  1 tablespoon unrefined sesame oil
  1 medium onion
  1 small head cauliflower
  1 tablespoon fresh lemon juice

1. Mince the garlic and mash with the salt. Place the garlic, coconut, sesame seeds, cumin seed, mustard seeds, cloves, peanuts, turmeric, cayenne and water in a blender and blend until smooth.
2. Mince the onion. Cut the cauliflower into small florets.
3. In a large skillet, heat the sesame oil. Add the onion and sauté over medium-low heat until translucent, about 5 minutes. Add the cauliflower. Stir in the garlic-coconut mixture. Cook, covered, over low heat until the cauliflower is tender, about 7 to 8 minutes, adding more water if the pan starts to dry out to avoid burning.
4. Add the lemon juice. Cook for a few minutes longer. Taste and adjust the seasoning. Serve immediately.

Millet and Cauliflower Puree

Major Phase: Metal

Yield: 8 servings

Some people call this millet mashed potatoes, and indeed it does resemble the dish made from the friendly tuber; it is less starchy, however, with more subtle taste gradations, and of course it's ideal for those who wish to avoid potatoes for health reasons.

     2 cups millet
     1 quart water or Light Vegetable Stock (page 72)
     ½ teaspoon sea salt, or to taste
     1 whole small cauliflower
     1 to 2 tablespoons unsalted butter or extra-virgin olive oil (optional)

1. Clean the millet (see page 38).
2. Place the millet in a 4-quart pot. Dry-roast over high heat, stirring continuously for about 10 minutes, or until the water has evaporated and the millet begins to change color slightly and turn fragrant. Add the water or stock and the salt.
3. Cut up the cauliflower into florets, discarding the tough core, and add to the millet. Cover, and simmer over low heat for 45 minutes, or until all the water is absorbed. At the end of cooking time, stir vigorously to further break up the cauliflower. Alternatively, mash the cooked millet and cauliflower with a fork, potato masher, or put through a food processor, to make a puree similar to mashed potatoes. Add a little butter or olive oil if desired. Serve immediately.

❧ • ☙

Braised Daikon with Mirin

Major Phase: Metal

Yield: 6 servings

The Japanese daikon radish is becoming increasingly popular and easy to find. This dish is flavorful and easy to prepare. It makes a fine side dish to a hearty stew, such as Locro (page 131).

1 small daikon (about 1 pound)
3 tablespoons mirin (sweet rice wine), sake, or dry sherry
   Pinch sea salt
1 tablespoon shoyu or tamari, or to taste

1. Wash the daikon and grate coarsely on the large holes of a grater or in a food processor. (You should have 2 to 3 cups.)
2. Place the daikon in a 3- to 4-quart pot and cook over medium heat, stirring, for 5 minutes, or until softened.
3. Add the mirin, sake, or sherry and the salt. Cover and let steam over very low heat for 10 minutes.
4. Add the shoyu or tamari, stir well, and steam for 10 minutes more. Serve immediately.

Braised Fennel on Radicchio

Phase: Metal

Yield: 6 servings

*O*ur version of this elegant dish was inspired by a recipe from Bert Greene's Greene on Greens.

2 medium onions
1 clove garlic
1 tablespoon extra-virgin olive oil
2 bulbs fennel
½ tablespoon anise seeds
½ teaspoon sea salt
  Freshly ground black pepper to taste
½ teaspoon finely grated orange rind
2½ cups water
1 tablespoon white miso
1 tablespoon kuzu
1 head radicchio*
2 teaspoons fresh lemon juice

---

* Use red cabbage if radicchio is not available.

1. Slice the onions into thin crescents. Mince the garlic.
2. In large skillet, heat the oil. Add the onions and garlic and sauté over medium heat until the onions wilt, about 3 to 4 minutes.
3. Meanwhile, slice the fennel bulbs lengthwise into thin slices. Mince the feathery green tops and set aside. Discard the stalks. Add the sliced fennel to the onions and garlic along with the anise seeds, salt, and pepper. Cook, uncovered, for 10 minutes, stirring occasionally.
4. Add 2 cups of the water, the lemon juice and the orange rind; cover the pan and simmer 20 minutes more. Mix the miso and kuzu with the remaining ½ cup water. When fennel is tender, remove with a slotted spoon and set aside.
5. Bring the liquid in the skillet to a boil and reduce to 1 cup. Add the miso/kuzu mixture and continue to cook, stirring continuously, until the mixture is clear and thickened, about 60 seconds. Remove from the heat.
6. Separate the radicchio leaves. Place about ⅓ cup of the fennel in each radicchio leaf. Arrange the leaves on a platter. Spoon a little fennel sauce over each leaf. Serve at room temperature or chilled, garnished with minced fennel tops.

❧ • ☙

Greens with Wild Mushrooms and Garlic

Major Phase: Fire
Minor Phase: Water

YIELD: 6 servings

Here is my favorite way of preparing these hardy but strengthening vegetables, one of the best vegetable sources of calcium. The cooking water—"pot likker"—is delicious to drink while hot with ½ teaspoon umeboshi vinegar or lemon juice per cup. Try it instead of soup, as a before-dinner drink.

1 bunch broccoli rabe
1 bunch mustard greens
1 cup sliced wild mushrooms (oyster, fresh shiitake, cremini, or other)

2 large cloves garlic
2 tablespoons extra-virgin olive oil
½ teaspoon minced fresh ginger root
Pinch sea salt
Freshly grated nutmeg

1. Prepare the greens (page 40). You should have 4 to 5 cups (loosely packed). Bring 2 quarts water to a boil in a 3- to 4-quart pot. Add the greens and boil, uncovered, for 5 to 10 minutes. Drain and chop well. Slice the mushrooms; peel and mince the garlic.
2. In a large skillet heat the oil and add the garlic and ginger; sauté over medium heat for 30 seconds. Add the mushrooms and sauté until they release some moisture, about 5 minutes. Add the greens. Sauté until heated through, about 5 minutes. Season with salt and a dusting of nutmeg. Serve immediately.

Four Greens and Walnut Sauté

Major Phase: Fire
Minor Phase: Metal

YIELD: 6 servings

1 cup beet greens or kale
1 cup collards   washed, picked over, and
1 cup dandelion greens   coarse stems removed
1 cup mustard greens
1 tablespoon extra-virgin olive oil
4 cloves garlic, minced
  Sea salt to taste
½ cup walnut pieces

1. Toast the walnuts in a 350° oven for 10 minutes, or until fragrant.
2. Boil the washed greens in 6 to 8 cups water for 10 minutes, uncovered; drain. When the greens are cool enough to handle, chop coarsely.

3. In a large skillet, heat the oil over medium heat. Add the garlic and sauté briefly. Add the greens and continue to sauté for 5 minutes. Add a pinch of salt, to taste.
4. Add the walnut pieces. Serve immediately.

Wilted Dandelion Greens with Navy Beans

Major Phase: Fire
Minor Phase: Metal

YIELD: 6 servings

A flavorful spring recipe for these strongly flavored greens. To make a salad out of it, toss it with a mustard vinaigrette, such as Mustard Cream Vinaigrette (page 213). Be sure to drink the "pot likker"!

2 quarts Light Vegetable Stock (page 72) or water
1 medium onion
2 pounds dandelion greens
3 sun-dried tomatoes, packed in olive oil
2 cups cooked navy beans (if unavailable, use pignolias or sunflower seeds)

1. In a 6-quart pot, bring the stock or water to a boil. Mince the garlic.
2. Trim and wash the dandelion greens. Add the greens and the whole onion to the pot and simmer, uncovered, for 10 to 15 minutes, or until the greens are tender; drain. Allow to cool. Remove and discard the onion.
3. Chop the tomatoes.
4. When the greens are cool enough to handle, chop them coarsely and toss with the tomatoes and beans. Serve either hot or at room temperature.

Buttered Green Beans
with Sunflower Seeds

Major Phase: Wood
Minor Phase: Fire

Yield: 4 to 5 servings

1 pound green beans
1 tablespoon unsalted butter
¼ cup sunflower seeds
Pinch sea salt, or to taste

1. Trim the beans. Place 1 inch of water in a medium saucepan, add the beans, and steam, covered, for 4 to 5 minutes; drain. (You may do this in advance.)
2. Just before serving, melt the butter in a skillet over medium-high heat and add the sunflower seeds. Let sizzle a bit until toasty, about 3 to 4 minutes. Stir into the beans, season with salt to taste, and serve immediately.

Green Beans with Ginger and Tomatoes

Major Phase: Wood
Minor Phases: Fire and Metal

Yield: 4 to 5 servings

Simple and delicious, this spirited dish goes well with spiced dishes like Aromatic Spiced Rice (page 112) and Cauliflower Curry (page 173).

1 pound green beans
2 medium tomatoes
2 large onions
4 cloves garlic
½ -inch piece fresh ginger root
2 tablespoons unrefined sesame oil
1 teaspoon whole black or brown mustard seeds
¼ teaspoon sea salt, or to taste

1. Wash the beans and trim the stem ends. Slice or snap into 1-inch pieces.
2. Peel and seed the tomatoes by dropping into boiling water for 10 seconds; pull off the skins, then slice in half crosswise and squeeze out and discard the seeds. Chop coarsely.
3. Chop the onions and mince the garlic. Peel and mince the ginger root.
4. In a medium skillet, heat 1 tablespoon of the oil. Add the tomatoes, onions, garlic, and ginger and sauté over medium heat for 5 minutes; set aside.
5. In a large skillet, heat the remaining oil. Add the mustard seeds and as soon as they begin to pop (about 30 seconds), add the beans and sauté over medium heat for 5 minutes. Sprinkle on the salt.
6. Add the tomato mixture. Cover the pan and cook, over low heat, stirring occasionally, for 20 to 25 minutes. Serve hot.

❧ • ❧

Green Peppers with Miso

Major Phase: Wood
Minor Phase: Water

YIELD: 4 to 6 servings

Green peppers and miso are a surprisingly felicitous combination, especially good for people who are not crazy about the vegetable: The salty tang of the miso eliminates the sharp edge of the pepper's flavor and mellows it delightfully.

2 large green peppers
1 tablespoon extra-virgin olive oil
1 tablespoon light unpasteurized miso (red, barley, or flint corn miso)*
2 tablespoons water

1. Wash and seed the green peppers and cut them into thin strips.
2. In a 2-quart saucepan, heat the oil. Add the peppers and sauté 10 minutes over medium heat, stirring. Cover, reduce heat, and cook for 10 minutes more, stirring occasionally.
3. In a small bowl, mortar, or suribachi, mix the miso and water. Add to the peppers, stirring once or twice. Cover and simmer for another 10 minutes, or until the peppers are well wilted. Serve immediately.

ᘓᘒ · ᘔᘓ

Potato-Cabbage Casserole with Dill

Major Phase: Metal

Yield: 6 to 8 servings

This hearty and filling dish is wonderful for a brunch. It can be prepared ahead of time and reheated in the oven just before serving. Try it with the Fish Timbales (page 229) and a green leafy salad.

1 large onion
1 tablespoon unrefined sesame oil
1 small cabbage (about 1½ to 2 pounds)
1 tablespoon vegetable seasoning salt or ½ teaspoon sea salt
3 pounds potatoes
½ cup chopped dill, plus additional fresh dill for garnish
¼ teaspoon white pepper
½ cup water

---

* Obtainable in health food stores that carry Oriental and macrobiotic products.

1. Preheat the oven to 350°F.
2. Chop the onion into large chunks. In a heavy 6-quart stovetop-to-oven casserole, heat the oil, then add the onion and sauté over medium-low heat until transparent, about 4 to 6 minutes.
3. While the onion is cooking, quarter the cabbage, cut out the core, cut each quarter in half again lengthwise, then across into 1-inch slices. Add the cabbage to the onion, stir, sprinkle on the vegetable seasoning or sea salt, and continue to sauté while you prepare the potatoes.
4. Peel, wash, and cube potatoes. Add them to the casserole along with the dill, pepper, and water. Cover and bake for 1 hour. Serve immediately, garnished with fresh dill.

Rutabaga-Yam Puree

Major Phase: Earth

Yield: 4 to 6 servings

This is my favorite Thanksgiving/Christmas vegetable dish. The butter makes all the difference.

> 1 small rutabaga
> 2 medium yams or sweet potatoes
> 2 cups water
> ¼ teaspoon sea salt
> 2 tablespoons unsalted butter, softened

1. Peel the rutabaga and cut into 1-inch chunks. Peel the yams or sweet potatoes and cut into large chunks.
2. In a 5-quart pot, bring the water to a boil. Add the rutabaga and yam chunks, reduce heat, cover, and simmer until the vegetables are soft, about 30 to 40 minutes.
3. Place the rutabaga and yam chunks in a food processor and process until smooth. Alternatively, pass the chunks through a food mill or potato masher,

or just mash with a fork. Add the salt and whip in the softened butter. Serve warm.

Creamed Spinach

Major Phase: Metal
Minor Phase: Wood

Yield: 4 to 6 servings

You won't miss the heaviness of dairy cream in this dish; if, however, you miss its flavor, the touch of butter should be sufficient to please your senses.

>   2 pounds fresh spinach
> 1 to 2 shallots
>   2 tablespoons unsalted butter or extra-virgin olive oil
>   3 tablespoons oat flour
> 1½ cups hot water
>   ½ teaspoon sea salt
>   Freshly ground black pepper to taste
>   Freshly grated nutmeg to taste

1. Wash the spinach by placing it in a large bowl or basin of water and swirling it around once or twice; then lift out; the dirt and sand will settle in the bottom of the bowl. Repeat two more times, using fresh water.
2. In a large covered pot, steam the spinach leaves in only the water that clings to their leaves until wilted, about 5 to 8 minutes. Drain the spinach thoroughly, pressing the leaves against a strainer with a wooden spoon to remove excess liquid. When cool enough to handle, chop finely.
3. Peel and mince the shallots. In a heavy 2- to 3-quart saucepan, heat the butter or oil and sauté the shallots over medium-high heat for 2 to 3 minutes, or until transparent.
4. Add the oat flour, stirring to mix well. Slowly pour in the hot water, stirring continuously to avoid lumps, until the mixture comes to a boil. Add the salt

and a good sprinkling of pepper. Reduce heat to medium and cook for 2 to 3 minutes longer.

5. Stir in the chopped spinach and grate a little fresh nutmeg into the pot. (Be judicious; a little nutmeg in this dish goes a long way.) Cook over low heat until spinach is hot, about 5 minutes. Serve immediately.

Spinach-Nori Rolls
with Tofu and Wild Mushrooms

Major Phase: Metal
Minor Phase: Water

YIELD: 4 to 6 servings as a side dish
8 to 10 servings as an appetizer

The spinach and nori provide an unusual marriage of flavors in this sensational vegetable sushi.

       2 pounds fresh spinach
     ⅔ pound soft tofu
       2 tablespoons umeboshi vinegar
       1 teaspoon wasabi powder
     ⅓ teaspoon sea salt
          Pinch freshly ground white pepper
     ⅓ cup black sesame seeds
     ⅓ pound fresh wild chanterelles and shiitake mushrooms
       1 tablespoon butter
       6 sheets toasted nori

1. Wash the spinach. Place in a 6- to 8-quart saucepan and cook, covered, in only the water clinging to its leaves, 3 to 4 minutes, until wilted; drain.

2. Place the tofu, vinegar, wasabi, salt, and pepper in a food processor and puree until smooth; set aside.

3. Dry-roast the sesame seeds over high heat in a small skillet or stainless saucepan until they begin to smoke a bit; set aside.
4. Remove the stems from the shiitake and reserve for stock. Chop the caps and the whole chanterelles. Sauté in the butter for 3 to 4 minutes over low heat.
5. *To assemble the nori rolls:* Place a sushi mat horizontally in front of you. Place a nori sheet on the mat, shiny side down. Spread a ¼-inch layer of spinach evenly over two-thirds of the nori sheet, leaving the one-third margin farther away from you. Spread evenly. Spoon a strip of tofu filling horizontally along the middle, then a strip of sauteed mushrooms. Roll up and tighten. (See Vegetarian Norimaki, page 62, for roll-up instructions.) Slice the rolls into 8 pieces each just before serving. Sprinkle with the sesame seeds.

Summer Squash Mirepois

Major Phase: Wood

Yield: 6 servings

½ pound zucchini
½ pound yellow summer squash
½ pound pattypan squash
 1 medium sweet red pepper
 2 tablespoons extra-virgin olive oil
¼ teaspoon sea salt
½ teaspoon dried marjoram

1. Wash the squashes and cut them into ½-inch cubes.
2. Seed the red pepper, cut it into strips, then cut the strips into ½-inch pieces.
3. In a medium saucepan, heat the oil, add the red pepper, and sauté over medium heat for 3 minutes.
4. Add the squashes, sprinkle with the salt and marjoram, and sauté for about 3 to 4 minutes, or until the zucchini turns bright green. Serve immediately.

Stuffed Acorn Squash

Major Phase: Earth
Minor Phase: Metal

YIELD: 6 servings

If you prefer a holiday meal without turkey, here's the classic vegetarian replacement. It's festive and delicious. For a really wonderful feast, try it with the Cranberry Aspic (page 198), Rutabega-Yam Puree (page 184), Holiday Stuffing (page 132), and Pecan Pie (page 256).

> 3 medium or 6 small acorn squashes
> 1 small yellow onion
> 1 tablespoon extra-virgin olive oil
> ½ teaspoon dried basil
> ½ teaspoon dried oregano
> 1 dried sage leaf, crushed or ¼ teaspoon ground sage
> 1 cup cooked brown rice (see page 38)
> ¼ cup currants
> ⅓ cup pumpkin seeds, roasted
> 1 tablespoon shoyu or tamari
> Sea salt to taste

1. Preheat the oven to 375°F. Wash the squash and slice off the tops. If using the acorn squashes, slice each one in half horizontally and make sure each half can stand on its own, cut side up. Take another thin slice off the bottom if necessary to make it stable. Do not remove the seeds. Bake the squash, cut side down, on a cookie sheet for 45 minutes.

2. Meanwhile, make the filling. Peel the onion and chop finely. In a 2-quart saucepan, heat the oil and sauté the onion over medium heat for 2 to 4 minutes, or until wilted. Add the basil, oregano, and sage and cook for 2 minutes longer. Add the cooked rice to the onion mixture, along with the currants and pumpkin seeds. Stir to combine well. Add the shoyu. Taste. Season with salt if necessary. Set aside.

3. Remove the squash from the oven and increase the oven temperature to 400°F.

4. When the squash is cool enough to handle, remove the seeds by scooping them

out with a spoon. Place ⅓ cup of the filling in each squash half. Return to the oven and bake for 20 minutes more. Serve immediately.

Pureed Buttercup Squash

Major Phase: Earth

YIELD: 6 servings

1½	pounds buttercup squash
1	tablespoon unsalted butter, or to taste
½	cup boiling water, or to taste
	Pinch ground mace
1	tablespoon chopped parsley for garnish

1. Preheat the oven to 400°F.
2. Cut the unpeeled squash in half. Do not remove the seeds.
3. Place the squash cut side down on cookie sheet and bake for 1 hour, or until the flesh is cooked through.
4. When cool enough to handle, remove the seeds with a spoon and scoop out the flesh. Put the flesh through a food mill or food processor or mash with a fork or potato masher.
5. Add the butter and the boiling water to squash; if necessary, add more until you reach the desired consistency. Stir in the mace.
6. Serve immediately, garnished with the chopped parsley.

Tomatoes and Peppers
Hungarian Style (Lecso)

Major Phase: Fire
Minor Phase: Wood

<small>YIELD:</small> 6 to 8 servings

This is a classic Hungarian vegetable side dish and a great accompaniment to stews.

> 5 large ripe tomatoes
> 2 medium yellow onions
> 3 tablespoons extra-virgin olive oil or sesame oil
> 3 large green peppers
> ½ teaspoon sea salt
> ½ teaspoon paprika

1. Blanch the tomatoes in boiling water for 10 to 15 seconds; peel. Cut the tomatoes in half crosswise and squeeze out the seeds. Chop coarsely. Peel and mince the onions.

2. In a 10-inch skillet or 4-quart saucepan, heat the oil. Add the onions and sauté over medium heat.

3. While onions are cooking, seed and chop the peppers. Add the peppers, salt, and paprika to the onions. Stir well to blend, then add the chopped tomatoes. Cook over low heat, uncovered, for 30 minutes or longer, stirring often. You can cook this dish as long as 1 hour and it will only get better. Serve hot.

Turnips au Gratin
with Kalamata Olives

Major Phase: Metal
Minor Phase: Wood

Yield: 6 to 8 servings

I first created this recipe as an alternative to scalloped potatoes, as turnips are a better complement to grain-based meals. It turned out to be a wonderful combination. The rich, full-bodied béchamel is enlivened by the earthy assertiveness of the turnips and olives. Try it with Red Lentil Pâté (page 144), fresh corn on the cob, and Four Greens and Walnut Sauté (page 179)

1½	pounds turnips
2	cups Béchamel Sauce (see below)
⅔	cup Kalamata olives
⅓	cup whole wheat bread crumbs

Béchamel Sauce

3	tablespoons cold-pressed safflower oil
⅓	cup whole wheat pastry flour
2	cups turnip-cooking water (approximately)
1	teaspoon sea salt, or to taste

1. *To prepare the turnips:* Bring a 3- to 4-quart pot of water to a boil. Slice off the tops of the turnips and discard; do not peel. Cut the turnips into ½-inch cubes. Drop into boiling water and simmer, covered, for 20 minutes. Drain, reserving the turnip water for the béchamel; set aside.
2. While the turnips are cooking, cut the olives off the pit, lengthwise; discard the pits. Preheat the oven to 350°F.
3. *To make the béchamel sauce:* In a 2- or 3-quart saucepan, heat the oil over medium heat. Add the flour and cook, stirring constantly, until it exudes a nutty aroma, about 5 to 6 minutes.

4. Whisk in 1 cup of the hot turnip water, stirring rapidly to avoid lumping. The mixture will begin to thicken immediately. Add enough additional turnip water to make a smooth sauce. (The consistency always varies slightly, depending on the flour.) Cover the pot and cook over low heat for at least 15 minutes. Taste and adjust the seasonings.
5. Oil a 4-quart casserole. Cover the bottom with a layer of turnips, then one of olives, and one of béchamel sauce; repeat. Top with the bread crumbs. Bake, uncovered, for about 25 minutes, or until the bread crumbs are lightly browned.

Baked Yams Sauté

Phase: Earth

Yield: 6 servings

For those with a sweet tooth who wish to stay away from desserts, here is the perfect solution. Bake a double batch of these, and just keep the cooked yams in the refrigerator. Whenever you are feeling frazzled and in need of a pick-me-up, you can take one and sauté it, steam it, or even eat it cold.

>   3 yams or sweet potatoes, about 5 to 6 inches long
> 2 to 3 tablespoons extra-virgin olive oil
>   Sea salt to taste (optional)

1. Preheat the oven to 400°F.
2. Scrub the yams well and cut out any dark spots. Bake them on an ungreased cookie sheet for 45 minutes to 1 hour, or until a thin knife penetrates easily.
3. When the yams are cool enough to handle, slice them into ½-inch slices. In a large skillet, heat the oil and add the yam slices. Fry them over medium heat until lightly browned, about 4 to 5 minutes. Using two forks, turn them over and brown on the other side. Serve immediately.

Carol's Vegetarian Carbonada Criolla (Argentina)

Major Phase: Earth
Minor Phases: Wood, Metal, and Fire

YIELD: 6 to 8 servings

*H*ere is a meatless version of a classic South American stew; the most distinctive thing about it is the inclusion of fruits among the roots and squashes. All you need with this is some plain brown rice and a green salad.

> One 6-pound calabaza (West Indian/Latin
> American pumpkin) or buttercup squash
> 2 large ripe tomatoes
> 2 medium onions
> 1 green bell pepper
> 1 sweet red pepper
> 2 cloves garlic
> 2 tablespoons extra-virgin olive oil
> 2 tablespoons mirin (sweet rice wine) or dry sherry
> 2 bay leaves
> 2 cups Rich Vegetable Stock (page 72)
> ¾ pound white potatoes
> 1 large yam
> 1 medium zucchini
> 6 dried prunes, pitted
> ¼ pound dried apricots
> 2 ears fresh corn
> 1 cup cooked red kidney beans
> Freshly ground black pepper to taste
> 2 large or 3 medium ripe peaches

1. Scrub the outside of the pumpkin clean, using a stiff vegetable brush. With a large, heavy, sharp knife, cut out a lid from the pumpkin top, about 5 to 6 inches in diameter, leaving the stem intact. Using a large metal spoon, scrape out the seeds and fiber from the pumpkin shell and lid.

2. Score the tomatoes with a small cross on the underside made with a sharp knife. Blanch the tomatoes in boiling water for 10 to 15 seconds. Remove to a colander with a slotted spoon. Cut the tomatoes in half crosswise and squeeze out the seeds. Cut into medium chunks.

3. Chop the onions coarsely. Chop the green and red peppers. Finely mince the garlic. In a 4-quart pot, heat the oil, add the onions, peppers, and garlic, and sauté over medium-low heat for about 5 minutes, or until the vegetables begin to soften.

4. Add the mirin or sherry, bay leaves, and the stock. Raise the heat and bring to a boil. Add the tomatoes, reduce heat, cover, and cook for about 10 minutes.

5. Peel and cube the potatoes and yams and add to the pot. Cover and cook for another 15 minutes, still over low heat.

6. Preheat the oven to 350°F. Wash the zucchini and slice them into ¼-inch rounds; add to pot. Coarsely chop the prunes and apricots; add to pot. Shuck the corn and cut with a very sharp knife into 1-inch rounds; add to pot. Cover and cook for about 5 minutes.

7. Add the cooked kidney beans to the vegetables and season with the pepper. Stir well, cover, and cook for 5 minutes longer.

8. Remove the pot from the heat. Peel and halve the peaches and stir in with the vegetables. Carefully ladle the stew into the hollowed-out pumpkin. Replace the lid. Place the pumpkin in a shallow baking pan and bake for 1 hour.

9. To serve, ladle the carbonada from the pumpkin onto individual serving plates. However, do not cut the pumpkin flesh until most of the stew has been removed, or the pumpkin will collapse. If you do not plan to eat the entire dish in one sitting, wait to cut the pumpkin until it is reheated as a leftover (in a 350° oven).

❧ Salads and Dressings ❧

Cool vegetables and a bit of a sour taste—these are the core elements of a salad. Thus, you can make them not just with leafy greens, but also with blanched vegetables, grains, beans, fish, fruit, and whatever else you fancy. A good green salad can lift and lighten a hearty meal. In the summer, a grain and bean salad can even be your entire meal. Add some raw onions, and you'll lower your cholesterol as well!

Beets and Onions Vinaigrette

Major Phase: Water
Minor Phase: Metal

YIELD: 6 servings

*T*his is a variation of a dish I always encounter on the table at my aunt and cousins'
home when I visit Buenos Aires. It's light and refreshing on a summer day and is terrific
with Savory Fish Stew (page 231) Try to buy beets with leaves; trim them to within
1 to 2 inches of the bulb and leave on the thin root. This will keep the beets from losing
their color during cooking.

    3 medium or 6 small beets
    2 medium onions
    ¼ cup brown rice or apple cider vinegar
    2 tablespoons umeboshi vinegar
    ½ cup extra-virgin olive oil
    1 to 2 bunches watercress

1. Boil the whole, unpeeled beets for 1 hour in water to cover.
2. Meanwhile, slice the onions into thin crescents. Bring water to boil in a 2-quart
   saucepan, drop in the sliced onions, then drain immediately in a strainer. Place
   the onions in a salad bowl. Combine the vinegars and oil and pour over the
   onions. Set aside to marinate while you prepare the beets.
3. When the beets are finished cooking, drain and set aside to cool. Working with
   wet hands, peel by slipping off their skins and stem end (it will come off easily)
   and running under cold water.
4. Slice the beets and add to the onions. Toss gently and let stand for 30 minutes
   more.
5. Serve on a bed of watercress.

Celery and Onion Salad
with Chimichurri Dressing

Major Phase: Metal
Minor Phase: Wood

YIELD: 4 to 6 servings

This tangy Argentine salad, made simply with celery and onion, is a welcome change from the standard leafy ones. It goes well in any heavy meal that includes greens. Try it with the Poached Salmon with Mock Hollandaise, Four Greens and Walnut Sauté, and Blueberry Couscous Cake.

    1 large Spanish onion
    ¼ cup brown rice or apple cider vinegar
    ⅓ cup extra-virgin olive oil
    ¼ teaspoon sea salt
    ¼ teaspoon dried oregano
    4 stalks celery

1. Peel the onion and slice into thin crescents. Place 2 cups water in a small saucepan and bring to a boil. Drop in the onion, count to ten then pour immediately into a colander to drain. Place onion in a medium bowl.
2. In a small bowl, combine the vinegar, oil, salt, and oregano. Add to the onion. Marinate for at least 30 minutes.
3. Slice the celery thinly. Add to the onion, mix thoroughly, and serve.

Cranberry Aspic

Major Phase: Water
Minor Phase: Wood

YIELD: 6 servings

*T*ry this on your Thanksgiving table! It's light, refreshing, and goes nicely with all the traditional dishes, including turkey or the Stuffed Acorn Squash (page 188).

> 2 cups fresh raw cranberries
> 2 pounds large red cooking apples, preferably Cortlands
> 1 bar agar-agar
> 1½ cups freshly pressed apple cider or unfiltered juice
> ¼ cup maple syrup
> 1 cinnamon stick
> Grated rind of 1 lemon
> Lettuce leaves

1. Wash and pick over the cranberries.
2. Wash, core, and finely chop the apples.
3. Run the agar under cold running water to soften; squeeze out the water. Place the cider or juice in a large saucepan and shred the agar into it. Add the maple syrup and cinnamon stick and cook over medium heat until the agar is dissolved.
4. Add the apples and cranberries. Continue cooking until the cranberries start popping and the apples are soft, about 8 to 10 minutes. Mix thoroughly with a wooden spoon, then remove from heat and add the lemon rind. Discard the cinnamon stick. Pour the mixture into a 1½-quart ring mold and chill until firm, about 2 hours.
5. To serve, line a plate with lettuce leaves. Unmold the aspic onto the leaves.

Crunchy Fennel Salad
with Lemon Dressing

Major Phases: Metal and Wood
Minor Phase: Wood

YIELD: 6 servings

This unusual salad combines several cool and crunchy vegetables; it's great for brunch with the Broccoli Tofu Quiche (page 157).

- 1 large carrot
- 1 medium bulb fennel
- 2 tablespoons fine, feathery leaves from center of fennel bulb
- ½ small bulb jicama, a small (4 to 6-inch) daikon, or ¼ pound white radishes

Lemon Dressing

- ¼ cup fresh lemon juice
- 3 tablespoons extra-virgin olive oil
- 1 teaspoon balsamic vinegar
- 1 teaspoon umeboshi vinegar
- Pinch sea salt

- 6 radicchios or red cabbage leaves
- ¼ pound brine-cured black olives for garnish

1. Peel the carrot only if the skin is dark or bitter. Quarter it lengthwise, then cut each length into ¼-inch chunks. Place in a large salad bowl.
2. Remove any imperfect or discolored parts of the fennel bulb and discard the tough top stalks. Mince 1 tablespoon of the very fine leaves from the center of the bulb. Cut the fennel into small pieces, about the size of the carrots. Add to the salad bowl.
3. Peel the jicama or radish and cut it into small chunks. Add to the salad bowl.
4. *To make the dressing:* Combine all the dressing ingredients in a small bowl. Pour

over the vegetables and toss gently. Set aside for 30 minutes. Serve in a cup-shaped piece of radicchio or red cabbage leaf, garnished with olives, or arrange the salad on a large platter and encircle with the leaves.

🐚 • 🐚

Herbed Marinated Vegetables

Salad Phases: Wood, Fire, Water
Marinade Phase: Wood

YIELD: 6 servings

1 sweet red pepper
6 ounces small fresh mushrooms
2 cups broccoli florets

Basil Marinade

2 tablespoons fresh lemon juice
3 tablespoons extra-virgin olive oil
½ teaspoon umeboshi vinegar (optional)
1 teaspoon dried basil
¼ teaspoon sea salt
  Freshly ground white pepper to taste

1. Roast the red pepper by placing it directly on top of the gas burner and turning it with metal tongs every few minutes until it is charred black. Place it in a paper bag or covered pot and let it sweat for 30 minutes while you prepare the rest of the dish.
2. Wipe the mushrooms with a damp towel and place them in a bowl. Add the broccoli florets.
3. *To make the marinade:* Combine all the marinade ingredients in a screw-top jar and shake vigorously—or whiz briefly in a blender—and pour over the vegetables. Toss gently to coat.
4. Remove the red pepper from the bag or pot and peel under cold running water.

Seed, slice into thin strips, and combine with the other vegetables. Allow to marinate in the refrigerator at least 2 hours; overnight is even better. Stir occasionally.

Chicory Salad with Lotus Root and Dressing

Salad Phases: Fire, Wood, Metal, and Earth
Dressing Phase: Wood

YIELD: 8 to 10 servings

The rich flavor of the sesame dressing makes an appealing contrast to the lightness of the vegetables. Thousand Sesame Dressing also makes a delicious hollandaise-type sauce for fish.

½ cup dried chick-peas, soaked
1 quart water
½ cup dried lotus root slices*
1 small red onion
1 large stalk broccoli (about ½ pound)**
1 head chicory
1 bunch watercress
1 cup radish sprouts

1. Drain the beans. Place them in a medium saucepan along with the water. Bring to a boil, reduce heat, cover, and cook until tender, about 1½ hours. (For quicker cooking, pressure-cook for 45 minutes.)

---

* Obtainable in Oriental or natural-foods stores.
** You may substitute any green vegetable in season for the broccoli. Asparagus or green beans are excellent.

2. Place the lotus root in a small saucepan. Add water to cover, bring to a boil, reduce heat, and simmer for 20 minutes. Cover and set aside.

3. Slice the onion thinly into half moons. Cut the broccoli into florets; peel the stems down to the pale tender center and cut into matchsticks. Place 1 inch of water in a large saucepan, bring to a boil, add the broccoli and cook, covered, for about 3 minutes, or until the florets are just tender and bright green. Drain, rinse with cold water, and set aside.

4. Wash and dry the chicory. Break it into bite-size pieces and arrange on a large platter. Remove the coarse stems from the watercress and layer on top of the chicory.

5. Sprinkle with the cooked chick-peas. Arrange the broccoli and the drained lotus root slices decoratively over the chick-peas. Spoon some Thousand Sesame Dressing over the vegetables, then top with radish sprouts and thinly sliced red onion rings. Pass the rest of the dressing around in a small sauce boat.

Thousand Sesame Dressing

YIELD: 1½ cups

¾ cup tahini
5 tablespoons white miso or light barley miso
⅔ cup brown rice or apple cider vinegar
¼ cup whole-grain mustard
Water as needed

1. Place the tahini in small mixing bowl. Blend in the miso, then add the vinegar and mustard. Thin to the desired consistency with water.

Green Salad with Miso-Coriander Dressing

Salad Phases: Wood and Metal
Dressing Phase: Wood

Yield: 6 servings

*F*resh green leaves clean the blood and cheer up the soul. This leafy salad brings together several flavorful greens that harmonize particularly well, and the red onion provides a welcome tang. Try it with Baked Whitefish with Scallion Stuffing (page 232).

½ small head Boston lettuce
½ head green leaf lettuce
1 bunch watercress
1 medium red onion

Dressing

½ cup fresh lemon juice
5 tablespoons plus 1 teaspoon white miso
2 teaspoons whole-grain mustard, preferably Pommery
3 tablespoons extra-virgin olive oil
1 bunch fresh coriander
Freshly ground pepper to taste (optional)

1. Tear the greens into bite-size pieces and place them in a bowl. Slice the onion thinly; add.
2. *To make the dressing:* In a small bowl, combine the lemon juice, miso, and mustard. Whisk in the oil, a few drops at a time, until the dressing is emulsified.
3. Remove the thick stems from the coriander and chop the leaves coarsely. Add to dressing. Season with the pepper.
4. Pour the dressing over the salad and toss gently. Serve immediately.

Janie's Leafy Salad
with Garlic-Parsley Vinaigrette

Salad Phases: Wood and Fire
Dressing Phase: Wood

YIELD: 6 to 8 servings

The technique of putting the dressing in the bowl first ensures that all the salad ingredients will pick some up during tossing. Toss the greens from the bottom up.

1 head romaine
1 head radicchio
1 Belgian endive

Garlic-Parsley Vinaigrette

1 bunch parsley
2 cloves garlic
2 tablespoons whole-grain mustard, preferably Pommery
2 tablespoons shoyu or tamari
¼ teaspoon freshly ground pepper, or to taste
½ cup extra-virgin olive oil

1. Tear the romaine, radicchio, and endive into bite-size pieces: set aside.
2. *To make the vinaigrette:* Chop the parsley and garlic and place in a large salad bowl. Mix in the mustard, shoyu, pepper, and oil.
3. Add the greens to the bowl just before serving. Toss gently to coat evenly with the dressing. Serve immediately.

Festive Salad
(Insalata Festiva)

Salad Phases: Fire and Metal
Dressing Phase: Wood

Yield: 6 servings

This colorful Italian salad goes well with either Pasta Primavera with Pesto (page 125) or Focaccia (page 118).

2 bunches arugula
1 head radicchio
1 large black radish
1 small red onion
1 bunch red radishes

Dressing

1 tablespoon grated lemon rind
3 tablespoons fresh lemon juice
5 tablespoons extra-virgin olive oil

1. Tear the arugula and radicchio into bite-size pieces, and place in a large salad bowl.
2. Cut the black radish into julienne strips. Add to the bowl. Thinly slice the onion and the red radishes. Add.
3. *To make the dressing:* Grate the lemon rind and mix with the lemon juice and oil in a small bowl. Pour over the salad and toss gently. Serve immediately.

Mixed Salad with Fennel

Salad Phases: Fire, Metal, and Water
Dressing Phase: Wood

YIELD: 6 servings

*T*ry this lively Italian salad with Black and White Bean Soup (page 102) and Stuffed Cabbage Rolls (page 129).

  1 medium head radicchio
  3 bunches arugula
  ½ red onion
  ½ head fennel
  ¼ pound oil- or brine-cured black olives, such as Kalamata, Sicilian, or Moroccan

Dressing

  ¼ cup balsamic vinegar
  ½ cup extra-virgin olive oil
  1 heaping tablespoon whole-grain mustard, such as Pommery

1. Arrange the whole radicchio leaves and the arugula leaves on a large platter.
2. Slice the onion thinly into ⅛-inch rounds. Slice the fennel into thin crescents. Arrange decoratively over the greens. Top with the olives.
3. *To make the dressing:* Combine all the dressing ingredients in a small bowl or screw-top jar and stir or shake well to blend. Drizzle the dressing evenly over the salad. Serve immediately.

Pico de Gallo Salad

Salad Phases: Wood, Fire, and Metal
Dressing Phase: Wood

Yield: 6 servings

A *traditional Mexican salad, terrific with Polenta (page 108) and Refried Beans, (page 149) or any other cormeal entrée.*

4 small kirby cucumbers, unwaxed
1 teaspoon sea salt
2 large ripe tomatoes, chopped
1 mild white onion, such as Vidalia
1 head Boston lettuce
1 bunch fresh coriander

Dressing

½ cup fresh lime juice
¼ cup extra-virgin olive oil
2 tablespoons rice syrup
½ teaspoon sea salt

1. Slice the cucumbers thinly. Sprinkle with the salt and set aside for 30 minutes.
2. Meanwhile, chop the tomatoes and peel and mince the onion. Tear the lettuce into bite-size pieces and place in a large salad bowl. Remove and discard the tough stems of the coriander. Chop the leaves and add them to the bowl.
3. Rinse the salt from the cucumbers and drain thoroughly. Add to the bowl.
4. *To make the dressing:* Combine all the dressing ingredients in a small bowl or screw-top jar and stir or shake to blend well. Pour over the salad and toss gently. Serve immediately.

Red and White Cabbage Salad
with Miso-Onion Dressing

Salad Phases: Water and Metal
Dressing Phases: Wood and Earth

YIELD: 6 servings

Easy, crunchy, and colorful!

¼ small head red cabbage
⅓ small head savoy cabbage
1 cup mixed bean sprouts

Miso-Onion Dressing

3 tablespoons cold-pressed sunflower
  or extra-virgin olive oil
3 tablespoons water
3 tablespoons white or yellow miso
2 teaspoons apple cider vinegar
2 teaspoons whole-grain mustard,
  preferably Pommery
1 tablespoon rice or maple syrup
½ small onion

1. Shred the cabbages finely and place in a large serving bowl.
2. *To prepare the dressing:* Combine all the dressing ingredients in a blender or food processor and puree until smooth. Alternatively, place the oil, water, miso, vinegar, mustard, and syrup in a bowl and whisk until well blended. Mince the onion finely and add.
3. Toss the cabbage with the dressing at least 1 hour before serving and allow to marinate.
4. Just before serving, add the sprouts and mix well. Serve immediately.

Radish-Watercress Salad
with Soy-Sesame Dressing

Salad Phase: Metal
Dressing Phases: Wood and Fire

Yield: 6 servings

*H*ere is a delicately piquant combination that goes especially well with mild-flavored or salty-tasting dishes. Try it with Turnips au Gratin with Kalamata Olives (page 191).

1 small daikon radish (about 6 inches)
1 bunch watercress
½ tablespoon black sesame seeds
6 whole radicchio leaves

Soy-Sesame Dressing

¼ cup fresh lemon juice
1 tablespoon shoyu or tamari
¼ cup toasted sesame oil
1 tablespoon umeboshi vinegar

1. Shred the daikon coarsely, using the large holes of a grater; set aside.
2. Remove the large, tough stems of the watercress and reserve for another use. Chop the leaves and small stems coarsely.
3. Place the radicchio leaves on 6 individual salad plates or arrange on a large serving platter.
4. Divide the watercress equally among the radicchio leaves and place a mound of grated daikon on top. Sprinkle the daikon with the sesame seeds.
5. *To make the dressing:* Combine all the dressing ingredients in a small bowl or jar and stir or shake to blend well. Pour a few tablespoons over each portion. Serve immediately.

Salad of Wilted Collard Greens
with Yellow Peppers
and White Miso Dressing

Salad Phases: Fire and Earth
Dressing Phase: Wood

YIELD: 6 servings

*H*ere is a refreshing new way to prepare these traditional greens. The yellow peppers provide a lovely visual contrast to the deep green of the collards.

2 to 3 quarts water
½ teaspoon sea salt
2 pounds collard greens
1 yellow bell pepper
4 red radishes

White Miso Dressing

3 tablespoons lemon juice
2 tablespoons umeboshi vinegar
1 tablespoon shoyu
1 tablespoon mellow white miso
1 teaspoon whole-grain mustard, preferably Pommery
3 tablespoons cold-pressed safflower oil

1. Bring a large pot of water to a boil. Add the salt.
2. Remove the tough stems of the collards and blanch them, uncovered, in the boiling water for 10 minutes; drain.
3. Chop the collards into bite-size pieces. Seed and slice the pepper into thin strips. Quarter the radishes. Place in a large serving bowl.
4. Place the dressing ingredients in a small bowl or screw-top jar and whisk or shake until well blended. Pour over the vegetables and toss gently to coat. Serve at room temperature. This salad may be dressed up to 2 hours before serving.

Watercress and Arugula Salad with Rosemary-Mustard Dressing

Salad Phases: Metal and Fire
Dressing Phase: Wood

YIELD: 6 servings

1 bunch arugula
1 bunch watercress
1 small red onion
1 Belgian endive

Rosemary-Mustard Dressing

¼ cup extra-virgin olive oil
2 tablespoons orange juice
2 tablespoons umeboshi vinegar
½ teaspoon whole-grain mustard, preferably Pommery
1 teaspoon crumbled dried rosemary

1. Cut or tear the arugula into bite-size pieces. Remove tough stems from the watercress. Arrange the greens attractively on a platter.
2. Thinly slice the onion crosswise and arrange the rings on top of the greens.
3. Separate the endive leaves and arrange them in spokes from the center of the platter.
4. *To make the dressing:* Combine all the dressing ingredients in a small bowl or screw-top jar and whisk or shake to blend well. Pour evenly over the salad just before serving.

Watercress–Sprout–Pumpkin Seed Salad with Creamy Lemon Dressing

Salad Phase: Metal
Dressing Phases: Wood and Metal

YIELD: 6 servings

The radish sprouts give this salad an unexpected tang.

> 2 bunches watercress
> ½ cup radish sprouts
> 6 tablespoons tamari-roasted pumpkin seeds* for garnish

Creamy Lemon Dressing

> 2 tablespoons avocado oil*
> 1 tablespoon umeboshi paste or 2 umeboshi plums, pitted
> 1 tablespoon fresh lemon juice
> ¼ cup soft tofu
> 6 tablespoons water

1. Remove the thick stems from the watercress. Place the leaves in a bowl with the sprouts.
2. *To make the dressing:* Combine all the dressing ingredients in a blender or food processor and blend until creamy.
3. Toss the watercress and sprouts with the dressing just before serving. Garnish each serving with 1 tablespoon pumpkin seeds.

---

* Obtainable in natural-foods stores

Vegetable Garden Salad
with Mustard Cream Vinaigrette

Phase: Wood

Yield: 6 servings

*T*his simple vegetable salad makes a nice contrast to hearty entrées. It is exceptional with any dish containing rice and mushrooms, or try it with the Red Lentil Pâté (page 144). Serve on a large platter, with a small bowl of sauce in the middle surrounded by individual mounds of the vegetables. The colors combine beautifully.

3 quarts water
1 teaspoon sea salt
2 stalks broccoli
2 small firm zucchini
½ pound carrots
½ pound green beans

Mustard Cream Vinaigrette

3 tablespoons brown rice or apple cider vinegar
2 tablespoons umeboshi vinegar
2 teaspoons whole-grain mustard, preferably Pommery
½ cup extra-virgin olive oil
1 tablespoon tahini

1. Bring 3 quarts of water to a boil in a large pot. Add the salt.
2. Meanwhile, cut the broccoli florets off the stalks; reserve the stalks for another use. Peel the carrots and dice them into ½-inch cubes. Trim the stem ends of the green beans (leave them whole). Cut the zucchini in half lengthwise, then slice each half into semicircles about ⅓-inch in thickness.
3. Cook the vegetables according to the following timetable: carrots, covered, 25 minutes; green beans, uncovered, 5 minutes; broccoli, uncovered, 1 minute; zucchini, uncovered, 30 seconds. Use the same cooking water each time; keep

the water for use as stock when done. Set the vegetables aside while you prepare the sauce.

4. Arrange the vegetables attractively on a platter. Serve with tongs, spooning the sauce over individual servings.

5. *To make the vinaigrette:* Mix the vinegars and mustard together in a small bowl. Whisk in the oil very slowly until the dressing emulsifies. Then whisk in the tahini. Alternatively, combine all the vinaigrette ingredients in a blender or food processor and process for 30 seconds.

❧ • ❧

Zesty Salad
with Toasted Sesame Dressing

Salad Phases: Fire, Wood, and Metal
Dressing Phases: Wood and Fire

YIELD: 6 servings

2 heads Belgian endive
1 bunch arugula
1 small head red leaf lettuce
1 medium black radish
½ package radish sprouts

Toasted Sesame Dressing

1½ tablespoons toasted sesame oil
3 tablespoons unrefined sunflower oil
3 tablespoons umeboshi vinegar
2 tablespoons brown rice or apple cider vinegar
½ teaspoon mellow white miso

1. Wash and dry the endive, arugula, and lettuce.
2. Wash the black radish, but do not peel. Cut into matchsticks. Trim the dirt end of the radish sprouts, if necessary.
3. Combine the greens, the black radish sticks, and the radish sprouts in a salad bowl.
4. *To make the dressing:* Combine all the dressing ingredients in a screw-top jar or small bowl and shake or stir well to blend. Just before serving, toss with the salad.

Black Bean Salad
with Corn and Red Pepper

Salad Phases: Water and Fire
Dressing Phase: Wood

YIELD: 6 servings

*T*he contrast of the yellow corn and red pepper with the beans makes this as gorgeous to look at as it is delicious to eat. It works especially well in a buffet; try it next to Orange Millet Pilaf (page 110) or the Rice-Spinach Timbales (page 127).

    1 cup dried black beans, soaked
    1 quart water
    1 bay leaf
    1 clove garlic
    2 ears corn
    ½ sweet red pepper
    2 whole scallions
    ¼ cup finely chopped parsley
    ¼ cup coarsely chopped walnuts
    1 bunch watercress (optional)
      Lettuce leaves (optional)

Dressing

2 tablespoons extra-virgin olive oil
2 tablespoons shoyu or tamari
3 tablespoons fresh lemon juice
1 tablespoon prepared whole-grain mustard,
   preferably Pommery

1. Drain the beans. Place them in a medium saucepan with the water, bay leaf, and garlic. Bring to a boil, reduce heat, cover, and cook for 1 hour, or until the beans are tender. Drain, discarding bay leaf and garlic.
2. *To make the dressing:* Combine the dressing ingredients and mix with the warm black beans.
3. Boil the corn in 1 quart water for 3 to 4 minutes. Remove from the water and allow to cool. Slice the corn kernels off the cob. Dice the red pepper. Slice the scallions thinly.
4. Add the corn kernels, red pepper, scallions, parsley, and walnuts to the beans. Toss to distribute the dressing and allow to marinate in the refrigerator or at room temperature for at least 1 hour. Serve on watercress, if desired, or on lettuce leaves.

❧ • ☙

Black-eyed Pea Salad with Sun-Dried Tomatoes and Balsamic Vinaigrette

Salad Phases: Wood and Fire
Dressing Phase: Wood

YIELD: 4 to 6 servings

*T*he tangy bite of the sun-dried tomatoes is a nice counter point to the earthiness of the black-eyed peas.

1 cup dried black-eyed peas, soaked
5 cups water
½ teaspoon sea salt
1 carrot
1 onion
4 whole scallions
⅓ cup sun-dried tomatoes, packed in oil
¼ cup chopped parsley

Vinaigrette

2 tablespoons whole-grain mustard
1 tablespoon lemon juice
3 to 4 tablespoons balsamic vinegar
¾ cup extra-virgin olive oil
1 teaspoon sea salt
Freshly ground black pepper to taste
1 tablespoon shoyu or tamari

1. Drain the beans. In a 3- to 4-quart saucepan, combine the black-eyed peas with the water, add the salt, carrot, and onion and bring to a boil. Skim off any foam that rises to the surface and cook, covered, over low heat, until tender but *not mushy*, about 45 to 50 minutes. Drain; discard carrot and onion.
2. *To make the vinaigrette:* While the beans are cooking, place all the vinaigrette ingredients in a screw-top jar or small bowl and shake or whisk to blend well.
3. Slice the scallions thinly. Drain the tomatoes, reserving the oil. (Some of the oil may be used in the vinaigrette if desired.) Slice the tomatoes into thin strips. Combine with the scallions and parsley in a large serving bowl.
4. Drain the cooked beans well and set aside to cool to room temperature.
5. Add the cooled beans to the serving bowl. Toss gently with the dressing. Taste and correct the seasoning. Marinate for 1 hour before serving. Serve at room temperature.

Brown Rice and Red Bean Salad with Cashews

Major Phase: Metal
Minor Phases: Water and Wood
Dressing Phase: Wood

YIELD: 4 to 6 servings

Since grain and bean salads are best made with leftovers, they are without a doubt the best way to consume high-fiber staples during the warm weather, when everyone likes to keep time spent over a hot stove to a minimum. This version is a meal all by itself; it will stick to your ribs for several hours. It makes a great addition to a picnic basket, since it stays fresh for several hours without refrigeration. If you wish, serve it with some carrot sticks or red pepper strips for a colorful accent.

Lemon-Garlic Marinade

2 tablespoons fresh lemon juice
1 tablespoon shoyu or tamari
3 tablespoons extra-virgin olive oil
1 clove garlic

2 cups cooked brown rice, cold
1 cup cooked red kidney beans, cold
¼ cup roasted cashews
3 whole scallions
2 stalks celery
    Handful parsley

1. *To make the marinade:* In a small bowl or screw-top jar, combine the lemon juice, shoyu, and oil. Smash the garlic clove with the side of your knife, remove the peel (it will come off easily), and add the garlic to the lemon juice mixture. Stir or shake once or twice to mix, then set aside for 30 minutes.

2. Place the rice and beans in a large bowl. Chop the cashews into large pieces and add. Chop the scallions, celery, and parsley and add to the bowl.
3. Remove the garlic clove from the marinade and discard. If you wish, you may chop it fine and put it back in. Whisk or shake until well blended and pour over the rice and beans. Toss and allow to marinate for at least 30 minutes. Serve cold or at room temperature.

Pasta Salad with Zucchini and Chick-peas

Major Phase: Wood
Minor phase: Earth
Dressing Phase: Wood and Metal

Yield: 6 to 8 servings

This robust pasta salad is a perfect one-dish summer meal. Try the Cantaloupe Soup (page 104) as appetizer.

   1 pound whole wheat pasta (spaghetti, elbow macaroni, or spirals)
   1 pound small zucchini
   2 cups cooked chick-peas
¼ pound pitted, sliced Kalamata olives
12 thin strips roasted red pepper (page 87), or bottled pimiento

Garlicky Mustard Vinaigrette

   3 tablespoons apple cider vinegar
¼ teaspoon sea salt
   1 tablespoon whole-grain prepared mustard
   2 cloves garlic
⅓ cup extra-virgin olive oil

1. Cook the pasta in boiling water for 15 minutes, or until *al dente*; drain. Place in a large bowl.
2. Trim the ends of the zucchini. Quarter them lengthwise, then slice the pieces across to make ¼-inch-thick quarter circles. Add to the pasta.
3. *To make the vinaigrette:* Place the vinegar, salt, and mustard in a bowl. Peel the garlic and squeeze it through a garlic press into the vinegar mixture. Whisk; add the oil in a slow trickle and continue whisking until it thickens.
4. Add the chick-peas, olives, and vinaigrette to the pasta and toss. Marinate for at least 1 hour. Serve cold or at room temperature. Decorate each serving with 2 strips of the red pepper or pimiento.

Pinto Bean Salad
with Chicory and Radishes
and Dill Dressing

Major Phase: Water
Minor Phase: Fire, Metal, and Wood
Dressing Phase: Wood

YIELD: 6 to 8 servings

I love bean salads! They're hearty, healthy, low in fat, and a great source of vegetable protein and complex carbohydrates. They also provide the revitalizing energy of raw vegetables.

2 cups dried pinto beans, soaked
1 small onion
1 small carrot
1 stalk celery
2 bay leaves
½ teaspoon sea salt

4 radishes, with tops
½ pound snow peas
1 small head chicory
1 bunch parsley

Dill Dressing

½ cup extra-virgin olive oil
½ cup brown rice or apple cider vinegar
2 tablespoons umeboshi vinegar
2 tablespoons water
¼ to ½ teaspoon freshly ground white pepper
3 tablespoons chopped fresh dill

1. Drain the beans. Place them in a 3- to 4-quart pot along with the onion, carrot, celery, bay leaves, and enough water to cover them by 1 inch. Bring to a boil, reduce heat, and cook covered, for 30 minutes. Add the salt and simmer for 20 to 25 minutes more, or until the beans are soft but not mushy.

2. While the beans are cooking, cut the tops off the radishes, wash them well, discarding ugly or yellowed leaves, and chop. Quarter the radishes. String the snow peas.

3. In a small saucepan, blanch the snow peas in boiling water for 30 to 60 seconds, just until they turn bright green. Drain immediately and run the snow peas under cold tap water briefly to stop the cooking.

4. *To make the dressing*: Combine all the dressing ingredients in a small screw-top jar or bowl and shake or whisk to blend well.

5. When the beans are done, drain them and remove the large chunks of vegetables, reserving these and the liquid for another use. Add the dressing to the hot beans, stirring to coat them. Allow to cool for 15 to 20 minutes.

6. Separate the leaves of the chicory, wash, and dry. Chop the parsley and set aside.

7. Add the radishes and their tops, snow peas, and parsley to the beans. Toss gently.

8. Arrange the larger chicory leaves, fluffy side out, over a large platter, or line a large bowl with them. Mound the bean mixture in the center. Place the small center leaves of the chicory on top. Serve immediately.

Wild Rice and Job's Tears (Hato Mugi) Salad with Lemon-Walnut Dressing

Major Phase: Water
Minor Phase: Wood
Dressing Phase: Wood

YIELD: 6 to 8 servings

Hato mugi, *marketed in this country by one or two natural-food companies under the name Job's tears, is a grain similar to barley. It can be found in gourmet, specialty, and natural-food stores. It has a rich, full-bodied texture and a mild flavor. It marries particularly well with our native wild rice in this recipe.*

1 cup wild rice
5 cups Rich Vegetable Stock (page 73)
⅔ teaspoon sea salt
1 cup Job's tears (hato mugi)
3 stalks celery
1 cup walnuts
1 cup parsley (tightly packed)
1 cup currants

Lemon-Walnut Dressing

¼ cup shoyu or tamari
¼ cup fresh lemon juice
¼ cup walnut oil

1. In a medium saucepan, combine the wild rice and 3 cups of the stock. Add ⅓ teaspoon of the salt, bring to a boil, reduce heat, cover, and simmer for 45 to 60 minutes, or until the kernels have opened. Spread in a shallow baking pan or on a platter to cool.

2. While the rice is cooking, place the hato mugi in a small saucepan with the remaining 2 cups stock and ⅓ teaspoon salt. Bring to a boil, reduce heat, cover, and simmer for 50 minutes, or until the grain is swollen and tender. Spread in a pan or platter to cool.
3. Slice the celery thinly. Quarter or crush the walnuts. Chop the parsley very finely.
4. *To make the dressing:* Whisk the dressing ingredients together in a small bowl, or shake them in a screw-top jar.
5. Place the cooled grain in a salad bowl; add the celery, walnuts, parsley, and currants and mix. Add the dressing, toss well, and allow to marinate for 30 minutes. Serve cold or at room temperature.

❧ Fish ❧

"Natural food" is often construed to mean vegetarian. Technically speaking, however, fish, fowl, beef, pork, and veal, are all "natural" as well. Unfortunately modern animal-husbandry techniques are anything but natural, including as they do the frequent and regular use of antibiotics, hormones, and artificial substances in the feed. In addition, the beef, pork, veal, and fowl we eat are often from weak, unhappy, mistreated, and sick animals. For those reasons—not only because they may be high in fat—countless consumers are cutting down on their intake of these foods, and we have avoided them in this book. Fish, more naturally raised, especially if from the ocean, then becomes the animal protein of choice.

Committed vegetarians can skip this chapter. However, most people have some trouble absorbing the protein from vegetable foods efficiently; therefore, a tasty fish dish several times a week is a must for good health and stamina. The sensualist and the epicure will also enjoy these dishes, especially when eating them within sight of the ocean!

Rolled Flounder Fillets
with Lemon-Dill Sauce

Fish Phase: Metal
Sauce Phase: Wood

YIELD: 4 servings

These are delightful chilled for a summer lunch. Serve with a flavorful grain salad and Nectarine-Nutmilk Ice Cream (page 272) for dessert.

  4 large flounder fillets
  2 tablespoons chopped dill
  ⅓ teaspoon sea salt
  ¼ teaspoon freshly ground black pepper
  1 teaspoon grated lemon rind
  1 cup water, fish stock (see page 228), or Light Vegetable Stock (page 72)
  ½ cup mirin (sweet rice wine), dry white wine, or apple juice
  3 tablespoons fresh lemon juice

Lemon-Dill Sauce

YIELD: 2 cups

  ¼ cup chopped dill
  ½ cup fresh lemon juice
  1⅓ cups cold water or fish stock (page 228)
  ½ teaspoon sea salt, or to taste
  ½ teaspoon ground turmeric
  2 tablespoons kuzu

1. Preheat the oven to 350°F. Rinse the fillets under cold running water and pat dry. In a small bowl, combine 1 tablespoon of the dill, the salt, pepper, and lemon rind. Rub ½ teaspoon of this mixture into each side of the fillets. Starting at the narrow end, roll up each fillet and secure with a toothpick. Place the rolls in a shallow baking pan with the seam side down.

2. Combine the water or stock, the wine or apple juice, and the lemon juice with the remaining tablespoon dill and pour over the fish. Cover, and bake for about 20 minutes, or until the fish is flaky.

3. *To make the sauce:* While the fish is baking, place all the sauce ingredients in a 1-quart saucepan. Stir well to blend. Bring to a boil, stirring continuously, until clear and thickened.

4. Serve the fish with the sauce either hot or chilled.

Poached Salmon Fillets
with Mock Hollandaise

Major Phase: Earth
Sauce Phase: Wood

YIELD: 4 servings

This light, delicately flavored dish may be served either hot or at room temperature. Best way to shop for fillets: get a whole fish, have it filleted, and keep the head and bones. Make stock with the latter and poach the fillets. It's ecological and nutritious—and delicious! This recipe works for any fillet of fish.

Fish Stock

1 carrot
1 stalk celery, with leaves
1 medium onion
¼ teaspoon dried thyme
10 peppercorns
1 large bay leaf
2 cloves garlic or 1 shallot
2 quarts water
3 sprigs parsley
3 -inch piece kombu seaweed
2 tablespoons shoyu or tamari
½ teaspoon sea salt
1 pound fish heads and bones
2 tablespoons brown rice, apple cider, or wine vinegar

4 fillets of fresh salmon (about 6 ounces each)
  Watercress, lemon wedges, and cherry tomatoes for garnish

1. *To make the fish stock:* Chop carrot, celery, and onion.
2. Tie the thyme, peppercorns, and bay leaf together in a piece of cheesecloth. Smash and peel the garlic.

3. In a large pot, combine the water, chopped vegetables, garlic or shallot, parsley, herb bundle, kombu, shoyu, salt, fish bones, and vinegar and simmer for 30 minutes. Strain.

4. *To poach the fish:* Oil a shallow flameproof baking pan large enough to hold the fish in a single layer. Pour the hot, strained stock over the fish and cover the pan with aluminum foil. Place the pan on 2 burners and simmer gently for 3 to 5 minutes.

5. Transfer the fish to a platter (but reserve liquid) and decorate with the watercress, lemon wedges, and cherry tomatoes. Serve Mock Hollandaise Sauce on the side (see below).

Mock Hollandaise Sauce

YIELD: About 2 ½ cups

2 cups Homemade Mayonnaise (page 283)
Fish-poaching liquid

1. Thin down the mayonnaise with the stock, 1 or 2 tablespoonfuls at a time, until it reaches sauce consistency. Serve in a sauceboat, so that each person can spoon a serving over the fish.

Fish Timbales
with Lemon Butter Sauce

Major Phase: Metal
Sauce Phase: Wood

YIELD: 4 servings

This elegant dish makes a lovely brunch, lunch, or a light summer dinner. Also, if you have been eating plain steamed vegetables for a while and can feel yourself gearing up for a major fat binge, try a tablespoon of this lovely sauce over broccoli or green beans. It may be just enough to satisfy and comfort you. Try it also on any type of poached fish.

    3 pounds spinach
    2 cloves garlic
    2 tablespoons light sesame oil
 1/4 teaspoon sea salt, or to taste
    Freshly ground black pepper
    Pinch ground nutmeg
 1 1/2 pounds fillets of flounder, sole, or any other flat fish

Lemon Butter Sauce

 1/4 cup fresh lemon juice
 12 tablespoons chilled, unsalted butter (about 1/3 pound)
    Sea salt and freshly ground black pepper to taste
    Finely grated rind of 1/2 lemon

1. Remove the tough stems of the spinach and wash the leaves well in several changes of cold water. Place the spinach in a large pot, cover, and steam it in its own moisture over medium-low heat for 5 minutes, or until completely wilted. Drain, and when it is cool enough to handle, chop finely.

2. Mince the garlic. In a large skillet, heat the oil, add the garlic and spinach, and sauté over medium heat until some of the moisture evaporates, about 8 to 10 minutes. Season with the salt, pepper, and nutmeg.

3. Butter four 10-ounce glass bowls (Pyrex is good). Cut the fish fillets lengthwise into 1/2-inch strips and score the outside flesh (the darker side). Divide into four equal portions and line the molds, placing the white fish against the outer side of the molds.

4. Preheat the oven to 400°F. Fill each mold with equal amounts of spinach. Set the molds into a shallow baking pan and add enough boiling water to reach halfway up the sides of the bowls. Cover the pan with aluminum foil. Bake for 15 to 20 minutes, or until the fish is opaque.

5. *To make the sauce*: bring the lemon juice to a boil in a small saucepan, and reduce to about 1 1/2 tablespoons. Cut the butter into 1/4-inch pieces.

6. Reduce heat to very low. Whisking constantly, slowly add the butter to the lemon juice one piece at a time, making sure each piece is thoroughly incorporated before adding the next. Season to taste with the salt, pepper, and lemon rind.

7. When the timbales are done, carefully invert each bowl onto a serving plate to

release the timbale. Serve at room temperature or chilled, lightly coated with the sauce.

Savory Fish Stew

Major Phase: Metal

Yield: 8 servings

This is a great low-fat, one-pot meal. Serve with a leafy salad and perhaps Spiced Glazed Pears (page 271) for dessert.

1 medium onion
1 carrot
1 stalk celery
3 cups cooked brown rice
6 cups water or fish stock (page 228)
1 pound scrod, whitefish, or haddock fillet (make sure there are no bones in it)
1 tablespoon grated fresh ginger root
2 tablespoons shoyu, or to taste, or 1 teaspoon sea salt
3 tablespoons chopped parsley for garnish

1. Mince the onion, carrot and celery. Place them in a 4-quart saucepan, along with the rice and water or stock. Cover, simmer for 20 minutes, stirring often. The rice will get very soft.
2. Rinse the fish under cold running water and pat dry. Cut each fillet into several large pieces and add to the rice, along with the ginger and shoyu or salt. Cover the pot and simmer for 10 to 15 minutes more. Stir to break up the fish pieces. Serve garnished with parsley.

Baked Whitefish with Scallion Stuffing

Major Phase: Metal

Minor Phase: Fire

YIELD: 8 servings

A lovely recipe for company, as well as for a hungry family. Some people don't like fish with bones—but since cooking fish on the bone may allow some of the calcium to be transferred to the flesh, it's perhaps not a bad idea.

Two 2-pound whole whitefish, cleaned, head and tail left on
½ teaspoon sea salt
1 bunch scallions (about 3 cups chopped, loosely packed)
1 cup parsley sprigs (firmly packed)
½ cup extra-virgin olive oil
1½ cups water
2 tablespoons shoyu or tamari, or ½ teaspoon sea salt

1. Preheat the oven to 350°F.
2. Rinse the fish under cold running water and pat dry. Place them head next to tail in a large shallow baking pan. Rub ¼ teaspoon of the salt into the cavity of each fish.
3. Chop the scallions and parsley. In a medium bowl, combine with the oil, water, and shoyu and stir to blend. Spoon about 1 cup of this mixture into the cavity of each of the whitefish; sprinkle the remaining mixture evenly over the top of the fish. Cover the pan with aluminum foil and bake for 25 to 30 minutes, or until the fish flakes easily and is white to the bone. Using a metal spatula, carefully transfer the fish to a serving platter. Pour the pan juices into a sauceboat. Serve immediately, spooning some of the juice onto each portion.

Seafood Yosenabe à la Janice

All Phases Present

Yield: 6 servings

*T*his is great fun to serve for company, as each guest dips his own seafood and vegetables into the stockpot to cook them. I always think of it as a culinary quilting bee. Serve this dish with Japanese Barley-Rice. (page 106) and the Watercress-Sprout Salad (page 212). For a vegetarian version, replace the seafood with seasoned seitan (wheat-gluten)* or tempeh (page 160).

                18 sea scallops
                12 shrimp
                 8 medium mushrooms
                ½ pound snow peas
                 1 sweet red pepper
                 2 leeks, white part only
                 2 ears corn
        12 to 18 white pearl onions
                 1 large carrot
                 2 medium zucchini
                 1 head broccoli
                 1 small cauliflower
                 2 tablespoons wasabi powder*
                 4 teaspoons water
                 6 tablespoons grated daikon
                 3 tablespoons thinly sliced scallion
                    Dipping Sauces (see below)

1. Peel and devein the shrimp. Wash the scallops under cold running water and pat dry. If using seitan or tempeh, cut into ¼-inch slices.
2. Remove the stems from the mushrooms. String the snow peas. Cut the red

---

* Obtainable in oriental and natural-foods stores

pepper into 1-inch squares. Wash the leeks and cut them crosswise into 2-inch lengths. Shuck the corn and slice the cobs into ½-inch rounds. Cut the carrot and zucchini diagonally into thin slices. Cut the broccoli from the top into 4-inch-long spears, including the florets; discard the remaining stems. Separate the cauliflower into florets.

3. *To prepare the wasabi*: In a small bowl or cup mix the wasabi powder with the water to make a smooth paste. Set aside. Place the daikon and scallions in separate bowls.

4. Prepare the dipping sauces (see below).

5. Arrange the fish on one platter, the vegetables on another. Place ¼ cup of dipping sauce in a small bowl for each person; daikon, scallion, or wasabi condiments can be mixed individually into the sauces.

6. In a 3-quart saucepan or wok, bring 2 quarts water to a boil. Place on a hot plate in the center of the table and keep on high heat. Have each person dip the vegetables and fish into the hot water using a fork, chopsticks, or bamboo skewers and cook to the desired degree of doneness. The seitan or tempeh is already cooked and only needs heating up. Snow peas and broccoli will take about 1 minute; mushrooms, zucchini, and cauliflower, about 2 minutes; scallops and shrimp will take 3 to 5 minutes; corn, peppers, leeks, carrots, and onions, about 4 minutes.

7. The broth left over from cooking the vegetables and fish is very rich. Add the leftover dipping sauces to it and ladle some over rice, which should accompany this dish.

Dipping Sauces for Seafood Yosenabe

Phases: 1) *Wood* and *Water*
2) *Water* and *Earth*

YIELD: 1½ cups

1) Ponzo Sauce

½ cup fresh lemon juice
½ cup shoyu or tamari
½ cup water

1 tablespoon mirin
2 tablespoons grated daikon

1. In a small bowl, combine all the ingredients.
2. Serve in individual bowls as a dipping sauce.

2) Ginger Sauce

¾ cup shoyu or tamari
½ cup water
2 tablespoons brown rice vinegar
1 tablespoon maple syrup
2 tablespoons grated fresh ginger root, or to taste

1. In a medium bowl, combine all the ingredients.
2. Serve in individual bowls.

❦Desserts❦

Here's to the sweet tooth! Healthful desserts may seem like a contradiction in terms—but the use of whole-grain flours gives these baked goods a depth and richness that create a *positive* addiction. Lightness is achieved by the careful blending of flours and the judicious use of sweet butter. (In the school we have found that both our tastebuds and our digestion are much happier when butter rather than oil is used in baking.) Fruit, juices, and maple syrup lend the most flavorful sweetness, without the excessive imbalance that white sugar can create.

You'll also find a delectable array of low-fat fruit-based desserts that will clear your palate and lift your spirits. Enjoy in good health!

Banana Layer Cake
with Carob Icing à la Minx

Major Phase: Earth

YIELD: One 9-inch cake

This beautiful, delicious cake, perfect for a birthday or special anniversary, is worth every bit of the time it takes to make. Its sweetness is attained by the use of concentrated apple juice and the overripe bananas. Remember to buy these several days before you plan to make to the cake. To make the bananas even sweeter, freeze them overnight and then defrost them before mashing.

Carob Icing

1½ cups very ripe mashed banana
 1 cup carob powder
 3 tablespoons unsalted butter, softened
½ teaspoon rose water or vanilla extract

Cake

 2 cups apple juice
½ cup water
 1 tablespoon almonds, blanched
 1 tablespoon cashews
 4 eggs, separated
 1 teaspoon vanilla extract
 2 cups very ripe mashed banana
½ cup (8 tablespoons) unsalted butter, softened
2½ cups whole wheat pastry flour
 2 teaspoons baking powder
¼ teaspoon sea salt
⅓ to ½ cup unsweetened raspberry preserves

1. *To make the icing:* Combine all the ingredients in a food processor and process until smooth. Transfer to a bowl and chill in the refrigerator to spreading consistency, about 2 to 3 hours.
2. Preheat the oven to 350°F. Butter two 9-inch springform cake pans.
3. *To make the cake:* In a 4-quart saucepan, simmer the apple juice over high heat until reduced to ½ cup. This may take 20 to 30 minutes.
4. Combine the water, almonds, cashews, and ¼ cup of the mashed banana in a blender and blend for 3 minutes. Add the egg yolks, reduced apple juice, and vanilla and blend until mixed. Then add the remaining mashed banana and puree until smooth. Add the butter, 1 tablespoon at a time, until incorporated.
5. Sift together the flour, baking powder, and salt into a large bowl. In a separate bowl, beat the egg whites until stiff.
6. Add the egg yolk/banana mixture to the dry ingredients in the bowl and stir until well mixed. Using a rubber spatula, gently fold in the beaten egg whites, one-third at a time.
7. Divide the batter evenly between the two 9-inch springform pans and bake for 30 to 40 minutes, or until a cake tester comes out clean and the cake springs back when pressed with a finger. Remove the cake from the pans and let cool completely on a rack.
8. Using a long serrated knife, carefully slice each layer in half to make 4 layers.
9. Spread the first layer with about one-quarter of the carob icing. Place the second layer over the first and spread with the raspberry preserves. Cover with the third layer and spread with another quarter of the carob icing. Top with the last layer and ice the whole cake with the remaining carob icing. Chill to set the icing for about 1 hour before serving.

Blueberry-Couscous Cake

Major Phase: Wood
Minor Phase: Water

YIELD: One 9-inch × 14-inch cake

This is a luscious cake, dense, moist, and rich tasting because of the blueberries, yet fat-free. Serve it topped with unsweetened raspberry or strawberry jam or orange marmalade, thinned with a little water. It's great the next morning for breakfast, too—with or without the topping.

> 6 cups apple juice
> 1 tablespoon vanilla extract
> 3 cups couscous
> 1 pint blueberries*

1. Pick over the blueberries and wash them gently under cold water. Set aside on paper towels to dry thoroughly.
2. Place the apple juice, vanilla, and couscous in a large pot, and bring to a boil. Stir continuously, until the couscous has thickened and all the juice has been absorbed.
3. Gently fold the blueberries into the hot couscous. Pour immediately into a 9-inch × 14-inch rinsed undried shallow baking pan. Chill until set, about 2 hours.

---

* If blueberries are not available, substitute strawberries. The next best choice is raisins.

Orange Loaf with Walnuts

Major Phase: Earth
Minor Phase: Wood

YIELD: One 9-inch × 5-inch loaf

A delectable and a romantic tea cake, excellent for a mid-afternoon pick-me-up.

⅔ cup chopped walnuts
2 cups whole wheat flour
4 teaspoons aluminum-free baking powder
1 tablespoon grated orange rind
½ tablespoon grated lime rind
1 egg
½ cup honey or maple syrup
1 cup fresh orange juice
1½ tablespoons fresh lime juice
¼ cup (4 tablespoons) unsalted butter, melted

1. Preheat the oven to 300°F. Grease a 9-inch × 5-inch loaf pan.
2. Toast the walnuts in the oven for 10 to 15 minutes. Turn up the heat to 350°.
3. In a large mixing bowl, sift together the flour and the baking powder. Add the fruit rinds and walnuts.
4. In a separate bowl, beat the egg. Add the honey or maple syrup, orange and lime juices, and the melted butter. Beat with a wooden spoon or electric mixer until thoroughly mixed.
5. Fold the liquid ingredients into the dry ones, stirring quickly just until all ingredients are completely moistened. Do not overmix, or the baking powder will begin to act.
6. Pour the batter into the prepared loaf pan, evening out the mixture with a rubber spatula. Bake for 40 to 45 minutes, or until a cake tester inserted into the center of the loaf comes out clean.
7. Remove from the oven. Allow to cool in the pan for a few minutes. Remove from pan and serve warm.

Almond–Lemon Cream Tart

Major Phase: Earth
Minor Phase: Wood

Yield: One 9-inch pie

This delicate tart makes a light and lovely ending to an elegant summer lunch.

Crust

½ cup almonds, roasted
1 cup whole wheat pastry flour
½ cup oat flour
Pinch sea salt
¼ cup cold-pressed vegetable oil
¼ cup maple syrup
¼ cup water

Filling

2 cups water
2 cups almonds, blanched
⅓ cup maple syrup
2 tablespoons kuzu
grated rind of ½ lemon
2 tablespoons arrowroot
1 tablespoon fresh lemon juice, or to taste
½ teaspoon almond extract

¼ cup almonds, roasted, for topping

Lemon Glaze

1 tablespoon kuzu
1 cup almond milk*
  Juice of 1 lemon
1 tablespoon maple syrup

1. Preheat oven to 350°F. Oil a 9-inch pie pan.
2. *To make the crust*: Finely grind the almonds in a nut grinder or food processor. Place in a medium mixing bowl, add the flours and salt, and mix well.
3. In a small bowl, whisk together the oil, maple syrup, and water until emulsified.
4. Add the liquid ingredients to the dry ingredients and mix until the dough has the consistency of wet sand. Press the dough evenly into the prepared pie pan. If you wish, you may line the pan with parchment paper to make serving easier.
5. Bake the crust for 20 minutes, or until lightly browned. If necessary, use the broiler to brown the crust lightly during the last 3 minutes.
6. *To make the filling*: Place all the ingredients in the container of a blender or food processor and blend until smooth. Pour into a medium saucepan and cook over high heat, stirring continuously with a whisk or wooden spoon, until the mixture reaches the thickness of pudding, about 6 to 8 minutes.
7. Remove from the heat and immediately pour the filling into the prebaked crust. Shake the pie plate gently to help spread the filling evenly.
8. Arrange whole roasted almonds decoratively over the top of the tart or chop and sprinkle them on top. Set aside while you prepare the glaze.
9. *To make the glaze*: In a small saucepan, dissolve the kuzu in the water. Add the lemon juice and maple syrup.
10. Cook over high heat, stirring continuously, until it is thickened and clear, about 2 to 3 minutes. Very slowly pour the hot glaze over the tart, making sure to cover the entire tart.
11. Chill for at least 2 hours before serving.

❧ · ☙

---

* Obtainable in natural-foods stores

Grated-Apple Tart

Major Phase: Wood
Minor Phase: Earth

Yield: One 9-inch tart

This is my version of a French peasant recipe presented by Richard Olney in his book Simple French Food.

> 3 cups grated peeled apples (about 1 pound)
> Juice of 1 lemon
> ½ teaspoon ground cinnamon
> 2 tablespoons maple syrup
> 5 tablespoons unsalted butter
> 3 cups fresh whole wheat bread crumbs
> ¼ cup maple syrup

1. Preheat the oven to 350°F.
2. Mix the apples with the lemon juice to prevent discoloring. Add the cinnamon. Stir in the maple syrup.
3. Warm ½ tablespoon of the butter in a 9-inch cast-iron skillet and rotate the skillet to coat thoroughly with the butter.
4. Place the bread crumbs, the remaining butter, and the maple syrup in a food processor and process for 2 to 3 minutes until thoroughly blended. Carefully pat the dough into the bottom and sides of the warm skillet. Cook over low heat until the crust sets, about 4 to 5 minutes.
5. Put the apples into the crust and pat down. Return to the stove and cook over low heat for another 10 minutes, then place in the oven and bake for 15 minutes, or until the apples are soft. Cool to room temperature before serving.

Apple-Cranberry Pie

Major Phase: Wood
Minor Phases: Earth and Water

YIELD: One 9-inch double-crust pie

*T*he filling of this pie can also be used as a relish in a Thanksgiving meal.

Crust

3 cups whole wheat pastry flour
¼ teaspoon sea salt
½ cup cold-pressed sunflower oil or unsalted butter
½ cup cold water
1 egg, beaten (optional)

Filling

2 pounds cooking apples (McIntosh or Cortland)
1 cup fresh cranberries
½ cup raisins
½ cup maple syrup or barley malt
Pinch sea salt
¼ teaspoon ground cloves
1 cinnamon stick
1 tablespoon arrowroot or kuzu
½ cup water

1. *To prepare the crust:* Place the flour in the container of a food processor and, with the machine running, slowly pour in the oil through the feed tube or drop in the butter a tablespoon at a time. (Alternatively, combine the flour and salt in a large mixing bowl. Mix in the oil or butter, working swiftly with a pastry cutter or two knives, until the mixture is crumbly.)

2. Add the cold water a little at a time, until a ball of dough forms. Squeeze the dough between your hands briefly to round out the ball. Wrap in wax paper and chill for 30 minutes.

3. *To make the filling:* Peel, core, and chop the apples.

4. Place apples, cranberries, raisins, syrup or malt, salt, and spices in a 4-quart pot and cook over medium heat, covered, for 15 minutes. Stir and mash the apples and cranberries with a wooden spoon to blend well. Cook for 15 minutes more.

5. Dissolve the kuzu or arrowroot in the water and stir into the cranberry mixture. Keep stirring over medium heat until it clears and thickens a little. Cover and keep warm over very low heat.

6. Preheat the oven to 375°F. Oil a 9-inch pie plate. Divide the dough into 2 pieces. Cut two 12-inch pieces of wax paper; dip your hand in water and run it over your work surface to moisten it slightly (this will keep the paper from slipping), then place one of the pieces of wax paper on it. Put one of the balls of dough on the paper, flatten it slightly with a rolling pin, and cover with the other sheet of wax paper. Roll out the dough evenly into a circle ¼-inch thick.

7. Peel off the top sheet of wax paper, then flip the dough into the pie plate, carefully pressing it into the bottom and sides of the pan. Remove the bottom wax paper and trim the edges. Poke with a fork a few times and prebake for 10 minutes. Remove from the oven and reduce heat to 350°F.

8. *To finish the pie:* Roll out the top crust following the directions above and remove the top layer of wax paper. Pour the filling into the prebaked crust, then invert the top crust over the pie. Remove the second sheet of wax paper, trim the edges with a paring knife, and press the edges together with the back of a fork. If you wish, you can cut a design out of the leftover dough and place it on the pie after moistening it slightly so that it will stick. Poke a few holes in the top crust with the fork and bake the filled pie for 35 to 40 minutes, or until the crust sounds hollow when tapped with a spoon.

9. For a nice glaze, brush the pie with the beaten egg 15 minutes before the end of cooking time, then finish baking.

Johnna's Best Cranberry Dream Pie

Major Phase: Water
Minor Phases: Earth and Wood

Yield: One 9-inch pie

*T*his refreshing pie is ideal for year-end holidays, not only because it's delicious, but also because it looks so very festive.

Crust

½ cup almonds or filberts
½ cup rolled oats
½ cup whole wheat pastry flour
    Pinch sea salt
¼ teaspoon ground cinnamon
 3 tablespoons cold-pressed sunflower oil
    or unsalted butter
 2 tablespoons maple syrup
¼ cup water

Filling

1½ cups fresh cranberries
 1 quart sweet apple cider,
    fresh-pressed if possible
 1 bar agar-agar
 5 tablespoons arrowroot
¼ cup maple syrup
    Grated rind of ½ lemon
 1 tablespoon fresh lemon juice

Meringue

4 egg whites
⅛ teaspoon sea salt
⅓ cup maple syrup
½ teaspoon vanilla extract

1. Preheat the oven to 350°F. Oil a 9-inch pie plate.
2. *To make the crust*: Finely grind the nuts in a food processor, coffee grinder, or blender. Mix thoroughly with the rolled oats, flour, salt, and cinnamon.
3. If using a food processor and the butter, cut the butter into the dry ingredients by pulsing the machine, then add the maple syrup and water. Otherwise, mix the oil, syrup, and water in a cup and blend into the dry ingredients. The dough should form a clump.
4. Press the dough evenly into the bottom and sides of the pie plate. Bake for 20 to 25 minutes, or until lightly browned. Let cool to room temperature.
5. *To make the filling*: Wash and pick over the cranberries. In a 2-quart saucepan, combine them with 3 cups of the cider. Bring to a boil, reduce heat to low, and cook, covered, until the cranberries are softened and begin to pop, about 10 to 15 minutes. Strain, pressing the cranberries well to extract their juice. Measure the liquid into a 4-cup measuring cup and add enough additional sweet cider to make 3⅓ cups. Reserve the cranberry pulp for another use or discard. Return the liquid to the saucepan.
6. Soften the agar under running water and shred it into the cranberry-apple liquid. Bring to a boil, reduce heat, and simmer until the agar dissolves, about 4 to 5 minutes.
7. Dissolve the arrowroot in ½ cup of the cold cider. Add it, along with the maple syrup, to the agar mixture. Cook over high heat, stirring constantly, until the mixture thickens and becomes clear, about 4 to 5 minutes.
8. Remove the saucepan from the heat and add the lemon rind and juice. Pour the mixture into the cooled, prebaked crust and set aside to cool in the refrigerator for 2 hours, or until set.
9. *To make the meringue*: One hour before serving, prepare the meringue. Preheat the oven to 350°F. Beat the egg whites with the salt until stiff. Fold in the maple syrup and vanilla.
10. Mound on top of the chilled cranberry pie. Bake for 10 to 15 minutes to brown the top of the meringue peaks. Serve either at room temperature or chilled.

Ice Dream Pie

Major Phase: Earth
Minor Phases: Wood and Fire

Yield: One 9-inch pie

A dramatic dessert, one of Lissa's creations, perfect for ice cream lovers who prefer the dairy-free version. The crunch of the crust contrasts nicely with the cool filling.

Crust

½ cup whole wheat flour
1½ cup rolled oats
    Pinch sea salt
½ teaspoon ground cinnamon
¼ cup cold-pressed vegetable oil
¼ cup maple syrup
2 teaspoons water

Filling

1 pint nondairy strawberry ice cream
1 pint nondairy orange ice cream
½ cup almonds, roasted and chopped
    (or ½ cup shredded unsweetened coconut, toasted)
½ pint strawberries
2 tablespoons kuzu
¾ cup apple juice

1. Preheat the oven to 350°F. Oil a 9-inch deep-dish pie pan.
2. *To make the crust*: In a medium bowl, stir together the flour, oats, salt, and cinnamon.
3. In small bowl, whisk the liquid ingredients together, then add to the dry ingredients and stir until thoroughly moistened.

4. Press the crust evenly into the bottom and sides of the prepared pan.

5. Bake for 25 to 30 minutes, or until slightly browned. Remove from the oven and allow to cool completely while you prepare the filling.

6. *To make the filling*: While the crust is baking, transfer the ice creams from the freezer to the refrigerator for 30 minutes to soften.

7. When the ice cream is soft enough to spoon easily and the crust is ready, spread a ½-inch layer of strawberry ice cream in the pie shell and sprinkle on the chopped almonds. Cover with a layer of orange ice cream and place the pie in the freezer.

8. Slice the strawberries and place in a small bowl. In a small saucepan, dissolve the kuzu in the apple juice; bring to a boil, stirring continuously, until thickened and clear, about 3 to 4 minutes. Fold in the strawberries and set aside for 10 minutes to cool and thicken a bit more.

9. Carefully pour an even layer of the apple-strawberry mixture over the top of the pie and return to the freezer. Place in the refrigerator to soften 30 minutes to 1 hour before serving.

Kiwi Fruit Tart with Almond Crust

Major Phase: Earth
Minor Phase: Wood

YIELD: One 9-inch tart or 8 individual tarts

Fruit and nuts are combined here in a most delectable and attractive dessert. Once I made one triple size, on a large cookie sheet, for a wedding; I was told it was the talk of the event.

Crust

     2 cups almonds
     ½ cup rolled oats
     ¼ cup maple syrup
     ¼ cup (4 tablespoons) unsalted butter
          or cold-pressed vegetable oil
     2 tablespoons water
          Pinch sea salt

Filling

     1 apple
     2 tablespoons fresh lemon juice
     1 ripe banana
     6 strawberries
     2 kiwi fruit
     8 ounces unsweetened raspberry jam
     1½ tablespoons kuzu
     1½ cups unfiltered apple juice
     ½ teaspoon vanilla extract

1. Preheat the oven to 375°F. Oil a 9-inch pie pan, an 8 × 8-inch shallow baking pan, or 8 individual tart pans.
2. *To make the crust*: Grind the almonds and oats together in a food processor or blender until pulverized.
3. In a small bowl, combine the maple syrup, butter or oil, water, and salt and whisk until emulsified.
4. With the motor running, add the liquid ingredients to the dry ingredients until a ball of dough forms in the bowl. Alternatively, blend dry and liquid ingredients in a medium mixing bowl. Press the dough evenly onto the bottom of the prepared pie pan and bake for 20 to 25 minutes, or until the crust sounds hollow when you tap it with a spoon and is lightly browned along the edges. Set aside to cool while you prepare the filling.
5. *To make the filling*: While the crust is baking, slice the apple thinly into a bowl; add the lemon juice, then slice the banana, strawberries, and kiwi onto separate plates. You should have about 2 cups sliced fruit.

6. When the crust has cooled, leave it in the pan and spread the jam over it. Arrange the fruit attractively over the jam, apple first, then the banana and strawberries. Finish with a layer of the kiwi.

7. In a small pan, dissolve the kuzu into the cold apple juice. Add the vanilla. Cook over high heat, stirring continuously, until the mixture thickens and becomes clear, about 3 to 4 minutes. Pour the glaze immediately over the fruit, making sure all of it is covered. Chill until set, about 30 minutes.

Mince Pie

Major Phase: Wood
Minor Phases: Water and Earth

YIELD: One 9-inch pie

This is an old favorite of mine. It contains no added sweetener, but thanks to the cooking method used, it is sweet enough to satisfy any sugar freak in town.

> 2 pounds cooking apples
> 1½ cups raisins, or 1 cup raisins and ½ cup currants
> ¼ cup cold-pressed vegetable oil
> Grated rind of 1 lemon
> 1 tablespoon lemon juice
> ¼ teaspoon ground allspice
> ½ teaspoon ground mace
> ½ teaspoon ground cinnamon
> ⅛ teaspoon ground cloves
> 2 cups apple juice
> ¼ teaspoon sea salt
> 1 rounded tablespoon kuzu or arrowroot
> 1 tablespoon rice or barley miso
> ½ cup cold water
> 1 recipe crust from Apple-Cranberry Pie (page 245)

1. Peel, core, and chop the apples.
2. In a 4-quart pot, combine the apples, raisins, currants, oil, lemon rind and juice, spices, apple juice, and salt. Cover, bring to a boil, reduce heat to low, and simmer gently for 1 hour, stirring occasionally. Remove the cover and simmer for 1 hour more, stirring often.
3. Dissolve the kuzu or arrowroot and miso in the water and add to the apple mixture, stirring continuously until thickened and clear, 1 to 2 minutes. Let cool. Mince filling can be refrigerated in tightly covered glass jars until needed. It keeps for several months.
4. Prepare piecrust according to instructions for Ice Dream Pie (page 249). Pre-bake the bottom crust for 8 to 10 minutes. Fill, cover with the top crust, and bake for 35 to 40 minutes at 350°F. Let cool completely before serving.

Peach Pie

Major Phase: Metal
Minor Phases: Wood and Earth

YIELD: One 9-inch pie

*T*his beautiful pie is a perfect way to use up bruised or slightly overripe peaches.

Crust

1½ cups whole wheat pastry flour
½ cup unbleached white flour
¼ teaspoon sea salt
¼ cup soymilk
½ cup cold-pressed vegetable oil or unsalted butter, melted

Filling

6 large or 8 medium peaches
2 tablespoons fresh lemon juice
2 tablespoons maple syrup
½ teaspoon ground cinnamon
⅓ cup unsweetened peach jam or preserves
½ cup slivered blanched almonds

1. Preheat oven to 375°F. Oil a 9-inch pie plate.
2. *To make the crust*: In a large bowl, sift together the flours and salt. Measure the soymilk into a liquid measuring cup, then add the oil or butter and whisk briefly with a fork. Add to the flour mixture, stirring with a fork until a ball is formed. Squeeze the ball between your hands, incorporating all the flour; don't over-knead, or the dough will be too stiff.
4. Roll out two-thirds of the dough between 2 sheets of wax paper, shaping a circle about ⅙-inch thick and large enough to fit the pie plate. Remove the top layer of wax paper and gently transfer the dough to the pie plate. Fit the dough in carefully and trim the edges. Decorate the border by pinching or scalloping if desired. Prick the dough several times with a fork and prebake in the oven for 5 minutes, or until set.
5. *To make the filling:* Peel, pit, and slice the peaches. Toss them in a bowl with the lemon juice. Gently stir in the maple syrup and cinnamon. Pile the filling high into the piecrust. Dot with the preserves or jam and sprinkle with the slivered almonds.
6. Roll out the remaining one-third of the dough between 2 pieces of wax paper as described above. Don't make it too thin, or it will break. Using a pastry wheel or sharp knife, cut the dough into strips about ¾-inch wide. Arrange crisscross on top of the pie. Pinch the ends to the bottom crust.
7. Bake at 375°F for 35 to 40 minutes, or until the edges look golden brown. (If you bake this pie in a glass dish, you can see the bottom turn golden, too!)

Pumpkin Pie

Major Phase: Earth
Minor Phase: Wood

Yield: One 9-inch pie

Crust

1½ cups rolled oats
½ cup brown rice flour
½ cup chopped almonds
⅓ cup cold-pressed vegetable oil
3 tablespoons maple syrup
¼ cup water
    Pinch sea salt

Filling

3 pounds butternut squash (1 large or 2 small squashes)
3 eggs, preferably organic or free-range
½ cup maple syrup
    Pinch sea salt
1 teaspoon ground cinnamon
¼ teaspoon ground ginger
¼ teaspoon ground cloves
¼ teaspoon freshly ground nutmeg

1. Preheat the oven to 400°F. Cut the squash in half. Place cut side down on a cookie sheet (seeds intact) and bake for 45 to 50 minutes, or until soft; set aside to cool. When cool enough to handle, scoop out the seeds and discard; scoop the pulp out of the skins. You should have 3 cups.
2. *To make the crust:* While the squash is cooking, oil a 9-inch deep-dish pie plate. Combine the oats, brown rice flour, and almonds in a large bowl. In a small bowl, whisk together the oil, maple syrup, water, and salt. Pour wet ingredients into dry, stirring well to mix.

3. With wet hands, press the crust evenly into the prepared pie plate, starting from the center outward, and going up the sides. Bake in the same oven, 5 to 7 minutes, or just until the crust is set. Do not let it brown.
4. *To make the filling:* Place the squash and the eggs, maple syrup, salt, and spices in the container of a food processor and process until smooth.
5. Pour the filling into the prebaked piecrust and bake at 400°F for 15 minutes. Reduce heat to 375°F and bake for 30 minutes more, or until set.
6. Let the pie cool to room temperature, then chill thoroughly before serving.

Pecan Pie

Major Phase: Earth
Minor Phase: Wood

YIELD: One 9-inch pie

*P*ecan *pie is always a holiday favorite, so here are two versions, one with eggs and one without. Try both. The flavor and texture of each one is quite different, and both are delicious.*

Crust

1½ cups rolled oats
½ cup whole wheat pastry flour
¼ cup water
¼ cup cold-pressed safflower oil or unsalted butter, melted
¼ cup maple syrup
Pinch sea salt

Kuzu Filling

2 cups pecans
1⅔ cups water or apple-strawberry juice
5 tablespoons kuzu
½ cup maple syrup
Grated rind of ½ lemon
1 teaspoon vanilla extract
1 tablespoon tahini

Egg Filling

2 cups pecans
3 large eggs, preferably organic or free-range
1 teaspoon vanilla extract
½ cup maple syrup
Pinch sea salt

1. Preheat the oven to 325°F. Oil a 9-inch deep-dish pie plate, or line it with parchment paper.
2. *To make the crust*: In a blender or food processor, grind the rolled oats to flour. In a 3-quart bowl, combine the oil or butter, maple syrup, and salt. Add the flour mixture and blend thoroughly with a fork until you have a soft dough.
3. Press evenly into the prepared pie plate and bake for 20 minutes if you are using Kuzu Filling, 10 minutes if you are using Egg Filling. Set aside and prepare one of the fillings.
4. *To make Kuzu Filling*: Toast the pecans in a 350°F oven for 10 minutes.
5. In a 2-quart saucepan, mix the water or juice, kuzu, maple syrup, lemon rind, and vanilla. Bring to a boil and cook, stirring continuously, until thickened, about 5 to 6 minutes. Remove from heat and swirl in the tahini until creamy.
6. Fold the toasted pecans into the kuzu cream. Pour the Kuzu Filling into the prebaked pie shell and chill until firm, about 2 hours.
7. *To make Egg Filling*: Toast the pecans in a 350°F oven for 10 minutes. Reduce oven temperature to 325°F.
8. In a 2-quart bowl, whisk together the eggs, vanilla, maple syrup, and salt.
9. Stir in the nuts and pour the Egg Filling into the baked pie shell.
10. Bake in the 325°F oven for 30 minutes, or until set. Allow to cool to room temperature before serving.

Ginger Lace Cookies

Major Phase: Wood
Minor Phase: Earth

Yield: 2½ dozen cookies

These tangy, crisp, and delicate cookies are a marvelous finale for an elegant meal.

- ½ cup (8 tablespoons) unsalted butter, softened
- ¾ cup rice syrup
- Juice and rind of 1 lemon
- ¼ cup maple syrup
- 1 teaspoon orange extract
- 3 to 4 ounce piece of fresh ginger root
- 1¼ cups whole wheat pastry flour
- 1 tablespoon ground ginger

1. Preheat the oven to 325°F. Line 2 cookie sheets with parchment paper.
2. Peel the fresh ginger root and grate it; you should have about ¼ to ⅓ cup. Place in a cheesecloth and squeeze, to extract the juice, or just squeeze by hand. Discard the pulp once it's been squeezed dry. You should have about 1 tablespoon of juice. (The fresher the ginger, the greater the amount of juice it will give up.) Set aside.
3. In a large bowl, cream the butter with the rice syrup. Grate the lemon rind and add to the butter/syrup mixture. Then cut the lemon in half crosswise and juice it. Add the lemon juice, maple syrup, orange extract, and 2 tablespoons of the ginger juice. Beat well with a whisk to blend.
4. Sift together the flour and ground ginger, then stir into the wet ingredients. The batter will be rather thick.
5. Drop by teaspoonfuls onto the prepared cookie sheets, leaving at least 2 inches between each cookie. The cookies will spread out and become thin during baking.
6. Bake for 12 to 15 minutes, taking care that the cookies don't burn. Remove the cookies from the oven as soon as the edges are slightly browned. Transfer to a rack to cool.

Lemon Cookies

Major Phase: Wood
Minor Phase: Earth

Yɪᴇʟᴅ: 3 dozen cookies

2½ cups oat flour
1 cup brown rice flour
½ teaspoon sea salt
⅓ cup maple syrup
¼ cup apple juice
⅓ cup (5⅓ tablespoons) unsalted butter, melted
   or ⅓ cup cold-pressed vegetable oil
1¼ teaspoons lemon extract
2 teaspoons vanilla extract
Grated rind of 1 lemon
2 teaspoons lemon juice

1. Preheat the oven to 375°F. Grease a cookie sheet or cover it with parchment paper.
2. In a 3-quart bowl, mix the flours.
3. In a smaller bowl, mix the salt, maple syrup, apple juice, butter or oil, extracts, lemon rind, and lemon juice.
4. Add the liquids to the flour, stirring well, until you have a moist, crumbly dough.
5. Working with 2 tablespoons, take a small quantity of the dough on one and shape it with the other one so that you have a spoon-shaped oval cookie. Using the other spoon, push the dough off the holding spoon onto the cookie sheet. Repeat until all the dough is used up. (Alternatively, you can just shape the cookies into ovals by hand.) It is okay to place the cookies close together, as they will not spread; they can almost touch.
6. Bake for 25 to 30 minutes, turning once, until lightly browned.

Diane's Macaroons

Major Phase: Metal
Minor Phase: Earth

<small>YIELD:</small> 35 to 40 cookies

Very simple to make, these scrumptious mouthfuls make a nice accompaniment to light, fruit-based desserts, such as the Pear-Raspberry Sorbet (page 274).

> 3½ cups shredded unsweetened coconut
> 1 cup whole wheat pastry flour
> ½ cup maple syrup
> 1⅓ cup water
> 1 teaspoon almond extract
> ¼ teaspoon sea salt

1. Preheat oven to 275°F. Grease a cookie sheet or line it with parchment paper.
2. In a large bowl, combine the coconut and flour.
3. In a small bowl, whisk together the maple syrup, water, almond extract, and salt.
4. Pour the liquid ingredients into the dry ones, stirring well, until you have a crumbly mixture.
5. With moistened hands, make small mounds and place them, side by side, on the cookie sheet (they will not spread). Bake for 25 to 30 minutes, or until lightly browned. Allow to cool to room temperature. These keep well stored in an airtight container.

Raisin Squares

Major Phase: Earth
Minor Phase: Wood

YIELD: 18 to 24 squares

These are delicious as an afternoon snack with mint tea or grain coffee, or as a quick breakfast (they're made of oatmeal and raisins, after all!)

Filling

3 cups seedless raisins
1½ cups water
1 cinnamon stick
3 tablespoons fresh lemon juice
¼ cup kuzu or arrowroot,
    dissolved in 2 tablespoons water

Crust

3 cups rolled oats
2 cups whole wheat pastry flour
¼ teaspoon sea salt
½ pound (2 sticks) unsalted butter, cut into small pieces
1 cup maple syrup or barley malt

1. *To make the filling:* In a 2-quart saucepan, combine the raisins, water, cinnamon stick, and lemon juice. Cover and cook over low heat for 10 minutes.
2. Discard the cinnamon stick. In a blender or food processor, puree the raisins and return them to the saucepan. Add the dissolved kuzu or arrowroot and cook over high heat, stirring, until thickened and clear; set aside.
3. Preheat the oven to 350°F. Oil a 9 × 14-inch cake pan.
4. *To make the crust:* Place the oats, flour, and salt in the container of a food processor. With the machine running, drop the pieces of butter in, one by one, until well mixed. (Alternatively, cut the butter into the flour in a bowl, using 2 knives or a pastry blender, until the mixture is crumbly.)

5. With the processor still running, slowly pour in the syrup or barley malt (or stir it into the flour in the bowl) until well mixed and you have a soft dough. Divide the dough in half.

6. Roll out one-half between two pieces of wax paper, to fit the cake pan. Remove the top paper. Invert the dough into the pan and carefully peel off the bottom paper. Gently press the dough into all the corners of the pan, then fold over or press down the edges so that the crust is flat with no border. Spread the filling evenly over the crust, smoothing with a rubber spatula.

7. Break up the remaining dough between your fingers until crumbly. Sprinkle the crumbly dough evenly over the raisin filling, covering it completely. Press down lightly.

8. Bake for 35 to 40 minutes, or until very lightly browned. Let cool, then cut into squares.

Sesame-Lemon Cookies

Major Phase: Wood
Minor Phase: Fire

YIELD: 30 to 35 cookies

These light, wonderfully crunchy cookies are popular with kids and grown-ups alike. They may be made in large quantities, although there is no guarantee that they will last very long.

  1½ cups oat flour
  1½ cups rolled oats, partially ground in a food processor
  ½ teaspoon sea salt
   1 teaspoon baking powder
  ⅓ cup sesame seeds, toasted
  ½ cup maple syrup
  ¼ cup unfiltered apple juice
  ½ cup tahini
   1 teaspoon lemon extract

2 teaspoons vanilla extract
Grated rind of ½ lemon
2 tablespoons fresh lemon juice
1 tablespoon water

1. Preheat the oven to 350°F. Grease a cookie sheet or cover with parchment paper.
2. In a large mixing bowl, combine the flour, oats, salt, baking powder, and sesame seeds.
3. In another, smaller bowl, whisk together the extracts, lemon rind, lemon juice, and water until blended.
4. Add the liquid ingredients to the dry ingredients, stirring well until you get a wet dough. Shape into cookies by dropping tablespoonsful on the baking sheet. Press down to flatten a bit with the spoon. Place them close to each other as these don't spread.
5. Bake for 10 minutes. Then turn over and bake for 5 to 10 minutes more, or until lightly browned. Watch carefully so as not to burn.

Walnut-Butter Cookies

Major Phase: Wood
Minor Phases: Earth and Metal

Yield: 25 to 30 cookies

Crunchy and with a surprising depth of flavor, these are certain to be crowd pleasers!

2 cups whole wheat pastry flour
1 cup walnuts
Tiny pinch sea salt
5 tablespoons unsalted butter, softened
1 tablespoon vanilla extract
⅓ cup maple syrup
¼ cup water

1. Place the flour, nuts, and salt in the container of a food processor and process for 15 to 30 seconds, or until well mixed. With the motor running, add the butter, 1 tablespoon at a time, then add the vanilla, maple syrup, and water. When the dough forms a ball, stop processing. Take the dough out of the processor and roll into a 1½-inch-thick log with aluminum foil or wax paper. Chill for 2 hours.
2. Preheat the oven to 350°F. Cut the cookie log into ½-inch slices and place on an ungreased cookie sheet (cookies will spread a little).
3. Bake for 15 minutes, then turn and bake on the other side for 5 to 10 minutes more, or until *lightly* browned.

Almond Flan with Raspberry Sauce

Major Phase: Metal
Minor Phases: Earth and Fire

Yield: 8 servings

For those who can't tolerate milk or eggs, here's a lovely dairy-free custard.

> 5 cups soymilk
> 2 bars agar-agar, rinsed, or ⅓ cup agar flakes
> ¼ cup arrowroot or kuzu
> ½ cup maple syrup
> 1 teaspoon almond extract
> 2 tablespoons vanilla extract
> 1 cup almonds
> 12 ounces raspberry jam
> ¾ cup water

1. In a 2-quart saucepan, combine 4 cups of the soymilk and the agar and simmer until the agar dissolves.

2. Combine the arrowroot or kuzu with the remaining soymilk, then add the maple syrup and extracts and add to the soymilk-agar mixture. Stir continuously over high heat until the mixture thickens slightly and comes to a boil, about 3 to 4 minutes. Pour into 1 large or 8 individual serving bowls. Chill until firm, about 1½ to 2 hours.

3. Preheat the oven to 350°F. Roast the almonds for 10 minutes. Allow to cool slightly, then chop.

4. Mix together the raspberry jam and the water to make a raspberry sauce. Just before serving, warm the sauce, and place 1 to 2 teaspoons on each serving dish. Place individual servings of the flan on top and garnish each with chopped almonds. If you have chilled the flan in small bowls, simply invert each bowl on top of the raspberry sauce. The flan should slip out easily; run a knife along edges if needed.

Blueberry Crunch

Major Phase: Water
Minor Phases: Wood and Earth

Yield: 6 to 8 servings

*T*ry this for breakfast some morning (it's not too sweet). It's an interesting variation on the cereal-and-fruit theme.

1½ cups rolled oats
½ cup whole wheat pastry flour
½ cup chopped almonds
¼ teaspoon sea salt
⅓ cup cold-pressed safflower oil
½ cup maple syrup
1 pint blueberries
2½ tablespoons kuzu
¾ cup cold water

1. Preheat the oven to 400°F.
2. In a large bowl, combine the oats, flour, almonds, and salt. In a separate, smaller bowl, whisk the oil and half the maple syrup and add to the oat mixture.
3. In a medium saucepan, bring the blueberries and the remaining ¼ cup maple syrup to a boil. Dissolve the kuzu in the water and add to the blueberries; cook, stirring constantly until thickened and transparent, about 2 to 3 minutes. Remove from heat and set aside.
4. Oil a 6 × 10-inch rectangular baking pan. With wet hands, press enough of the oat crust (about two-thirds) into the bottom of the dish to form a solid layer. Pour blueberry mixture evenly over the crust. Sprinkle the remaining crust over the blueberries.
5. Bake for 20 to 25 minutes, or until the top is nicely browned.
6. Allow to cool slightly. Then chill in the refrigerator until the filling is set, at least 1 hour. Cut into squares and serve.

Compote of Dried Fruits with Cashew-Almond Cream

Major Phase: Earth
Sauce Phase: Earth

YIELD: 6 servings

1 pound mixed dried fruit
  (prunes, apples, apricots, peaches, pears)
½ cup raisins
2 cinnamon sticks
1 lemon

1. In a 3-quart pot, combine the dried fruit, raisins, and cinnamon sticks. Cover with 3 inches of water, bring to a boil, and simmer, covered, for 20 minutes.
2. While the fruit is cooking, grate the lemon rind and set aside. Juice the lemon. Add the lemon juice and grated rind to the fruit during the last 10 minutes of cooking.

3. Allow the compote to steep in its juice for at least an hour before serving. Serve either hot, cold, or at room temperature, with a large dollop of Cashew-Almond Cream (see below).

Cashew-Almond Cream

YIELD: 2 cups

1 cup cashew pieces
1 cup almonds
2 tablespoons maple syrup
1 teaspoon vanilla extract
¼ to ⅓ cup water
2 tablespoons mirin (sweet rice wine) (optional)

1. In a food processor or blender, grind the nuts until pulverized. With the machine running, add the maple syrup, vanilla, optional mirin and enough water to make a creamy consistency. (This cream has a tendency to thicken as it sits; add some water as needed to thin it out.)

Fruit Crisp

Major Phase: Earth
Minor Phases: Wood, Water, and Metal

YIELD: 6 to 8 servings

6 ripe peaches
6 plums
1 pound cherries
½ cup maple syrup
1 teaspoon ground cinnamon
½ teaspoon ground ginger
Pinch sea salt
¼ cup arrowroot

Topping

1½ cups dry whole wheat bread crumbs
¼ cup (4 tablespoons) unsalted butter, softened
½ teaspoon ground cinnamon
⅓ cup maple syrup
½ cup almonds, chopped

1. Preheat the oven to 350°F. Oil a 6-inch × 9-inch shallow baking pan.
2. Pit the peaches and plums, then slice them and place them in a large bowl.
3. Pit the cherries and cut them in half, adding them to the bowl.
4. Toss the fruit with the maple syrup, cinnamon, ginger, salt, and arrowroot. Spread the mixture into the prepared baking pan.
5. *To make the topping:* In another bowl, combine all the topping ingredients and spread over the top of the fruit. Bake for 35 to 45 minutes, or until the topping is nicely browned. Serve either warm or chilled.

Stuffed Oranges

Phase: Earth

Yield: 6 servings

These are lots of fun to make, and to eat as well. They take a bit of work, but their refreshing and unusual flavor make the effort absolutely worth it.

1 cup apple juice
1 cup raisins
7 large, thick-skinned sweet oranges (not waxed)
½ cup almonds, roasted and coarsely chopped (not waxed)
¼ cup kuzu
1 cup freshly squeezed orange juice

Topping

    ⅔ cup almonds, roasted
    ⅓ cup malted rice syrup*
     1 teaspoon mirin (sweet rice wine) or sweet sherry
     2 teaspoons tahini
    ¼ cup fresh orange juice

1. *To prepare the oranges:* In a small saucepan, combine the apple juice and raisins and simmer, covered, for 8 minutes. Puree in a blender or food processor; transfer to a large bowl and set aside.
2. Slice ½ inch off the tops of 6 of the oranges. Line a large strainer with cheesecloth and place it over a bowl. Using a teaspoon, carefully scoop the pulp out of the oranges into the strainer. Squeeze well to extract all the juice; set aside. Discard the cheesecloth and pulp.
3. Grate the rind of the remaining orange and then juice it. Add the rind and juice to the raisin puree, with the juice from the rest of the oranges and the roasted almonds.
4. In a saucepan, dissolve the kuzu in the additional cup orange juice and bring it to a boil, stirring continuously, until clear and thickened, about 2 to 3 minutes. Combine with the raisin mixture. Spoon into each hollowed-out orange. Allow to cool until set. Make this at least 2 or up to 24 hours before serving. Make the topping just before serving.
5. *To make the topping:* Place the almonds in the container of a food processor or blender and grind well. Add the syrup and other ingredients and process until creamy.
6. Spoon about 2 tablespoons of the topping over each stuffed orange. Serve immediately.

---

* Obtainable in natural-foods stores.

Raspberry Parfait

Major Phase: Fire
Minor Phase: Earth

YIELD: 8 servings

Luscious tasting but refreshing, this summer dessert would be a wonderful ending to an evening meal in the country.

1½ cups apple-raspberry juice
½ cup water
1 bar agar-agar or 3 tablespoons agar flakes
1 teaspoon vanilla extract
2 teaspoons tahini
1½ cups amasake*
2 teaspoons almond extract
3 to 4 tablespoons kuzu, dissolved in ½ cup water
8 very thin orange slices for garnish
8 raspberries for garnish

1. In a small saucepan, heat the apple-raspberry juice along with the water, agar, and vanilla until it comes to a boil and the agar has melted. Pour into a shallow pan or bowl and let cool until set, 1½ to 2 hours.
2. Place half the jelled agar in a blender and blend until smooth; set aside. Blend the other half the same way with the tahini; set aside in a separate bowl.
3. In a small saucepan, heat the amasake and almond extract. Add the dissolved kuzu and simmer, stirring, until clear and thickened, about 1 to 2 minutes. Allow to cool for 10 minutes.
4. Using 8 tall parfait glasses, layer the parfait in the following order: tahini, agar mix, amasake-almond pudding, plain agar. Top each serving with an orange slice and a fresh raspberry. Chill in the refrigerator for 2 hours, or until set.

❧ • ☙

---

* Sweet rice drink, obtainable in natural-foods stores.

Spiced Glazed Pears
with Tofu Cream

Major Phase: Metal
Minor Phase: Earth

YIELD: 6 servings

The reducing of the pear-cooking juices creates a most delicious syrupy glaze for this sophisticated dessert.

8 firm pears, preferably Bosc
1½ cups unfiltered apple juice or cider
2 teaspoons ground cardamom
¼ teaspoon ground cloves
¼ teaspoon ground ginger

Tofu Cream

8 ounces soft tofu
¼ cup rice syrup
¼ to ½ cup water
Ground cinnamon for garnish

1. Preheat the oven to 350°F.
2. *To prepare the pears*: Quarter the pears, slicing off the core. Slice each quarter in half lengthwise to make 8 slices. Place in a 9-inch × 14-inch shallow baking dish.
3. In a small saucepan, heat the apple juice or cider. Stir in the spices, pour over the pears, and bake, covered with aluminum foil, for 35 to 40 minutes, or until the pears are tender when pierced. With a slotted spoon, remove to a bowl and allow to cool to room temperature.
4. To make a glaze, pour the pan juices into a 3- to 4-quart saucepan, leaving the spice residue behind to discard. Bring to a boil over high heat and keep boiling, uncovered, for about 40 minutes, or until the juice is reduced to about ½ cup. Spoon 1 tablespoon glaze over each serving.

5. *To make the Tofu Cream:* Place the tofu and rice syrup in a blender and blend until smooth, adding water as needed to reach a consistency similar to whipped cream.

6. Serve over the spiced glazed pears, with a dusting of ground cinnamon for garnish.

Nectarine-Nutmilk Ice Cream

Major Phase: Metal
Minor Phases: Earth and Wood

YIELD: 6 cups

*T*his is no pallid ice cream imitation—it is a genuinely mouth-watering fruit-and-nut frozen dessert. You can invent a thousand variations on this theme and say good-bye to artificial ice creams forever.

Nutmilk

¾ cup cashews or blanched almonds
2¾ cups water
1 tablespoon maple syrup

6 ripe nectarines or peaches
¾ cup natural pear or apple juice
1½ cups fresh orange juice
¼ to ⅓ cup maple syrup, to taste
1 tablespoon vanilla extract

1. *To make the Nutmilk:* Place all the ingredients for the Nutmilk in the container of a blender and blend until very smooth.

2. *To complete the ice cream:* Peel and pit the nectarines or peaches and puree in

a blender or food processor. You should have about 1½ to 2 cups puree. Add the rest of the ingredients, including the Nutmilk, and process again until smooth. Adjust taste for sweetness with maple syrup.

3. Freeze in an ice-cream machine according to the manufacturer's instructions. Alternatively, freeze in ice-cube trays or a shallow baking pan for 1 hour. Transfer to a blender or food processor and process briefly. Refreeze to reach a sorbet consistency, about 1½ to 2 hours.

Apple-Raspberry Ice

Major Phase: Fire
Minor Phase: Wood

YIELD: 4 cups

This is a simple but delicious and refreshing treat. It can be made with any juice and unsweetened jam or preserve.

¼ cup unsweetened raspberry jam
1 quart apple-raspberry juice
¼ teaspoon ground nutmeg
Fresh raspberries for garnish

1. In a large bowl, whisk together the jam, juice, and nutmeg until well blended.
2. Freeze according to the directions for your ice-cream machine. Alternatively, freeze in ice-cube trays or a shallow baking pan for 1 hour; blend or process briefly and refreeze to reach sorbet consistency, about 1½ to 2 hours.
3. Decorate each serving with 2 to 3 fresh raspberries for garnish.

Pear-Raspberry Sorbet

Major Phase: Metal
Minor Phase: Fire

Yield: 8 to 10 servings

Pears and raspberries are a uniquely refreshing and satisfying combination, but try others as well. Apricots and apples are wonderful together, as are strawberries and fresh oranges.

> 1 lemon (unwaxed)
> 5 large pears, preferably Comice or Bartlett
> 1 bar agar-agar or 3 to 5 tablespoons agar flakes
> ⅔ cup water
> 1 cup pear juice
> 1 pint fresh raspberries

1. Grate the lemon rind into a large bowl, then juice the lemon and add the juice to the bowl.
2. Core and slice the pears and add to the bowl, tossing them with the juice and rind.
3. Rinse the agar bar under running water until softened. In a small saucepan, combine the water, pear juice, and agar bar or flakes and bring to a boil. Simmer for a few minutes, or until the agar has dissolved.
4. Combine the pears, agar mixture, and ¼ cup of the raspberries. In a blender or food processor, process in two batches until very smooth, then recombine.
5. Freeze in an ice-cream machine according to the manufacturer's instructions. Alternatively, freeze in ice-cube trays or a shallow pan for 1 hour. Transfer to a blender or food processor and process briefly. Refreeze to a sorbet consistency, about 1½ to 2 hours. Serve garnished with the rest of the raspberries.

Strawberry-Mint Sorbet

Major Phase: Fire

Minor Phase: Metal

YIELD: 4 servings

1 cup apple-strawberry juice
1 pint strawberries
1 teabag mint tea
½ cup boiling water
½ bar agar-agar or 2 tablespoons agar flakes
Juice and rind of 1 lemon
Pinch sea salt
4 sprigs mint

1. In a small saucepan, bring the apple-strawberry juice to a boil. Boil, uncovered, for about 20 to 30 minutes, or until liquid is reduced to ½ cup.
2. Clean and stem the strawberries; set aside. Reserve 4 whole berries for garnish.
3. In another small saucepan, steep the mint tea in the boiling water for 3 minutes. Remove and discard tea bag. Soften the agar bar under running water; shred the bar or sprinkle the flakes into the mint tea and simmer until the agar dissolves. Remove from heat and set aside to cool slightly.
4. Grate the lemon rind and add it to the mint tea; then juice the lemon and add 1 tablespoon of the juice.
5. In a food processor or blender, puree the strawberries along with the reduced apple juice and the agar mixture. Pour into small dessert bowls and freeze for 1 hour. Remove from the freezer 10 minutes before serving to soften slightly. Garnish each serving with a whole strawberry and a mint sprig.

Watermelon Sorbet
with Fruit Skewers

Major Phase: Water
Minor Phases: Earth and Fire

Yield: About 6 cups

A most delightful summer cooler, perfect after a spirited game of tennis or an invigorating run.

½ medium watermelon
¼ cup fresh lemon juice,
    crème de cassis, or champagne
8 to 12 very ripe fresh figs
12 to 16 large strawberries

1. Remove the thick rind and seeds from the watermelon.
2. In a food processor fitted with the steel blade, puree the watermelon in batches along with the lemon juice or liquor.
3. Freeze the mixture in an ice-cream machine according to the manufacturer's directions. Alternatively, freeze in trays in the freezer, scraping up the mixture with a fork until mushy every 45 to 50 minutes until done to sorbet consistency.
4. Thread the whole figs and strawberries alternately onto 6 to 8 thin skewers.
5. Serve the sorbet in a large wineglass accompanied by a fruit skewer.

Zen Punch

Phase: Wood

YIELD: 2 servings

Cool and refreshing, this is an excellent party drink to balance various rich appetizers.

- 1½ cups apple-strawberry juice
- 1½ tablespoons fresh lemon juice
- 3 ounces seltzer or sparkling mineral water
- 1 sliced lemon or orange for garnish
- 1 sliced strawberry for garnish

1. Mix all the ingredients together and serve in tall glasses with lemon slices and strawberries floating on top.

Dips, Sauces, and Condiments

Here are various accents and adornments that will help enhance your meals.

Curry Mixes

You've never tasted good curry until you've made your own mix. These two versions are purposely mild, but intensely aromatic and totally unlike anything commercial you may have tasted.

Once you've tried them, you'll hesitate to go back to the commercial kind. Use whenever curry powder is called for. Curry Blend I is aromatic, sweet, and only mildly spicy. Curry Blend II is less sweet. Remember that aromatic spices help you assimilate complex carbohydrates better, so they're also good for your digestion. These keep well, so make up a batch to have on hand. Add to your favorite sautéed or stir-fried vegetables as the spirit moves you.

Curry Blend I

Phase: Earth

Yield: ½ cup

6 tablespoons coriander seeds
1 tablespoon cumin seeds
1 tablespoon mustard seeds
2 teaspoons sweet paprika
2 teaspoons ground turmeric, or more to taste
1 teaspoon ground ginger
½ teaspoon anise seeds or fennel seeds
½ teaspoon whole white or black peppercorns
½ teaspoon cardamom seeds
½ teaspoon celery seeds
¼ teaspoon freshly grated nutmeg
⅛ teaspoon cayenne pepper
8 whole cloves
12 fenugreek seeds
2 -inch piece cinnamon stick

1. Preheat the oven to 250°F.
2. Combine all the ingredients together and distribute evenly in a shallow baking pan. Bake for 15 minutes, stirring often. Grind in a coffee or spice grinder. Store in a covered jar.

Curry Blend II

Phases: Metal and Wood

YIELD: ½ cup

2 tablespoons coriander seeds
2 tablespoons cumin seeds
½ teaspoon fennel seeds or anise seeds
½ teaspoon whole white peppercorns
½ teaspoon cardamom seeds
1 teaspoon dill seeds
6 fenugreek seeds
1 teaspoon ground ginger
2 tablespoons ground turmeric
⅛ teaspoon asafetida or "Hing"*

1. Preheat the oven to 250°F.
2. Combine the first 7 ingredients (the *whole* spices) and distribute evenly in a baking pan. Bake for 15 minutes, stirring frequently. Allow to cool.
3. Combine with the remaining ingredients (the powdered spices) and grind in a blender, coffee grinder, or spice mill. Store in a tightly closed container. A screw-top jar is best.

---

* Obtainable in Indian spice stores.

Garam Masala

Phase: Earth

YIELD: ⅓ to ½ cup

A sweet spice mix terrific for cookies or desserts; try it also in Dates with Almonds.

> 1 tablespoon cardamom pods
> ¼ cup ground cumin seeds
> 3 tablespoons coriander seeds
> 3 tablespoons black peppercorns
> 2 to 2½ -inch cinnamon stick, crushed
> ½ whole nutmeg, crushed
> 1 teaspoon whole cloves

1. Remove the cardamom seeds from their pods; discard pods.
2. Heat a dry, heavy skillet over moderate heat. Place the cardamom seeds and the remaining ingredients in the skillet and toast until golden, about 3 to 4 minutes. Shake the pan gently but constantly to prevent burning.
3. Remove from heat and pulverize in a spice or coffee grinder.
4. Store in airtight jars until ready to use.

Coriander Chutney

Phase: Wood

YIELD: 2 cups

This chutney will cool the palate after a spicy curry.

½ bunch coriander
1 fresh hot green chili
2 cups plain low-fat yogurt
Pinch sea salt
⅛ teaspoon freshly ground black pepper
½ teaspoon ground cumin
2 tablespoons fresh lemon juice

1. Remove the tough stems of the coriander and chop the leaves fine. (If you wish, you may chop the coriander and the chili in a blender. Simply seed the chili first, then add ⅓ cup water along with the coriander leaves and chili and blend.) Place in a medium bowl.
2. Slice the hot green chili lengthwise (if not already blended with coriander) into thin strips. Remove the small white seeds and slice the strips very thinly crosswise. Add to the bowl, then add the remaining ingredients. Blend well. Chill until ready to use.

❦ · ❦

Homemade Mayonnaise

Phase: Wood

YIELD: 1¼ cups

If the idea of making mayonnaise has never crossed your mind, try this one. It's surprisingly easy, and foolproof.

1 egg, preferably organic or free-range
1 tablespoon whole-grain mustard, such as Pommery
¾ teaspoon sea salt
2 tablespoons fresh lemon juice
1 tablespoon brown rice or balsamic vinegar
¾ cup cold-pressed soy or sunflower oil
¼ cup extra-virgin olive oil

1. In a blender, combine the egg, mustard, salt, lemon juice, and vinegar and blend for 30 seconds, or until completely mixed.
2. With the blender running on low speed, add the oil very slowly in a thin stream, until the mixture has emulsified. The last ⅓ cup can be added a bit faster. Taste and adjust the seasonings. Transfer to a screw-top jar. Refrigerate until ready to use.

Oil-Free Salad Dressings

If you are trying to reduce your fat intake, here are three oil-free salad dressings that may be used in place of the ones indicated in the recipes. All are full-bodied and flavorful. You won't miss the oil.

No-Oil Parsley Dressing

Phase: Wood

Yield: ½ cup

1 cup Light Vegetable Stock (page 72)
1 tablespoon fresh lemon juice
1 tablespoon red wine or balsamic vinegar
¼ cup chopped parsley
¼ teaspoon sea salt

1. In a 1-quart saucepan, boil down the stock to reduce it to 5 tablespoons.
2. In a small bowl or screw-top jar, combine all the ingredients and whisk or shake thoroughly to blend.

Spa Dressing (Oil and Salt-Free)

Major Phase: Wood

Minor Phase: Metal

YIELD: 1 cup

2 cups Light Vegetable Stock (page 72)
2 cloves garlic
⅓ cup fresh lemon juice
⅓ cup fresh coriander or dill

1. In a 1-quart saucepan, boil down the stock to ½ cup. Let cool.
2. Peel garlic and squeeze through a garlic press into a blender. Add the rest of the ingredients and blend until well mixed.

White Miso and Orange Dressing

Major Phase: Earth

YIELD: 1¼ cups

*T*his dressing is lovely over bitter greens, such as arugula, chicory, and radicchio.

½ cup fresh orange juice
½ cup white miso
¼ cup Light Vegetable Stock (page 72) or water
½ teaspoon grated orange rind

1. Place all the ingredients in a small bowl and whisk until creamy.

Spicy Peanut Sauce

Major Phase: Wood
Minor Phase: Metal

YIELD: 1 cup

This delectable sauce simply can't be beaten for enlivening whole grains! A tablespoon on rice or kasha is just right for an average serving. We also serve this sauce as a dip at parties, with vegetables or whole-grain crackers.

1 tablespoon unrefined sesame oil or unsalted butter
1 teaspoon Szechuan peppercorns, crushed
¼ teaspoon ground cumin
¼ teaspoon ground coriander
½ cup natural peanut butter
1 tablespoon shoyu or tamari
1 tablespoon maple syrup
4 to 6 tablespoons water, as needed
2 to 3 cloves garlic (optional)
¼ to ½ teaspoon cayenne pepper or Tabasco, to taste

1. In a small skillet, heat the oil or butter and add the spices, stirring briefly. Remove the pan from the heat.
2. In a medium bowl, combine the peanut butter and the sautéed spices. Slowly add the shoyu and maple syrup, whisking constantly. Add the water, a tablespoon at a time, until desired consistency is reached.
3. Peel the garlic and mince it very finely, or put it through a garlic press, and add it to the sauce, if desired.
4. Season to taste with the cayenne or Tabasco.

❧ • ☙

Clear Mushroom Sauce
with Shallots

Major Phase: Water
Minor Phase: Metal

Yield: 2½ cups

*H*ere's a light sauce that goes well over noodles, millet, and especially kasha. Plan to use it all at once, since it does not reheat well.

- ¾ pound fresh mushrooms
- 3 large shallots
- 4 cloves garlic
- 2 tablespoons extra-virgin olive oil
- 2 tablespoons kuzu
- 2 cups cold water or Light Vegetable Stock (page 72)
- 2 tablespoons shoyu or tamari, or to taste

1. Wipe the mushrooms and slice them thinly; chop the shallots and the garlic.
2. In a medium saucepan, heat the oil, then sauté the garlic, shallots, and mushrooms over medium heat for 8 to 10 minutes.
3. Dissolve the kuzu in the water or stock, add to the mushroom mixture, and bring to a boil, stirring continuously until thickened and clear. Stir in the shoyu. Serve immediately.

Jicama Pickles

Major Phase: Metal
Minor Phase: Water

YIELD: 6 to 8 servings

An unlikely combination: the Mexican vegetable and the Oriental soy sauce—but it works! Try this also with daikon or black radish.

　1　large jicama
　$\frac{2}{3}$　cup shoyu or tamari
1$\frac{1}{3}$　cups water
　3　tablespoons brown rice or apple cider vinegar

1. Peel the jicama and cut into matchsticks.
2. In a medium bowl, combine the jicama with the shoyu, water, and vinegar. There should be enough liquid to completely cover the jicama. Marinate for an hour or two at room temperature.
3. Serve as a condiment, only a small amount for each person. This will keep for 3 weeks in a covered jar in the refrigerator.

❦Menus❧

It's not enough to have great recipes—you need to combine them harmoniously in order to derive maximum well-being and comfort from your meals. The menus that follow are examples of how you can put together delicious balanced meals according to the Five-Phase Theory as we do it at the school. You'll also find the individual presentation menus of each of the graduates of the first Teachers' Training Program.

To see if meals are balanced, just read off the phases and you'll see if they're all there: wood, fire, earth, metal, and water. In meals with five or more dishes, I've only mentioned the major phase. However, if one of the phases is not represented (that is, there are two or more dishes of the same phase) I'll get the missing phase among the minor ones. In meals with less than five dishes, I include both the major and the minor phase to insure energy balance.

Individuals can create their own automatic balance by choosing those dishes that most appeal to them. More often than not, their subconscious body wisdom will draw them to those phases that suit them best.

SPRING SUPPER

Bean-of-the-Orient Miso Soup (*Water*)
Pinto Bean Salad with Chicory and Radishes (*Metal—Fire*)
Mediterranean Pasta Garni (*Wood*)
Pear-Raspberry Sorbet (*Earth*)

FALL WEEKEND

Vegetable-Barley Soup (*Wood*)
Cauliflower Curry (*Metal*)
Black Bean Log with Fresh Coriander (*Water*)
Festive Salad (*Fire*)
Raisin Squares (*Earth*)

WINTER TUESDAY

Garden Green Soup with Chick-peas (*Fire*)
San Franciscan Pizza (*Wood*)
Red and White Cabbage Salad (*Metal—Water*)
Baked Yams Sauté (*Earth*)

LISSA'S SUMMER LUNCH

Vegetable-Tofu Sauté (*Metal*)

Lissa's Homemade Black-Pepper Pasta with Scallion Butter
Sauce (*Wood—Fire*)

Beets and Onions Vinaigrette (*Water*)

Ice Dream Pie (*Earth*)

FRENCH VEGETARIAN WINTER DINNER

Mushrooms Stuffed with Garlic and Rosemary (*Water*)

Leek and Potato Soup (*Wood*)

Red Lentil Pâté (*Fire*)

Vegetable Garden Salad with Mustard Cream Vinaigrette (*Wood*)

Turnips au Gratin with Kalamata Olives (*Metal*)

Compote of Dried Fruits with Cashew-Almond Cream (*Earth*)

NATURAL GOURMET
MEALS FOR ENTERTAINING

Baked Garlic on Pita Toasts (*Metal*)

Clear Soup with Shiitake and Mustard Greens (*Fire*)

Baked Beans with Miso and Apple Butter (*Water*)

Rice-Spinach Timbales with Mushroom Sauce (*Metal*)

Summer Squash Mirepois (*Wood*)

Walnut-Butter Cookies (*Wood—Earth* and *Metal*)

Avocado Mousse (*Wood*)
Shoyu Consommé with Enoki Mushrooms (*Water*)
Avocado Mousse (*Wood*)
Pico de Gallo Salad (*Wood*)
Mamaliga (*Fire*)
Refried Beans (*Water*)
Peach Pie (*Metal—Wood* and *Earth*)

Aduki Bean Dip with Crudites (*Water—Wood*)
Escarole-Miso Soup (*Fire*)
Orange Millet Pilaf (*Earth*)
Braised Daikon with Mirin (*Metal*)
Watercress and Arugula Salad (*Metal—Fire*)
Almond-Lemon Cream Tart (*Earth*)

HOLIDAY SUPPER

Black and White Tofu Aioli Dip (*Metal*)
  Sesame Crackers (*Wood*)
Black Bean Soup (*Water*)
Stuffed Acorn Squash (*Earth*)
Creamed Spinach (*Metal*)
Zesty Salad with Toasted Sesame Dressing (*Fire*)
Cranberry Aspic (*Water*)
Pecan Pie (*Earth*)

GRADUATION PARTY BUFFET

Bernie's Gravlax (*Earth*)
Focaccia with Fresh Tomatoes and Rosemary (*Wood*)
Spicy Guacamole with Corn Chips (*Wood*)
Daikon Radish Canapés (*Metal*)
Corn Soup with Pimiento Puree (*Fire*)
Mediterranean Pasta Garni (*Wood*)
Black-eyed Pea Salad with Sun-Dried Tomatoes (*Wood—Fire*)
Apple-Raspberry Ice (*Fire*)
Nectarine-Nutmilk Ice Cream (*Metal—Earth*)

AMERICAN NATURAL

Bulgur Pilaf with Mushrooms (*Wood*)
Saffron Beans with Tomato (*Metal*)
Crunchy Fennel Salad with Lemon Dressing (*Metal—Wood*)
Broccoli Rabe with Garlic (*Fire*)
Johnna's Best Cranberry Dream Pie (*Water—Earth*)

—Johnna Albi

INTERNATIONAL MENU FOR
WARM WEATHER

Spicy Guacamole (Mexico) (*Wood*)
Aromatic Spiced Rice (India) (*Metal—Earth*)
Insalata Mista con Finocchio (Italy) (*Fire—Metal and Water*)
Vegetarian Carbonada Criolla (Argentina) (*Earth*)
Orange Loaf (Barbados) (*Earth*)

—Carol Amoruso

A LADIES' LUNCH

Curried Apple-Squash Bisque (*Earth*)
Wild Rice and Job's Tears (Hato Mugi) Salad
   with Lemon-Walnut Dressing (*Water—Wood*)
Vegetable Pâté (*Wood*)
Wilted Dandelion Greens with Navy Beans (*Fire—Metal*)
Banana Layer Cake with Carob Icing à la Minx (*Earth*)

—Minx Boren

TABLETOP COOKING

Seafood Yosenabe à la Janice with Dipping Sauces
   (*Mixed—all phases present*)
Japanese Barley-Rice (*Metal*)
Radish Watercress Salad with Soy Sesame Dressing
   (*Metal—Wood* and *Fire*)
Ginger Lace Cookies (*Wood—Earth*)

—Janice Florendine

JAPANESE MACROBIOTIC FEAST

Vegetarian and Fish Norimaki (*Metal—Water*)
Barley Croquettes with Shiitake Mushroom Sauce (*Wood*)
Chicory Salad with Lotus Root (*Fire—Wood* and *Metal*)
   Thousand Sesame Dressing (*Wood*)
Hiziki with Snow-Peas, Ginger, and Radish (*Water*)
Almond Flan with Raspberry Sauce (*Metal—Earth* and
   Fire)

—Gail Vandy Bogurt Hansen

❧ • ❧

BRUNCH

Cantaloupe Soup with Blueberries (*Earth—Water*)
Fish Timbales with Lemon-Butter Sauce (*Metal*)
Potato-Cabbage Casserole with Dill (*Metal*)
Janie's Leafy Salad with Garlic-Parsley
   Vinaigrette (*Wood—Fire*)

—Janie Jacobson

❧ • ❧

LATIN AMERICAN LUNCH

Tomato-Coriander Soup (*Fire*)
Black Bean Feijoada (*Water*)
Yellow Corn Bread (*Fire*)
Watercress-Sprouts-Pumpkin Seed Salad with
   Creamy Lemon Dressing (*Metal—Wood*)
Diane's Macaroons (*Metal—Earth*)

—Diane Korzinski

❧ • ❧

HINDU CURRY DINNER

Joan's Red Lentil-Lemon Soup (*Fire*)
Cauliflower Curry (*Metal*)
Brown Rice Pilaf (*Metal*)
Coriander Chutney (*Wood*)
Green Beans with Ginger and Tomatoes (*Wood—Fire*)
Spiced Glazed Pears with Tofu Cream (*Metal—Earth*)

—Joan R. Kupetsky

FAMILY DINNER

Clear Broth with Garlic and Escarole (*Fire*)
Vegetable-Tofu Stroganoff (*Metal—Wood*)
Black Bean Salad with Corn and Red Pepper (*Water—Fire*)
Blueberry Crunch (*Water—Wood* and *Earth*)

—Jenny Matthau

ITALIAN PEASANT CELEBRATION

Bean Soup with Arugula (*Metal—Fire*)
Mushroom-Stuffed Artichokes (*Wood*)
Pasta Primavera with Pesto (*Wood*)
Insalata Festiva (*Fire—Metal*)
Stuffed Oranges (*Earth*)

—Phyllis Johnson Owen

MAIL ORDER SOURCES

ARKANSAS

SHILOH FARMS (nuts, legumes, fruit, flour mixes)
P.O. Box 97
Sulphur Springs, AK 72768
(501) 298-3297

EAGLE AGRICULTURAL PRODUCTS (beans, grains, fresh and dried produce)
Rt. 4, Box 4-B
Huntsville, AK 72740
(501) 738-2203

MOUNTAIN ARK TRADING COMPANY (produce, grains, Oriental products, soyfoods,
sea vegetables)
120 South East Avenue
Fayetteville, AK 72701
AK: (501) 442-7191 US: (800) 643-8909

GOLD MINE NATURAL FOOD COMPANY (whole grains, beans, Oriental items)
1947 30th Street
San Diego, CA 92102
CA: (800) 647-2927 US: (800) 647-2929

GRAVELLY RIDGE FARMS (organic produce, grains)
Star Route 16
Elk Creek, CA 95939
(916) 963-3216

JAFFE BROTHERS (dried fruit, nuts, grains, beans, assorted goods)
P.O. Box 636
Valley Center, CA 92082-0636
(619) 749-1133

LUNDBERG FAMILY FARMS (Lundberg rice and rice products)
P.O. Box 369
Richvale, CA 95974
(916) 882-4551

MARIN ORGANIC NETWORK (dried and fresh produce, herbs, garlic)
P.O. Box 7037
Corte Madera, CA 94925
(415) 285-6907

MENDOCINO SEA VEGETABLE COMPANY (wildcrafted sea vegetables)
P.O. Box 372
Navarro, CA 95463
(707) 895-3741

FLORIDA

OAK FEED (grains, legumes, Oriental products)
3030 Grand Ave.
Coconut Grove, FL 33133
(305) 448-7595

IOWA

PAUL'S GRAINS (whole grains and grain products, chicken, turkey, dried fruits, honey, nuts and seeds)
2475-B 340 Street
Laurel, IA 50141
(515) 476-3373

MAINE

MAINE COAST SEA VEGETABLES (alaria, kelp, dulse, nori)
Shore Road
Franklin, ME 04634
(207) 565-2907

MARYLAND

ORGANIC FOODS EXPRESS (produce, grains, beans, assorted goods)
11003 Emack Rd.
Beltsville, MD 20705
(301) 937-8608

THE MACROBIOTIC MALL (whole grains, beans, tofu, tempeh, Oriental products)
18779 Frederick Rd.
Gaithersburg, MD 20879
LOCAL: 963-9235 US: (800) 533-1270

MASSACHUSETTS

BALDWIN HILL BAKERY (wholegrain sourdough bread)
Baldwin Hill Road
Phillipston, MA 01331
(508) 249-4691

MICHIGAN

SPECIALTY GRAIN COMPANY (grains, beans, seeds, dried fruit, nuts)
Box 2458
Dearborn, MI 48123
(313) 561-0421

MINNESOTA

DIAMOND K ENTERPRISES (grains and products, nuts, dried fruit)
R.R. 1, Box 30A
St. Charles, MN 55972
(507) 932-4308

NATURAL WAY MILLS, INC. (whole grains, flours, other products)
Rt. 2, Box 37
Middle River, MN 56737
(218) 222-3677

NEBRASKA

M & M DISTRIBUTING (amaranth and blue corn products)
R.R. 2, Box 61A
Oshkosh, NE 69154
(308) 772-3664

NEW HAMPSHIRE

WATER WHEEL SUGAR HOUSE (organic maple sugar)
Rt. 2
Jefferson, NH 03583
(603) 586-4479

NEW YORK

COMMUNITY MILL AND BEAN (flour, mixes, beans, grains, cereals)
RD 1, Rt. 89
Savannah, NY 13146
(315) 365-2664

DEER VALLEY FARM (produce, grains, wide variety of products)
R.D. 1
Guilford, NY 13780
(607) 764-8556

OHIO

MILLSTREAM MARKET (produce, nuts, grains, cereals)
1310A East Tallmadge Ave.
Akron, OH 44310
(216) 630-2700

PENNSYLVANIA

KRYSTAL WHARF FARMS (grains, beans, nuts, dried fruit, fresh produce, and other
products)
R.D. 2, Box 191A
Mansfield, PA 16933
(717) 549-8194

RISING SUN DISTRIBUTORS (produce, dried fruit, nuts, beans, grains, other items)
P.O. Box 627
Milesburg, PA 16853
(814) 355-9850

WALNUT ACRES (full line of cereals, flours, grains, many other items)
Penns Creek, PA 17862
(717) 837-0601

VERMONT

HILL AND DALE FARMS (organic apples, cider)
West Hill-Daniel Davis Rd.
Putney, VT 05346
(802) 387-5817

TEAGO HILL FARM (organic maple syrup)
Barber Hill Road
Pomfret, VT 05067
(802) 457-3507

VIRGINIA

GOLDEN ACRES ORCHARD (organic apples in season, cider vinegar, juice)
Rt. 2, Box 2450
Front Royal, VA 22630
(703) 636-9611

KENNEDY'S NATURAL FOODS (nuts, seeds, dried fruits, legumes, grains, flours, herb teas, jams and jellies, juices, pastas)
1051 West Broad St.
Falls Church, VA 22046
(703) 533-8484

WASHINGTON

CASCADIAN FARM (organic fruit butters and conserves, pickles)
5375 Highway 20
Rockport, WA 98283
(206) 853-8807

REFERENCES AND FURTHER READING

GENERAL

Butt, Gary and Frena Bloomfield. *Harmony Rules.* New York: Samuel Weiser, 1987.

Carper, Jean. *The Food Pharmacy.* New York: Bantam Books, 1988.

Colbin, Annemarie. *The Book of Whole Meals.* New York: Ballantine Books, 1983.

———. *Food and Healing.* New York: Ballantine Books, 1986.

Estella, Mary. *Natural Foods Cookbook.* Tokyo-New York: Japan Publications, 1985.

Flaws, Bob and Honora L. Wolfe. *Prince Wen Hui's Cook.* Brookline, MA: Paradigm Publications, 1985.

Schmid, Ronald F., N.D. *Traditional Foods Are Your Best Medicine.* New York: Ballantine Books, 1989.

Schneider, Elizabeth. *Uncommon Fruits and Vegetables: A Commonsense Guide*. New York: Harper & Row, 1986.

Wilson, Jane W. *Eating Well When You Just Can't Eat the Way You Used To*. New York: Workman Publishing, 1988.

Wittenberg, Margaret M. *Experiencing Quality: A Shopper's Guide to Whole Foods*. Austin, TX: Whole Foods Market, 1987.

Wood, Rebecca. *The Whole Foods Encyclopedia: A Shopper's Guide*. New Jersey: Prentice Hall, 1988.

FIVE PHASES

Note: The classification of foods according to the five phases is based, with some modifications, on the work of John Garvy, N.D., D.Ac., director of the Foundation for Energetic Medicine in Black Mountain, N.C. For more information on this, as well as on the complete Five-Phase theory, a list of references follows:

Connelly, Diane M., Ph.D., M.Ac. *Traditional Acupuncture: The Law of Five Elements*. Columbia, MD: The Center for Traditional Acupuncture, 1979.

Garvy, John W., N.D., D.Ac. *The Five Phases of Food: How to Begin*, Second edition. Brookline Village: Wellbeing Books, 1983.

Haas, Elson M., M.D. *Staying Healthy with the Seasons*. Millbrae, CA: Celestial Arts, 1981.

Kaptchuk, Ted J., O.M.D. *The Web that Has No Weaver: Understanding Chinese Medicine*. New York: Congdon & Weed, 1984.

Muramoto, Naboru. *Healing Ourselves*. New York: Avon Books, 1974.

Index

Horseradish:
    sauce; tempeh with creamy, 163
Hungarian asparagus soup, 80–81

Ice cream:
    apple-raspberry ice, 273
    in ice dream pie, 249–50
    nectarine-nutmilk, 272–73
    pear-raspberry sorbet, 274
    strawberry-mint sorbet, 275
    watermelon sorbet with fruit skewers, 276
Ice dream pie, 249–50

Jalapeño peppers: *see* Peppers, jalapeño
Janie's leafy salad with garlic-parsley vinai-
    grette, 204
Japanese barley-rice, 106
Japanese red bean soup, 96–97
Jicama pickles, 288
Joan's red lentil-lemon soup, 103–4
Job's tears (hato mugi):
    about, 222
    and wild rice salad with lemon-walnut
        dressing, 222–23
Johnna's best cranberry dream pie, 247–48

Kale:
    in four greens and walnut sauté, 179–80
    in garden green soup with chick-peas,
        98–99
Kanten: *see* Agar
Kasha:
    cooking, 39
Kitchen equipment, 33–38
Kiwi fruit tart with almond crust, 250–52
Knives, 34
Kuzu, 30
    filling, for pecan pie, 257

Lactovegetarian diet, 9–10
Lee, Karen, 169
Leeks:
    cleaning, 41
    and potato soup, 88
    in rich vegetable stock, 73–74
Legumes: *see* Beans and legumes
Lemon(s):
    almond cream tart, 242–43
    butter sauce, 230
    cookies, 259–60
    dill sauce, 227
    dressing
        creamy, 212
        for fennel salad, 199–200
    garlic marinade, 218
    glaze, 243
    in ponzo sauce, 234–35
    red lentil soup, 103–4
    sesame cookies, 262–63
    walnut dressing, 222–23
Lentils:
    croquettes, 146–48
    puree, 142
    red
        lemon soup; Joan's, 103–4
        pâté, 144–45
        pâté en croute (in the crust), 145–
            46
Lettuce:
    Belgian endive
        in leafy salad with garlic-parsley vinai-
            grette, 204
        in zesty salad with toasted sesame dress-
            ing, 214–15
    Boston
        in green salad with miso-coriander
            dressing, 203
        in Pico de Gallo salad, 207
    green leaf

in green salad with miso-coriander dressing, 203

radicchio

braised fennel on, 177–78

in festive salad, 205

in leafy salad with garlic-parsley vinaigrette, 204

in mixed salad with fennel, 206

red leaf

in zesty salad with toasted sesame dressing, 214–15

romaine

in leafy salad with garlic-parsley vinaigrette, 204

Light vegetable stock, 72

Lissa's homemade black pepper pasta with scallion-butter sauce, 121–25

Lissa's rolled flounder fillets with lemon-dill sauce, 226–27

Locro (Argentine vegetable stew), 131–32

Lotus root:

and dressing; chicory salad with, 201–2

Macrobiotic diet, 3–4

Mamaliga polenta (with cheese), 108–9

Mayonnaise, homemade, 283–84

Meal balancing, 12–13, 20–22

Mediterranean pasta garni, 126–27

Melon: see Cantaloupe; Watermelon

Menus, 289–96

Metal phase (charts), 17, 19

Milk products, 10

Millet:

and cauliflower puree, 176

cooking, 39

orange pilaf, 110

and quinoa pilaf, 111

Mince pie, 252–53

Mint:

strawberry sorbet, 275

Mirin, 30

Miso, 30

barley

and apple butter; baked beans with, 136

soup; bean-of-the-orient, 74–75

in thousand sesame dressing, 202

green peppers with, 182–83

mugi

and apple butter; baked beans with, 136

onion dressing, 208

white

collard soup, 78–79

coriander dressing, 203

dressing, 210

and orange dressing, 285

in thousand sesame dressing, 202

Mixed salad with fennel, 206

Mock hollandaise sauce, 229

Mousse, avocado, 52–53

Mushrooms:

in broccoli-tofu quiche with wild mushrooms, 157–58

bulgur pilaf with, 107

in chunky cream of mushroom soup, 90–91

in herbed marinated vegetables, 200–201

in rich vegetable stock, 73–74

sauce

clear, with shallots, 287

rice-spinach timbales with, 127–28

soup; simple cream of, 89

stuffed artichokes, 166–67

in stuffed grape leaves, 60–61

stuffed with garlic and rosemary, 58–59

tofu stroganoff with bulgur, 155–56

in vegetable pâté, 54–55

in vegetable-tofu sauté, 154–55

see also Mushrooms, wild

in San Francisco pizza, 120–21
in white bean chili, 150–51
TTP: *see* Teacher's Training Program
Turnips:
    au gratin with Kalamata olives, 191–92
    and coriander; black-eyed pea soup with, 100
Turnovers:
    tofu and spinach, 66–67

Udon pasta: *see* Pasta
Umeboshi plums, 30
Umeboshi vinegar, 30
    substitute for, 30
Uncooked tomato sauce, 153
Utensils, small, 34–35

Vegetables, 165–94
    about, 27–28
    barley soup, 95–96
    cleaning and peeling, 40–41
    cutting (illus.), 41–44
    garden salad with mustard cream vinai-
        grette, 213–14
    herbed marinated, 200–201
    pâté, 54–55
    stew; Argentine (locro), 131–32
    stock
        light, 72
        rich (salt-free), 73–74
    tofu sauté, 154–55
    vegetarian carbonada criolla (Argentina),
        193–94
    white bean terrine, 151–53
    see also Vegetables, sea; individual names
Vegetables, sea:
    about, 28
    agar, 30

arame or hiziki with ginger and garlic,
    167–68
hiziki with snow peas, ginger, and radish,
    168–69
soaking water, 168
Vegetarian norimaki (illus.), 62–64
Vinaigrettes: *see* Salad dressing; Salads
Vinegars:
    brown rice, 30
    umeboshi, 30

Wafers: *see* Crackers
Walnut(s):
    butter cookies, 263–64
    and four greens sauté, 179–80
    and green bean pâté; celery stuffed with,
        57–58
    lemon dressing, 222–23
    orange loaf with, 241
    toasting, 179
Water phase (charts), 17, 19
Watercress:
    and arugula salad with rosemary-mustard
        dressing, 211
    in green salad with miso-coriander dress-
        ing, 203
    radish salad with soy-sesame dressing,
        209
    sprout-pumpkin seed salad with creamy
        lemon dressing, 212
Watermelon sorbet with fruit skewers,
    276
White beans: *see* Beans and legumes
White miso: *see* Miso
Whitefish:
    in savory fish stew, 231
    with scallion stuffing; baked, 232
Whole foods, 11–12
Wild rice: *see* Rice, wild

ABOUT THE CONTRIBUTORS

JOHNNA ALBI has a background in European cooking and has studied natural-foods cooking and holistic health since 1975. She founded her own school, Natural Foods Cookery, in 1984 in Marshfield, Mass., and teaches cooking at Bread and Circus, a natural supermarket, as well as in local schools and adult education programs in the Boston area.

CAROL AMORUSO is a dancer and has been a vegetarian for many years. She teaches classes in nutritious vegetarian meal preparation, caters vegetarian food for private and office parties through her company, Amorosa, and offers luncheons for senior citizens through East Village Visiting Neighbours, a non-profit organization in New York City.

MINX BOREN has taken over 200 classes in the art and science of good cooking. In 1987 she completed her studies with Gary Null's Health and Nutrition program at SAV to become a nutrition and life-style consultant in private practice in New York City. She occasionally teaches cooking classes at the Natural Gourmet Cookery School and other institutions.

LISSA DE ANGELIS studied natural-foods cooking with Michio and Aveline Kushi and Melanie Melia, and completed the apprenticeship with Annemarie Colbin in 1982. She owned a bakery in Illinois before that, and eventually ran a lucrative private cooking and catering business. Lissa joined the NGCS staff in the fall of 1983, and ran the Long Island branch of the school for five years. She is currently Associate Director of the school.

GAIL VANDY BOGURT HANSEN got her B.F.A. at the Cleveland Institute of Arts. With a partner, she founded Laughing Gull Natural Food Deli, in Long Island, New York, in 1983, where she teaches natural-food cooking classes regularly. The company prepares healthful salads, sandwiches, and desserts, and caters for all occasions.

JANIE JACOBSON studied with Annemarie Colbin from 1980 until 1985, rounding out her education with classical and Pritikin-style cooking classes. She cooks privately for people with serious health conditions in her hometown of Virginia Beach, Va., and was the director of cooking classes at the Kitchen Barn, a local kitchen and cookware store, for four years.

DIANE KORZINSKI is vice-president of Paul's Motors, in Hawthorne, N.J. She is also a certified Masters Psychophysical teacher, and regularly teaches Masters Body Awareness seminars, where she incorporates discussions about diet and health and offers lunch along the principles taught at the Natural Gourmet Cookery School.

JENNY MATTHAU has a B.A. in psychology from UCLA, and has been cooking with natural foods since 1975. After graduating from the Natural Gourmet Cookery School's Apprenticeship and Teacher Training Program in 1985, she was the chef for the Judson Cancer Help Project, and joined the teaching staff at the school in the winter of 1986.

PHYLLIS JOHNSON OWEN studied cooking and natural-foods cuisine in both the U.S. and France. She has been a natural-foods chef since 1975, and served as the nutritional consultant for the Boston Food Coop. She currently teaches whole-foods cooking classes at the Boston Adult Education Center and does private catering.

JOAN RUTKOWSKI-KUPETSKY, R.N., has studied food and nutrition since 1963 and natural-foods cooking since 1980. She began teaching cooking classes on Long Island in 1983, and since her graduation from the NGCS's Teacher Training Program has given numerous presentations on whole-foods cookery to organizations. A member of the American Holistic Nurses Association, she teaches wellness and nutrition to her clients in her nursing practice. She contributed a section on natural recipes to a cookbook published by the Wellness Committee at Brookhaven Memorial Hospital, Patchogue, N.Y.

❧ • ☙

For information about *The Basics of Healthy Cooking: Grains and Beans* videotape (101 minutes) VHS or Beta. Contact:

The Natural Gourmet Cookery School
48 West 21st Street, Second Floor
New York, N.Y. 10010.
(212) 645-5170